Victorian Fashion Accessories

Victorian Fashion Accessories

Ariel Beaujot

London · New York

English edition
First published in 2012 by
Berg
Editorial offices:
50 Bedford Square, London WC1B 3DP, UK
175 Fifth Avenue, New York, NY 10010, USA

Berg is an imprint of Bloomsbury Publishing Plc.

Library of Congress Cataloging-in-Publication Data

A catalogue record for this book is available from the Library of Congress.

British Library Cataloguing-in-Publication Data

A catalogue record for this book is available from the British Library.

ISBN 978 1 84788 683 5 (Cloth)
978 1 84788 682 8 (Paper)
e-ISBN 978 0 85785 319 6 (institutional)
978 0 85785 320 2 (individual)

Typeset by Apex Publishing, LLC, Madison, WI, USA
Printed in the UK by the MPG Books Group

www.bergpublishers.com

**To my mentors
Tim Blackmore and Pat Skidmore-Skuce**

Contents

List of Figures ix

Acknowledgments xiii

Introduction 1

1 "The Beauty of her Hands": The Glove and the Making
of Middle-Class Womanhood 31

2 "The Language of the Fan": Pushing the Boundaries
of Middle-Class Womanhood 63

3 "Underneath the Parasol": Umbrellas as Symbols
of Imperialism, Race, Youth, Flirtation, and Masculinity 105

4 "The Real Thing": The Celluloid Vanity Set and the Search
for Authenticity 139

Conclusion 179

Bibliography 183

Index 213

List of Figures

INTRODUCTION

0.1 Ephemera showing a flirtatious Victorian lady with her
fan/calendar open. 1897.   2

0.2 The fan/calendar is closed revealing the lady's bosom. 1897.   15

CHAPTER 1

1.1 A woman signs the register after her wedding with gloveless
hands. Circa 1880.   35

1.2 Afternoon tea was a time when women revealed their hands
to an intimate circle of friends. 1892.   36

1.3 The "awful effects of too much lawn-tennis by the sea" is
experienced by women once they return to Society events
in the city. 1883.   37

1.4 Bridal Bouquet Bloom was advertised as a hygienic liquid;
however, many of these mail-order beauty products
contained dangerous ingredients like lead or arsenic. 1892.   39

1.5 Actress Sarah Bernhardt brought opera gloves back into
fashion because she was embarrassed to show her
thin arms. 1887.   41

1.6 Fashion plates throughout the nineteenth century demonstrate
passive hand gestures meant to be emulated by middle-class
women. 1880.   42

1.7 In this 1897 family photo, lax hands imitate the fashion
plates of the day.   43

1.8 The glove stretcher's pointed tips (center object) helped
keep the fingers of gloves tapered. Circa 1900.   44

1.9 Working-class women, possibly actresses, solicit wealthy
gentlemen at the Victoria Theatre, a popular music hall of
the 1870s.   45

1.10 Male glovemakers at work in Grenoble, France. Late
nineteenth century.   47

1.11 Hanna Cullwick, maid-of-all-work and wife of Arthur Munby,
showing off her large working hands and bicep. 1867.   50

1.12 Victorians believed that a person's temperament could
be read by observing certain aspects of their skulls and
hands as demonstrated on this phrenological drawing
of a head. 1854.   53

CHAPTER 2

2.1 A young woman paints a fan. 1891.   68

2.2 A pretty young woman surrounded by six male admirers uses
her fan to communicate her chosen companion for the
last waltz. Circa 1875.   79

2.3 The vast majority of the fashion plates picture women with
their fans closed and their gazes passive. 1881.   80

2.4 The open fan of fashion plates is never the fan of a
coquette. 1880.   81

2.5 Three images of women flirting their way into men's hearts.
1857, 1882, 1858.   82

2.6 Lovers communicate behind a fan. 1894.   84

2.7 Sada Yacco was a Japanese actress who toured Europe and
America in the late nineteenth and early twentieth centuries.   89

2.8 The three little maids from *The Mikado* pose coyly with
their fans. 1885.   90

2.9 *Carte de visite* for Berlin production of *The Mikado*. Actress
from the first production of *The Mikado* in Germany poses in
what purports to be the Japanese style. 1886.   91

CHAPTER 3

3.1 The King of Ashanti under his official umbrella surrounded
by his retinue. 1873.   108

3.2 Procession of state umbrellas at the emperor's marriage
in Peking. 1888.   110

3.3 King Prempeh's royal umbrella from when he ruled
Ashanti. 1873.   111

3.4 Image of first primitive parasol (that looks like a fan) to protect royalty from the sun in India. Late nineteenth century.   112

3.5 The umbrella worship of the Santal Hill peoples. 1898.   113

3.6 A royal parasol as used by the Assyrians, compared with Jonas Hanway's umbrella of 1786.   114

3.7 A lady in court dress with her fashionable parasol. 1715.   115

3.8 Jonas Hanway pioneers the first umbrella in London. 1756.   117

3.9 As umbrellas became more common they were sold on the street by hawkers. 1823.   118

3.10 A woman uses her white parasol to maintain a pale complexion. 1906.   121

3.11 A gentleman gallantly offers a woman shelter from the rain. 1913.   123

3.12 The Earl of Hardwicke leans on his slim umbrella. 1843.   126

3.13 How to properly fold an umbrella. 1900.   127

3.14 An umbrella-mender at work. Circa 1890.   128

3.15 Music-hall entertainer George Robey poses as a working-class upstart with his misshapen umbrella. Circa 1905.   130

3.16 Knife grinder working at a street market under an umbrella. 1950.   131

CHAPTER 4

4.1 An advertisement for a range of hairbrushes in ivory and erinoid from Harrods's toilet-brush department. 1929.   142

4.2 Three men stand in front of a store of ivory in Congo. 1889.   143

4.3 Edward VII, when Prince of Wales, shooting a tiger from the safety of his howdah on the back of an elephant in India. 1877.   144

4.4 A group of Bengalis carving ivory in a live exhibit at the Great Exhibition of 1851.   145

4.5 Male accessories made out of ivory. May 1937.   146

4.6 Women's accessories made out of ivory. May 1937.   147

4.7 Trademark image of the British Xylonite Company. 1936.   149

4.8 Women threading bristles into ebony brushes. 1930s.   153

4.9   This cartoon entitled "Cause and Effect" shows that a
maid's crinoline is too large and misshapen to wear while
she works. 1864.   161

4.10 Advertisement for Ivory Pyralin. 1920.   162

4.11 Advertisement for Ming pattern vanity set showing a white
woman's hand and a reflection of imagined China.
Late 1920s.   165

Acknowledgments

I would first like to thank the many archivists and curators who helped me navigate the collections that have allowed me to do this study: Julie Anne Lambert from the John Johnson Collection of Printed Ephemera at Oxford University; Oriole Cullen at the Museum of London; Valerie Reilly at Paisley Museum; Emma Luker, Assistant Curator of Furniture, Textiles and Fashion, at the Victoria and Albert Museum; Rosemary Crill of the Indian Department at the Victoria and Albert Museum; Eleanor Summers at the Museum of Costume at Bath; Sheila Hughes at Axminster Museum; Mrs. Alexander at the Fan Museum in Greenwich; Allison Pollard at the Science Museum Library in London; Sandy Paul at Trinity College Library at Cambridge University; Nancy Shawcross, Curator of Manuscripts at the University of Pennsylvania; Walter Zimmerman of Weldon Library at the University of Western Ontario; Caitlin Tillman at Robarts Library at the University of Toronto; Regina Lee Blaszczyk, Roger Horwitz, Linda Gross, Marge McNinch, and Debra Hughes, all from Hagley Museum and Library in Delaware; and the Mary Evans Picture Library. Je tiens finalement à remercier vivement l'Association de Sauvegarde et de Promotion du Gant de Grenoble (ASP2G) pour son aide.

I am grateful for the support of many colleagues and friends. I am lucky to have had two dedicated and loving mentors, Pat Skidmore-Skuce and Tim Blackmore. Pat, you guided my academic path since my undergraduate studies until today; my PhD and the topic that I chose were thanks to your suggestions and insight. Tim, you have always been willing to walk with me through the challenges of academic life; besides this you have a brilliant mind, always encouraging me to draw together ideas that are seemingly unrelated. A sincere thank you also goes to Barbara Todd and Frances Timbers for reading and rereading my chapters and each time asking insightful questions that led my work into new and better directions. Your honesty and commitment to research and writing were an inspiration to me throughout this process. To Len van der Meer and Wendy Pascoe with whom I shared many long conversations about collecting and objects. Len, you have a breadth of knowledge any academic would envy. Wendy, your wide-ranging interests and never-failing enthusiasm are my motivation. I also want to thank the wonderful colleagues from the University of Toronto whom I did my doctoral studies alongside: Amy Milne-Smith, Sarah Amato, Mike Petit, Alexia Yates, Ruth Percy, Steve Maddox, Jeff

Bowersox, Cara Spittal, and Nathan Smith. Your humor, support, intellect, and savvy were much appreciated. Also thanks to Todd Webb, my friend and colleague from Laurentian@Georgian. Your ongoing help is much appreciated. Thanks also goes to Annette, Andrew, and Meghan Gun for opening their warm home to me as I did research in England. Your laughter, good food, and generosity touch my heart.

Thanks must also go to my thesis committee at the Department of History of the University of Toronto. As a PhD student writing on the topic of women's accessories, I was fortunate to have supervisors who were both enthusiastic about my project and thoughtful in their suggestions. I am particularly grateful to my supervisor, Lori Loeb, who offered encouragement and advice at every stage of the writing process. Committee members Sidney Aster, Adrienne Hood, and Carol Chin all enriched my work with their helpful comments. And my external examiner, Erika Rappaport, offered many fascinating lines of inquiry. Supportive from the day I met him at Hagley Museum and Archives was Steve Zdatny. A debt of gratitude also goes to my editor, Anna Wright, whose unfailingly positive and encouraging responses to the book kept me going.

I also wish to thank Jennifer Levin-Bonder for her help as a Research Assistant and for working with me on the exhibition that accompanied the launch of this book. To Jessica Clyburn, my Teaching and Research Assistant at Laurentian, thank you for the great work you did transcribing articles. To Matthew Capel and Anderson Todd, thanks for your help sourcing images and primary sources. I experienced the wonderful opportunity of working with enthusiastic students at the Abbey Program in Pontlevoy, France (2010) and at Laurentian University. The fresh perspectives that you brought to my topic influenced the writing of this book.

My sincerest appreciation goes out to my loving friends Alison v. Krause, Hilary Tranter, Stephanie Cairns, Jessica Lamb, Cheryl Richardson Andrea Ledvinka, Jenny Dixon, Jacky Hamilton, and Kristen Aspevig for reminding me to maintain balance in my life. I also want to thank my family: Rod, Liz, Damien, and Natalie Beaujot. Mom and Dad, thanks for your guidance and belief in me. Also, to my love, Matthew Hodkinson, what would I do without you?

I want to express my sincere appreciation to the following sources of academic support: the Ontario Graduate Scholarship, Hagley Museum and Library, Laurentian University Research Fund, and the Department of History and School of Graduate Studies at the University of Toronto.

Introduction

The glove, the fan, the parasol, and the vanity set have been largely over-looked by previous scholars.[1] These objects helped women create a sense of who they were, with important consequences for how they experienced gender, class, and race in the Victorian period. By accentuating the hands, face, and head, accessories marked the significance of the female body. In this book I will show that womanhood changed from the eighteenth century, in which women were characterized by their actions and attitude, to the nineteenth century when middle-class women began to express themselves through con-sumerism.[2] In a world that could increasingly purchase the trappings of class, a woman's performance of gender moved away from what she did toward what she could buy (figure 0.1).

Victorians continued to believe, along with their early modern forebearers, that the moral character of a woman was communicated through her body and therefore could be read by those around her. According to this model, to change her appearance for the better a woman had to go through a moral reeducation. The anonymous author of *The Ladies' Hand-Book of the Toilet*, written in England in 1843, reassured women that they could improve their external beauty by cultivating a good character: "From this mode of reasoning, it results that the fair one, who would become really beautiful, must make the cultivation of her mind—of those intellectual and moral powers with which her Creator has endowed her—her first and principal care. Pure affections must be cherished"; the author explains "amiable dispositions encouraged; use-ful knowledge acquired, and a mild, even, and obliging temper assiduously cultivated; or all her endeavours, to obtain real beauty," the author warns "will prove nugatory and vain. If, however, a due regard be paid to this 'inward adorning', her external appearance will be by no means neglected."[3] This at-titude was surprisingly persistent. Again an example appeared in an 1877 guide authored by the American Elisa Bisbee Duffery. Writing about beautiful eyes she says "those who would have their eyes bear a pleasing expression must cultivate pleasing traits of character and beautify the soul, and then this beautiful soul will look through its natural windows."[4] Over thirty years later this attitude, though expressed more plainly, continues to grace the pages of etiquette manuals suggesting that one must "be nice and you will look nice."[5]

Figure 0.1 I open this book with my favorite piece of ephemera showing a flirtatious Victorian lady with her fan/calendar open. 1897. John Johnson Collection of Printed Ephemera.

The warnings that women must be kind to look beautiful abound in the introductions to Victorian etiquette manuals. Surprisingly, however, as readers flipped through the chapters they found practical advice on how to properly coif the hair, what creams to use to keep skin white, what colors of parasols to purchase to maintain the appearance of a youthful complexion, and which glove fabrics made hands appear small and dainty. Advice manuals can be characterized by their practical suggestions for improving a lady's exterior, negating the introductory remarks that suggested that the soul will shine through. While emphasizing the importance of moral character on the one hand, on the other Victorians were constantly focused on the outer changes that they could achieve through consumerism.

A typical example of the practical advice found in manuals is contained in *Etiquette for Ladies; with Hints on the Preservation, Improvement, and Display of Female Beauty* (1840). As the title implies, this book suggests that a woman must maintain healthy skin in order to be seen as beautiful: "though heaven has given us a complexion which vies with the flowers of the field, we yet have it in our power to render it dingy by neglect, coarse through intemperance, and sallow by dissipation. Such excesses must therefore be avoided," the author suggests, using language that shows a strong Protestant work ethic must prevail over personal indulgences, "for, though there may be something in the pallid cheek which excites interest, yet, without a certain appearance of health, there can never be an impression of loveliness." The manual goes on to explain how to avoid the effects of a harsh climate by covering the face and head, engaging in light exercise, fanning one's self when overheated rather than bathing the face with cold water, and washing the face with "French or white brandy, and rose water" every night and morning.[6] There are vestiges of the introduction's suggestion that one's private life, that might include intemperance and neglect, could be reflected on the skin. But, we also see the idea that a woman who is disciplined and regularly uses consumer products can create a desired pallor through protective clothing, fans, and mixtures for washing the skin.

I selected the glove, fan, parasol, and vanity set (personal grooming items typically consisting of a comb, brush, and handheld mirror)[7] as my accessories for this study because they were items that were involved in tensions that existed in the Victorian mind. Had there not been a push toward a leisured lifestyle for middle-class women, gloves would not have been employed to hide the labor done by ladies. Had there not been restrictions regarding contact between lovers, fans would not have been used as a way of communicating subtle messages to men. Had Britain not been an imperial nation, parasols would not have become symbols of British superiority. And, finally, had ivory not been a representation of the colonial spoils bought by the rich in the form of vanity sets, the middle class would not have aspired to acquire an imitation of this rare material. Putting these objects in their historical context has made this a particularly productive inquiry for a historian of material culture.

This study spans the period 1830 to 1920. It begins in a decade where four phenomena that were important for the development of middle-class women's fashion came together. These were (1) the solidification of the social category of middle class, (2) an increase in consumption, (3) the democratization of luxury, and (4) a proliferation of the press. Many of these developments have antecedents in the eighteenth century, which will be elaborated in the following sections, but all of these trends became especially pronounced in the nineteenth century. My accessories are all particularly Victorian, and did not last long after the period because of changing concepts of leisure, gender, and class in the post–World War I period.[8]

IMAGINING THE MIDDLE CLASS

In order to write this book, I had to think about who the middle class were, and what people who identified themselves as "middle class" thought they had in common. These questions, that seem simple at first, turned out to be quite complex. The middle class was a very diverse grouping in the nineteenth century. It was both an economic classification and an imaginary social category. It included people ranging from the ill-paid spinsters, who made a meager salary designing fashionable objects, to rich factory owners. The category "middle class" was defined by what the head of the family did. A typical middle-class husband and father could be a sales clerk, banker, office worker, physician, lawyer, engineer, teacher, shop owner, factory manager, civil servant, artist, doctor, author, clergyman, and much more. The middle-class status extended from the breadwinner of the family to his immediate relations: his wife, sons, and daughters. It is generally agreed that middle-class households lived on incomes ranging from £100 to £1,000 a year,[9] but because the social category was both real and imagined, individuals continued to consider themselves middle class even if they fell below this income bracket.[10]

In this book I show that class is not a given, rather it is a social position that was "made real" through actions and relationships.[11] Many British historians, including Leonore Davidoff and Catherine Hall, consider the middle class to be a defined group of people that can be studied for its particular class characteristics.[12] These historians argue that between 1780 and 1850 the middle class became a distinct group that was based on a specific set of moral, family, and gender values. Studying the same time period, Dror Wahrman proposes that the middle class was an imagined category established by politicians to diffuse moments of potential revolution in Britain brought on by the French Revolution, the Napoleonic Wars, the Peterloo Massacre, and the Great Reform Act.[13] I argue a middle ground between these historians. While I agree with Davidoff and Hall that the middle class took ownership of a distinct set of values, I do not see the class as a natural category. Here I look to Wahrman's concept of the middle class as an imagined grouping that the middling sort sought to embody. I contend that class should be conceived of as an ongoing accomplishment. My argument, then, is that Victorians performed their class roles on a daily basis according to the values that were imagined as middle class, aristocratic, or working class. My work looks at accessories as consumables that help to differentiate the middle class from other classes. I argue that middle-class women took symbols originally associated with the aristocracy and modified them to help make their class position real through consumption. This is Thorstein Veblen's "trickle down" argument with a twist.[14] The middle class appropriated such aristocratic symbols of refinement as the made-to-order leather glove, the silk parasol, and the ivory vanity set. However, the women could not afford to have their gloves made to fit their particular hands, so they bought gloves ready-made. Similarly, middle-class parasols were typically made of cotton rather than silk, and vanity sets were fabricated in a way that looked like ivory even though they were made of plastic. However, middle-class adjustments to aristocratic style were not seen as shams or imitation, but as modifications that allowed the middle class to see itself as a class apart; distinct from the aristocracy while still appropriating its symbols of refinement.

People of the middle class shared certain values that were often predicated on the difference between themselves and the other classes.[15] They thought of themselves as the moral center of society—a group separate from the drunken, lazy, uncouth working class, and the debauched, womanizing aristocracy.[16] To some historians, who see this class as emerging from the evangelical revival of the late 1700s, it is understood as particularly Christian.[17] Embodying Christian values such as a work ethic, self-restraint, and modesty, this class was seen as the segment of society that could bring morality to the wider British public. Later in the century the middle class shed its evangelical roots and became the major power behind such initiatives as public museums, art galleries, schools, and parks. It believed that these institutions could act as an example of respectability for the working class and would reorganize the national landscape, allowing middle-class values to suffuse the nation.[18]

Another abstract concept that separates the middle class from the other classes is its belief in merit-based employment and the idea of the self-made man. It was believed that once the nation rid itself of such unfair pro-aristocratic advantages as religious tests for political office, the purchase of army commissions, and favoritism in appointments, anyone could achieve respectable employment if only he worked hard enough. The ideal of the self-made man, famously articulated by Samuel Smiles in his 1859 book *Self-Help; with Illustrations of Character and Conduct*, is a man who worked hard, was thrifty, and had a good moral outlook. Anyone who practiced these tenets, argued Smiles, would become prosperous.[19] By the 1880s, however, the ideal of thrift was replaced by a preference for consumption. The acquisition of such showy material goods as pianos, oriental carpets, Wedgwood pottery, and Kashmir shawls was a more immediate way of demonstrating one's class than abstract values, which only became apparent through a person's words and actions over time. The transition from thrift to consumption became particularly evident with the women of the middle class who adorned their bodies in beautiful, expensive-looking clothing and accessories, which acted as a symbol of their status and that of their family.

The emergence of the middle class has traditionally been examined as a masculine/public phenomenon, especially by historians writing in the 1950s to mid-1990s.[20] More recently, historians such as Davidoff and Hall, Mary Ryan, David Kuchta, and Simon Gunn and Rachel Bell have looked at how women, the home, and writings about domesticity were sites of class formation.[21] However, these works do not look at the specifics of how middle-class women helped create their class through seemingly mundane decisions made on a day-to-day basis. In the nineteenth century, certain fabrics, colors, sizes, and even the complexion of the skin became markedly middle class. The material that is presented here shows that middle-class women used fashion as an outward symbol of rank that helped them express pride in their social status and allowed them and their families to advance socially.[22]

CONSUMPTION AND THE MIDDLE CLASS

A number of financial and social trends that became evident by the mid-nineteenth century made it possible for women to contribute to their class formation and differentiation through consumption. The middle class forsook its earlier ideology of thrift and saving, which was evident in the middling sort at the beginning of the century, and replaced it with consumption. This was made possible because middle-class incomes rose by as much as £100 per person between 1850 and 1870. To make this trend in income growth even more pronounced, prices during this period increased slowly, by only 16 percent, a figure well below income growth. Economic expansion was coupled with a decrease in family size and later age of marriage. Couples began married life in a higher income bracket and sustained their lifestyle by having fewer children.[23] Finally, in the 1850s there was a dramatic increase of white-collar employment due to the growth of clerical jobs, which led to an expansion of the lower middle class (whose yearly incomes were £100–£200).[24] Though most women tended not to make money, they were the ones who spent much of the household income. As part of their roles as conspicuous consumers, women bought clothing and accessories to show off their husbands' wealth.[25]

Though dramatic changes in consumption became evident in the mid-nineteenth century, due to the faster production of the factory system and improved transport, the shift in consumption patterns had begun in the early modern period as more people gained access to luxury goods of all kinds.[26] Also in the early modern period there was a change in people's attitudes toward consumption. What came to be termed "the luxury debate" spurred a shift in economic philosophy making it a moral economic good to consume. Maxine Berg, a leading scholar of luxury, suggests that before the eighteenth century the term *luxury* had negative connotations: it was associated with the sin of excess and the debauchery of the very rich.[27] Discussions of lavishness in this earlier period often reflected fears about whether or not social hierarchies would remain if everyone was allowed to consume the same things. By the eighteenth century, such sumptuous objects as silk, porcelain, mahogany, sugar, tea, and chocolate, which were once considered luxuries of the rich, began to be available to the middling classes. "The appearance of these goods," Berg suggests, "coincides with a new civility in middling and upper-class society which was conveyed in new ways of eating and socializing."[28]

As a result of the increased availability of opulent goods and the new trend toward civility, moralists, economists, and novelists debated whether luxury goods were signs of extravagance and self-indulgence that would corrupt the populace, or if they were an improving force that acted as an instrument and indication of progress in Britain. Mercantilist tracts such as Dudley North's *Discourses upon Trade* (1691), Nicholas Barbon's *A Discourse of Trade* (1690), and Adam Smith's *An Inquiry into the Nature and Causes of the Wealth of Nations* (1776) were influential in putting forward the argument that extravagant consumption was not a question of morality; rather increased consumption would benefit all classes by providing jobs for workers, and a reason for people to save so that they might be able to afford extra comforts.[29] It was not until the later 1820s, however, that Smith's ideas were taken up by a larger community.[30] In the beginning decades of the nineteenth century, then, and progressively more throughout the century, the middle class believed itself to be part of a mass-market economy that incorporated an abundance of goods available to all classes rather than an economy based on scarcity and hierarchy. This shift in thinking about opulence as a social and economic benefit helped spur the nineteenth-century middle-class consumption of luxury goods that originated in such far-off places as Japan, China, India, and Africa.

The 1830s was also a revolutionary moment for the press. Between 1800 and 1830 the number of newspaper stamps, a special type of stamp used to send newspapers and periodicals in the regular postal system, doubled from sixteen to thirty million. This trend continued into the nineteenth century; between 1868 and 1900 provincial dailies increased from 43 to 171. At the same time, printing became less expensive because of steam power and the mechanization of paper making.[31] These changes allowed the women's press, which began at the end of the eighteenth century, to proliferate and provide practical fashion advice for the well-off middle-class lady.[32] Further, by the 1880s advertisements had become visually and textually persuasive. This new advertising was directed specifically at middle-class women.[33]

All of these phenomena—the creation of a middle-class consciousness, the expansion of consumerism, the changing concepts of luxury, and the greater availability of fashion news—produced an environment where advertisers, authors, and women wrote and thought about the meaning of newly available women's accessories.

MATERIAL CULTURE, GENDER, CLASS, AND RACE

What makes a study of women's accessories so interesting is that they were embroiled in many of the controversies of the day. The accessories I have chosen acted like lightning rods for larger issues; they were props that helped women perform their gender, they played a central role in helping women sustain their class status (which was fraught with tension because of the contradictions of a leisured housewife who had to do manual labor), and they helped show women's interest and involvement in British colonialism. The type of analysis that puts accessories into their historical context and views them as an entrée into the beliefs, dreams, and anxieties of Victorians is a relatively new form of analysis within fashion history. This analysis has been encouraged by the advent of material culture studies.

Between 1960 and 1980 a new way of studying historical objects emerged that came to be called "material culture."[34] One of the movement's founding members, Jules Prown, defines material culture as "the study through artifacts of the beliefs—values, ideas, attitudes and assumptions—of a particular community or society at a given time."[35] By the 1980s historians of fashion began to incorporate the ideas of material culture into their work by taking into account the role that clothing played in the society that produced it. Valerie Steele, for example, documents the meaning of fashion for Victorians. She looks at fashion in nineteenth and early twentieth century Britain to determine how ideals of beauty, respectability, and class became manifest at any given moment through clothing.[36] Material culture has also had an impact on the study of accessories. Historians have looked at specific objects—corsets, makeup, collars, handkerchiefs—as important cultural symbols in their own right. Because they are human-made artifacts these accessories unconsciously reflect the ideals of the individuals who manufactured and consumed them, and by extension they reveal the concerns and beliefs of the culture at large.

The advantage of thinking with objects is that we can discover contradictions between what people said and what they did. As I researched I began to see specific ideas and narratives appearing again and again. I started to understand that language was used to create distinct ways of seeing the world, which made Victorian ways of thinking distinct from our own. While I present the stories that Victorians told about their objects I also describe the everyday practices of using and consuming accessories. Discourses of democracy appear in the primary sources specific to objects like gloves and umbrellas. These narratives suggest that objects are democratic agents used by all classes, the accessories proclaiming a kind of egalitarianism across class lines. Though this written discourse exists, in everyday practice, there are major differences in what people bought based on what they could afford. As conspicuous consumers, Victorians were well versed in decoding the quality of the objects, and in turn, the class of those who owned and used the articles.

British historians have yet to study women's accessories for what they reveal about the Victorians in terms of gender, class, and race. The present study is unique because it opens a window into the minute practices of everyday life. It asks such questions as: how did women brush their hair, what did they put on their hands, why were parasols popular? The Victorian interaction with their accessories reveals a rich cultural nexus. Analyzing the way middle-class women used these objects shows very clearly the intimate entanglements among race, class, and gender. Anne McClintock's *Imperial Leather* argues that "race, gender and class are not distinct realms of experience, existing in splendid isolation from each other; nor can they be simply yoked together retrospectively. . . . Rather, they come into existence *in and through* relations to each other."[37] I reexamine McClintock's claims in relation to seemingly innocuous aspects of daily life; in doing this, the book reinterprets and expands her analysis. The work sketches a loose arc from the early Victorian period to the Edwardian period, demonstrating the interconnectedness of race, class, and gender across different materials and artifacts.

Accessories helped women show off their position as feminine; in the Victorian period this meant creating a pronounced gender difference between men and women. The feminist scholar Judith Butler suggests that femininity is an identity constructed through a series of gestures and movements that come to represent "womanhood."[38] In Butler's work the female body "becomes its gender through a series of acts which are renewed, revised and consolidated through time."[39] Victorian women were encouraged to use accessories as props that helped them perform passivity, asexuality, innocence, coyness, and leisure. Perfectly white gloves worn by a woman in public demonstrated to onlookers that she was a leisured lady who had servants who cooked and cleaned for her. A young woman used the vanity set to keep her hair long and flowing, proclaiming her innocence. Her married mother employed the same accessories to create a well-kept updo demonstrating respectability and sexual unavailability. The soft flutter of the fan near another woman's cheek, her gaze cast downward, gave the impression of shyness, but the same woman on promenade with her parasol playfully twirling and framing her pretty face with the colorful silk was considered flirtatious. Women used their accessories to perform the bodily acts that made up middle-class femininity.

Performance was not only about femininity, the buying of clothes and use of accessories was also highly enmeshed in questions of social class. Writing in the late nineteenth century, American economist Thorstein Veblen argued that middle-class women were supposed to establish their family's status by buying and using more and more extravagant fashions that helped show they led a leisured lifestyle.[40] Davidoff and Hall demonstrated that an ideal middle-class household had a working husband and a domestic wife.[41] The men of the family worked in professional jobs and women were imagined as leisured household managers who employed servants to do the manual labor around the house. Victorians themselves believed that keeping a domestic servant marked the division between the middle and working classes.[42] However, necessity dictated that many middle-class women, especially those of the lower middle class who could only afford one maid-of-all-work, had to do housework and gardening alongside their servants. The bind in which women found themselves—acting leisured while participating in unpaid work—created anxiety that became evident in etiquette manuals and fashion plates, but was also played out across the bodies of women. Women were acutely aware that their class was not automatically evident, but that it had to be constantly maintained, demonstrated, and proven by adjusting their outer appearance.

The lower middle class was desperately in need of accessories to maintain its status. By the end of the century the reality for many lower-middle-class households was that they were generating less income than their unionized working-class counterparts, especially since working-class women were economic contributors to the household. The strain on lower-middle-class wives to perform unpaid household labor was enormous and women who could not find husbands were in a similar situation, being forced to find some small wage for themselves, while restricted to work that was suited to their gender and class. Women who found themselves in these situations still maintained a separation from the servant class by buying expensive clothing and presenting their bodies in culturally sanctioned ways. Accessories such as gloves and parasols helped to hide the effects of women's labor by protecting their skin—the primary surface where labor becomes evident in the form of chapping, tanning, and dirt. And etiquette manuals, short stories, and phrenology advocates warned women that an overexposure to sun and dirt would transform their bodies from that of a middle-class lady to a working-class laborer. Being part of the middle class required secrecy when it came to household labor and performance when it came to fashion and leisure.[43]

The fear of appearing to be of the working class was exaggerated because there was more at stake than a simple fall in social rank. Throughout the nineteenth century there was a conflation of race and class fears.[44] Social workers who entered London's poor East End often imagined that they were headed into Africa or some other unexplored colonial territory. The people in these areas, though they were British citizens, were seen as a race apart; their habits studied and judged as if they were part of an anthropological study. Upper- and middle-class men and women such as Henry Mayhew, Jack London, Andrew Mearns, Beatrice Webb, and Olive Christina Malvery published investigative reports of their travels into "Unknown England," often likening the metropolitan poor to savages.[45]

The most famous example of the racialization of the poor was Mayhew's *London Labour and the London Poor* (1851–1852) where the term *vagabond savage* first appeared.[46] Mayhew's schema separates the world into "two distinct and broadly marked races, viz., the wanderers and the settlers—the vagabond and the citizen—the nomadic and the civilized tribes." He then grafts the "socially, morally and perhaps even physically" distinct racial characteristics of the vagabond nomad onto the poor of London.[47] Mayhew uses the term *vagabond savage* to describe street sellers and costmongers within the city:

"these two classes may be used to describe the *natives* of the streets—the tribe *indigenous* to the paving stones—imbibing the habits and morals of the gutters almost with their mother's milk. To expect that children thus nursed in the lap of the kennel, should when men not bear the impress of the circumstances amid which they have been reared, is to expect to find costermongers heroes instead of ordinary human beings." Mayhew's writing then slips from a class description to a racial one: "We might as well blame the various races on the face of the earth for those several geographical peculiarities of taste, which constitute their national characteristics. Surely there is a moral acclimatization as well as a physical one, and the heart may become inured to a particular atmosphere in the same manner as the body; and even as the seed of the apple returns, unless grafted, to its original crab, so does the child, without training, go back to its parent stock—the vagabond savage."[48] The term that Mayhew so dramatically ends with, "the vagabond savage," combines class and race to describe the poorest of the poor in the colonial capital. To Mayhew the roguish element of the vagabond was comparable to those of foreign nomads. Along the same lines, London's *The People of the Abyss* depicts the East End as a social pit. He believed that Anglo Saxons had become separated into two white races due to industrialization: the ghetto race and the master race. "If this is the best that civilization can do for the human," London lamented, "then give us howling and naked savagery. Far better to be a people of the wilderness and desert, of cave and squatting place than to be of the machine and the Abyss."[49]

These depictions likening the London poor to Africans were not only found in the books written by social workers but also in etiquette manuals of the period. Beads made of colored pastes, or mosaic gold overlaid onto wood or metal, should never be seen in women's jewelry, claimed the author of *Etiquette for the Ladies* (1837). "Nothing can more severely or more truly satirize this taste than the fancy of the Negro chief in the interior of Africa, who received an Englishman's visit of ceremony in a drummer's jacket and judge's wig!"[50] Here again we see an author slipping from a description of a British citizen into an African simpleton; the shift is brought to mind because of something as simple as a fake gold necklace. Due to depictions such as these, the working class was linked in the popular imagination with the colonized other. This conflation of race and class helped solidify the more tenuous distinctions between the classes.

The apprehension that English people felt about race stemmed from the status of Britain as a colonial world power.[51] In 1891, the population of Britain was 37,880,764 and the population of Europeans (mostly British) in India was 165,000, which meant that there was one European in India for every 230 in Britain.[52] Though women would have been a fraction of those who lived in the empire, they participated in the British colonial project by consuming objects that were represented in the Victorian imagination as imperial spoils. By looking at women's accessories we can see that in the smallest ways empire infused the everyday lives of Victorian women. Objects sourced in the colonies were incorporated into women's lives in catalogues that emphasized the imperial origin of ivory brushes, popular magazines that featured articles about the oriental history of umbrellas, and fans that were painted in Japanese patterns. Other objects, like the parasol and the glove, were involved in maintaining white skin. According to the narratives of scientific racism that abounded in the period, whiteness represented a racially superior complexion. There was a scientific justification for imperial rule, which was dependent on the skin color and the "civilized" practices of different colonies. It was imperative that women, especially, kept their pale complexion because they were highlighted as representatives of the British race.[53] These findings challenge the work of Bernard Porter, which deemphasizes the place of imperialism in Victorian society. Porter argues that many Britons were unaware of their imperial stature in the nineteenth century, and only a small number of citizens were committed to it in any way. Porter asks: "In what ways can [Britain] be said to have been an imperial *society*, as well as an imperial nation?"[54] I and other historians show that contrary to Porter's thesis, middle-class Britain was an imperial society that incorporated physical reminders of the empire into novels, the education system, Boy Scouts, public entertainment, architecture, and even in simple household objects.[55]

This book also contributes to the debate about women's role in imperialism. According to Antoinette Burton, such nineteenth and early twentieth century feminists as Josephine Butler, Millicent Garrett Fawcett, and Mary Carpenter Burton, blindly accepted British imperial thinking.[56] These authors suggest that oriental womanhood represented sexual difference, primitive society, and colonial backwardness. My research shows that these characterizations extended beyond feminist debates. They became part of average women's lives in the form of accessories. In terms of sexual difference, the fan in the hands of a Japanese woman represented innocence and submissiveness while in the hands of a British woman it represented emancipation from the domestic sphere, because British women were paid to design and paint fans, and it represented women's active participation in the marriage market through fan flirtation. Umbrellas, also, became part of the story that British people used to see themselves as different from their colonial subjects. In the colonial context the umbrella was used mainly by royalty. The British interpreted this as a sign of despotism and therefore politically backward in comparison to their own tradition of democratizing the umbrella and the people of their nation. By using accessories women entered the debate about Britain's geopolitical supremacy over its colonies. In their everyday use of objects, they subdued the great beasts of Africa into dainty ivory combs. They used fans to emphasize the difference between the emancipated woman of the West and the submissive women of the East. And they read about the umbrella as a sign of despotism of the non-Western nations.

THE SOURCES OF A MATERIAL CULTURALIST

The sources used for this project were widely available at the time and helped me to capture a thorough understanding of the objects under study. I have looked at a wide selection of images and documents, all of which generated different perspectives on the accessories and helped to broaden their cultural meaning. In order to decipher how women interacted with their accessories on a day-to-day basis, prescriptive literature (instructive manuals and essays) and direct observation of the objects were particularly useful. Etiquette manuals,[57] women's magazines,[58] and fashion plates[59] give historians a sense of the way women were ideally supposed to relate with their accessories and when and how they wore them. Etiquette manuals often provide step-by-step details about how to make the hair shiny and smooth, women's magazines explained what type of parasol to take on a promenade as opposed to a carriage ride, and fashion plates helped women see an entire ensemble so that they might understand what accessories were needed with which outfits.

Personal interaction with Victorian accessories was important for confirming or rethinking the claims presented in Victorian publications or by historians. To complete my understanding of women's day-to-day relations with their accessories I visited various museums to view the accessories firsthand. Explorations of the collections at the Museum of London, Axminster Museum, the Fan Museum, and the Museum of Costume at Bath allowed me to observe and handle the accessories as a Victorian woman might have done. In this way the historian can interact with the past by touching what others have touched, wearing what others have worn, and even feeling what others have felt. This is a very different interaction with the past than when we use written sources. With recorded words, we interact with the minds of the past, whereas with material culture our senses interact with the past to understand it in new ways. At the museums I observed, for example, the way that the sun shone through brightly colored parasols casting different shades and tones onto my skin as I stood underneath them. I fluttered fans of various constructions and found out which ones were used for cooling and which were only for show. I observed the minute sizes of kid gloves that gave me a sense of the proportions of the ideal hand. And I handled plastic and ivory vanity sets to get a sense of the different weight and feel of the two and how they would encourage a sense of beauty in the user.

For background on the manufacture and promotion of accessories, I examined trade journals, company records, union records, and government reports. These types of sources helped me to see the early stages of the fashion system as they indicate the meanings that manufacturers, unions, and governments placed onto objects before they entered the consumer market. These sources provide the behind-the-scenes trends in procuring materials and manufacturing products, and they give further details about consumption such as seasonal buying patterns. For example, *The Brush Journal*, the trade journal that covered the bristle, brush, and comb trades, reported consistently on the price and volume of ivory and boar's bristle coming into British ports.[60] The editors of *The Bag, Portmanteau and Umbrella Trader* bemoaned the fact that fewer parasols were sold when fashionable hats became larger and better able to protect the complexion.[61] The United Society of Brushmakers controlled such issues of manufacture and professionalization as which master brushmakers were able to work for, how long boys must apprentice, and what tasks required greater payment.[62] Government reports such as *Report of the Departmental Committee on Celluloid* or "The Case of the Fann-Makers Who Have Petitioned the Honorable House of Commons, against the Importation of Fanns from the East-Indies [sic]" show the government's concern for individuals when it came to potentially flammable plastics, and issues of free trade when it came to the deluge of inexpensive fans flooding the British market from the East Indies.[63] Finally, company records such as the Xylonite Company Archives, housed at the Science Museum and Library, delineate the early history and financial standing of the first plastic manufacturer in England.[64] All of these developments, from union rulings to manufacturer concerns to government interference, helped to create the circumstances under which the accessories were consumed and understood in the wider world.

By simply typing "umbrella" or "fan" into library catalogues I found that accessories had a place in more generalized popular sources of the Victorian period. These searches helped me to find fictional representations in plays, novels, songs, and short stories, which then helped me to tap into the subconscious meanings that objects carried for the culture at large. In short stories such as "A Study about the Umbrella-Mender" (1889), umbrellas were used as metaphors for the personalities of various characters.[65] Stage directions and lyrics in musical plays like *The Mikado* (1885) delineate the movements and the coy looks that made fans devices of flirtation.[66] Songs such as "Rotten Cotton Glove" satirically drew the line between the middle-class lady's kid glove and working-class women's cotton glove.[67] Finally, novels like *The Little Green Glove* (1920) show the intimate connections between women and their accessories (in this story a spurned lover kept his girlfriend's glove and used it to trigger memories of their time together).[68] Popular fiction tapped into various areas that other sources could not—it allowed class and character to come to the forefront, it made visible the specific (if exaggerated) ways that women flirted, and it drew out the intimate connections between women and their accessories. In these ways, writers of popular fiction both created and developed the collective unconscious that surrounded accessories.

To get a sense of the objects' purported histories, I looked at such contemporary publications as articles in periodicals and newspapers and small books dedicated to specific accessories. These are somewhat fanciful histories that helped prop up existing understandings of British history and the country's position as a world power. Books and articles like *Fans: A Brief Sketch of Their Origin and Use* (1896) and "Umbrella Evolution: The Umbrella and Parasol in History" (1909) make up a history of fans belittling "the orient," where the accessories originated, and praising the British for their innovation and perfection of the items.[69] In the books like *A Brief Description of the Manufacture, History and Associations of Gloves* (1890s) the story is concentrated in England's past. The history of the glove went back to the days of knightly chivalry when ladies lent their gloves to soldiers in battle to ensure their safety, and courtly rule when gloves were thrown down in front of new kings to demonstrate support for their monarchy.[70] While the histories are not accurate, they are useful in helping to understand the way that Victorians saw themselves and their past, and the way that they viewed their role in the wider world.

Figure 0.2 To end this introduction we return to the young lady that we started with; here the fan/calendar is closed revealing the lady's bosom. 1897. John Johnson Collection of Printed Ephemera.

Finally, there was a great amount of ephemera surrounding these objects. For research in this area I visited the John Johnson Collection at the Bodleian Library, which included advertisements, pamphlets, song sheets, fashion plates, department store catalogues, a collection of paper fans, and exhibition catalogues. One of my favorite pieces of ephemera is a calendar that opens and closes this introductory chapter (figure 0.1 and figure 0.2). A beautiful young woman coyly looks over her fan into the eyes of her onlooker, her head is slightly tilted and she has a smile on her face, as if she is in the process of seducing the one who uses the calendar printed on her fan leaves. The image reminds me of the pin-up calendars of the 1940s, especially when the fan/calendar is closed and the woman's bosom is revealed. Sources like this one, that incorporate objects like the fan in a whimsical way, create a sense of the deluge of imagery surrounding accessories that appeared at the very moment that these objects became widely bought and consumed. The varied selection of primary sources used for this project helped me form an understanding of the meaning these objects had at different moments of their life cycle from manufacture, to consumption, to daily use, to the object as a referent with grand cultural implications.

The study of accessories helps to demonstrate how the larger interests of the Victorian culture were reflected in common household objects. When studied in their context, women's accessories open up lines of inquiry that lead to questions of how the category "middle class" became manifest through consumption, how whiteness, leisure, and femininity were performed on an everyday basis, and how concepts of empire and British superiority became incorporated into women's dress. Additionally, the study of everyday objects used by Victorians can help us to understand the subconscious ideals of the culture that created them (figure 0.2).

NOTES

1. There has been considerable work done on shoes, hats, and bags. See for example: Georgine De Courtais, *Women's Headdress and Hairstyles: In England from* A.D. *600 to Present Day* (London: B.T. Batsford, 1973); Vanda Foster, *Bags and Purses*, The Costume Accessories Series, ed. Aileen Ribeiro (London: B.T. Batsford, 1982); Anne Buck, *Victorian Costume and Costume Accessories*, 2nd ed. (Carlton: Ruth Bean, 1984); Giorgio Riello and Peter McNeil, *Shoes: A History from Sandals to Sneakers* (London: Palgrave, 2006); Valerie Steele, *Shoes: A Lexicon of Style* (London: Scriptum Editions, 1998); and June Swann, *Shoes* (London: B.T. Batsford, 1982).
2. Michael Curtin, *Propriety and Position: A Study of Victorian Manners* (New York: Garland, 1987); Nancy W. Ellenberger, "The Transformation of London 'Society' at the End of Victoria's Reign: Evidence from the Court

Presentation Records," *Albion* 22 (1990): 633–53; Marjorie Morgan, *Manners, Morals and Class in England, 1774–1858* (Houndmills: Macmillan, 1994).

3. Anon., *The Ladies' Hand-Book of the Toilet: A Manual of Elegance and Fashion* (London: H. Gt. Clarke and Co., 1843), vii.

4. Elisa Bisbee Duffery, *The Ladies' and Gentlemen's Etiquette: A Complete Manual of the Manners and Dress of American Society* (Philadelphia: Porter and Coats, 1877), 236.

5. Mrs. Robert Noble, *Every Woman's Toilet Book* (London: George Newnes, 1908), 80.

6. Anon., *Etiquette for Ladies; with Hints on the Preservation, Improvement, and Display of Female Beauty* (Philadelphia: Lea & Blanchard, 1840), 118–23.

7. The brush, comb, and mirror are the elements that constitute the most basic vanity sets. Some sets had dozens of add-ons such as cuticle pushers, glove stretchers, and perfume bottles.

8. Gloves were used into the 1950s but no longer worn constantly after 1920. Vanity sets lasted into the interwar period. For more information on this see: Ariel Beaujot, "Coiffing Vanity: A Study of the Manufacture, Design, and Meaning of the Celluloid Hairbrush in America, 1900–1930," in *Producing Fashion*, ed. Reggie Balszczyk, Hagley Perspectives on Business and Culture (Philadelphia: University of Pennsylvania Press, 2007), 229–54.

9. Branca argues that the lower-middle-class minimum income in 1867 should be in the £100–£300 range. In this she argues with Banks who puts the minimum income at £300. Branca suggests the change in minimum income because the advice manuals seem to reflect a lower income. Banks considers £900 the lower limit of the upper-middle-class income in 1851, but Musgrove argues that £1,000 is the lower limit for this social strata. Joseph Ambrose Banks, *Prosperity and Parenthood: A Study of Family Planning among the Victorian Middle Classes, International Library of Sociology and Social Reconstruction* (London: Routledge & Paul, 1954), 48; Patricia Branca, *Silent Sisterhood: Middle-Class Women in the Victorian Home* (London: Croom Helm, 1975), 38–59; F. Musgrove, "Middle-Class Education and Employment in the Nineteenth-Century," *Economic History Review*, 2nd series XII (August 1959): 91–111.

10. In their definition of the English middle classes Roy Lewis and Angus Maude argue that the family is the basis for social class. Any individual who technically falls out of the class could still consider herself middle class due to her family background. The problem of "redundant" women is a case in point. Many women formerly of the middle class could not find husbands and therefore fell below middle-class income levels. However, Victorians concerned with "The Surplus Women Question" continued to

consider these women middle class. Roy Lewis and Angus Maude, *The English Middle Classes* (London: Phoenix House, 1949), 15.

11. The idea of class was invented by Karl Marx who was especially concerned with the formation of the working class. In the Marxist tradition once the working class became conscious of its mutual oppression it came to consider itself a social class. Postmodern scholars, such as Gilmore and Dimock, have moved beyond the concept of class as a definite and definable social category arguing instead that class is an identity that needs to be achieved and maintained. In this view a person is not working class or middle class until she defines herself as such and acts and consumes in a way that will put her into her desired class position. Michael T. Gilmore and Wai Chee Dimock, *Rethinking Class: Literary Studies and Social Formations* (New York: Columbia University Press, 1994), 2–3.

12. Leonore Davidoff and Catherine Hall, *Family Fortunes: Men and Women of the English Middle Class, 1780–1850*, Women in Culture and Society (Chicago: University of Chicago Press, 1987).

13. Dror Wahrman, *Imagining the Middle Class: The Political Representation of Class in Britain, c. 1780–1840* (Cambridge: Cambridge University Press, 1995).

14. Veblen was an American economist and sociologist of the late nineteenth and early twentieth centuries. His most famous book, *The Theory of the Leisure Class*, is often seen as a satire about the upper middle class who consumed extravagant clothing and participated in time-wasting leisure activities in order to show that they had an abundance of money. Thorstein Veblen, *The Theory of the Leisure Class: An Economic Study of Institutions* (New York: New American Library, [1899] 1953).

15. I disagree with Patrick Joyce who suggests that culturally, the middle class shared much with the aristocracy and even workers. In *Democratic Subjects,* Joyce shows that a radical parliamentarian and an artisan engaged in a rhetoric of populism, which was not antagonistic but instead suggested that all people are part of an organic whole. In *Visions of the People* Joyce argues that the working class is not a separate entity, but shares middle-class concerns for respectability, patriotism, piety, liberty, and peaceful reform. Patrick Joyce, *Visions of the People: Industrial England and the Question of Class, 1848–1914* (Cambridge: Cambridge University Press, 1991); Patrick Joyce, *Democratic Subjects: The Self and the Social in Nineteenth-Century England* (Cambridge: Cambridge University Press, 1994).

16. Dror Wahrman argues that the middle class was an idiom before it was a group of people. He states that revolutionary threats between 1790 and 1840 necessitated the emergence of a "middle-class idiom," which was a repository for all the virtues of society and acted as the glue that

held the rest of society together. Wahrman believes that the idiom later became attached to the middling sort who increased in numbers throughout the nineteenth century. Wahrman, *Imagining the Middle Class.*

17. Davidoff and Hall, *Family Fortunes.*

18. Dianne Sachko Macleod, *Art and the Victorian Middle Class: Money and the Making of Cultural Identity* (Cambridge: Cambridge University Press, 1996); Alan Kidd and David Nicholls, eds., *Gender, Civic Culture and Consumerism: Middle-Class Identity in Britain 1800–1940* (Manchester: Manchester University Press, 1999).

19. Samuel Smiles, *Self-Help; with Illustrations of Character, Conduct, and Perseverance* (New York: Allison, 1859).

20. Men of the middle class became more visible in government and administration in the early Victorian period. Middle-class men received voting rights due to the Great Reform Act of 1832, and they put pressure on the government to protect their money resulting in the New Poor Laws of 1834, and the Repeal of the Corn Law in 1846. Perkin explores the rise of the middle class through the new professions of the nineteenth century. Searle explores how Victorians tried to reconcile their economic convictions with their ethical principles; partly they did this by identifying the boundaries of what was right and wrong (slavery, addictive drugs, and pornography), partly by protecting certain occupations from the pressures of market competition (doctors, lawyers), and partly by separating the market from family. Harold James Perkin, *The Rise of Professional Society: England since 1880* (London: Routledge, 1989); G. R. Searle, *Morality and the Market in Victorian Britain* (Oxford: Clarendon Press, 1998).

21. David Kuchta, *The Three-Piece Suit and Modern Masculinity: England, 1550–1850* (Berkeley: University of California Press, 2002); Simon Gunn and Rachel Bell, *Middle Classes: Their Rise and Sprawl* (London: Cassell, 2002); Mary P. Ryan, *Civic Wars: Democracy and Public Life in the American City during the Nineteenth Century* (Berkeley: University of California Press, 1998).

22. I refer here to the theoretical concept of "cultural capital," which is put forth by Bourdieu, who writes about 1960s France. Cultural capital refers to nonfinancial social aspects that might increase mobility such as education, accent, intelligence, and appearance. Pierre Bourdieu, *Distinction: A Social Critique of the Judgment of Taste*, trans. Richard Nice (Cambridge, MA: Harvard University Press, 1984). Fashion and consumption have long been considered unmanly sites and practices. J. C. Flugel and D. Kuchta attribute the somber dress of aristocratic and middle-class men to what they call "the Great Masculine Renunciation" of 1688, a moment when men gave up their finery for the more

authoritative dress of the three-piece suit. Along with the sober style of clothing that emerged after the Glorious Revolution came a rhetoric that separated men and women in terms of the equation of character, fashion, and authority. While men's characters were now interpreted through their actions, the argument goes, women continued to display their inner selves through their garments. My forthcoming book about male accessories in the Victorian period argues that, like women, men's characters were represented in their clothing and accessories. Historians have often thought otherwise because men inconspicuously consume their accessories rather than conspicuously buying showy, colorful objects as do women. An aristocratic man and a middle-class man might both carry a black umbrella, for example, but the astute observer could distinguish the gentleman from the middle-class professional by the material that was used to construct the accessory (silk vs. cotton, silver vs. bone). J. C. Flugel, *The Psychology of Clothes* (New York: International University Press, 1969). David Kuchta, "The Making of the Self-Made Man: Class Clothing and English Masculinity 1688–1832," in *The Sex of Things: Gender and Consumption in Historical Perspective*, ed. Victoria De Grazia and Ellen Furlough (Berkeley: University of California Press, 1996), 55–62.

23. Banks, *Prosperity and Parenthood*.

24. Gregory Anderson, *Victorian Clerks* (Manchester: Manchester University Press, 1976). McBride confirms the increase in white-collar employment but also argues that the middle class in general was increasing during this period. She states: "the number of people who fell into the middle income bracket of 200 to 500 pounds per year doubled between 1851 and 1871, while total population increased only 11.9 per cent by 1861 and 13.2 per cent by 1871." Eeresa M. McBride, *The Domestic Revolution: The Modernisation of Household Service in England and France 1820–1920* (New York: Holmes and Meier, 1976), 19.

25. Veblen, *The Theory of the Leisure Class*.

26. Linda Levi Peck, *Consuming Splendor* (Cambridge: Cambridge University Press, 2005); Jean-Christophe Agnew, "Coming up for Air: Consumer Culture in Historical Perspective," in *Consumption and the World of Goods*, ed. John Brewer and Roy Porter (London: Routledge, 1993), 19–39; Helen Berry and Jeremy Gregory, eds., *Creating and Consuming Culture in North-East England, 1660–1830* (Aldershot: Ashgate, 2004); Jan de Vries, *The Industrious Revolution: Consumer Behavior and the Household Economy, 1650 to the Present* (Cambridge: Cambridge University Press, 2008); Elizabeth Kowaleski-Wallace, *Consuming Subjects: Women, Shopping, and Business in the Eighteenth Century* (New York: Columbia University Press, 1997); Beverly Lemire, "Second-Hand Beaux and 'Red-Armed

Belles': Conflict and the Creation of Fashions in England, c. 1660–1800," *Continuity and Change* [Great Britain] 15, no. 3 (2000): 391–417; Beverly Lemire, *Dress, Culture and Commerce: The English Clothing Trade before the Factory, 1660–1800* (London: Macmillan, 1997); Beverly Lemire, *Fashion's Favourite: The Cotton Trade and the Consumer in Britain, 1660–1800* (Oxford: Oxford University Press, 1991); Carole Shammas, *The Pre-Industrial Consumer in England and America* (Oxford: Clarendon Press, 1990); Joan Thirsk, *Economic Policy and Projects: The Development of a Consumer Society in Early Modern England* (Oxford: Clarendon Press, 1978).

27. Maxine Berg and Elizabeth Eger, eds., *Luxury in the Eighteenth Century: Debate, Desires and Delectable Goods* (New York: Palgrave Macmillan, 2003), 1. Maxine Berg, *Luxury and Pleasure in Eighteenth-Century Britain* (Oxford: Oxford University Press, 2005); Maxine Berg and Helen Clifford, eds., *Consumers and Luxury: Consumer Culture in Europe 1650–1850* (Manchester: Manchester University Press, 1999). For other works on luxury see: Carolyn Brucken, "In the Public Eye: Women and the American Luxury Hotel," *Winterthur Portfolio* 31, no. 4 (1996): 199–203; Christopher J. Berry, *The Idea of Luxury: A Conceptual and Historical Investigation* (Cambridge: Cambridge University Press, 1994); John Sekora, *Luxury: The Concept in Western Thought, Eden to Smollett* (Baltimore: Johns Hopkins University Press, 1977).

28. Berg and Eger, *Luxury in the Eighteenth Century*, 1.

29. Other British political economists writing in the late eighteenth and early nineteenth centuries like Archibald Alison, J.R. McCulloch, and Nassau Senior suggested that the intensifying global exchange of goods, increased availability of luxuries to all classes, rising wages, and the decrease in family size were all signs of the evolution and progress of the British peoples that would benefit the nation as a whole.

30. M.J.D. Roberts, "The Concept of Luxury in British Political Economy: Adam Smith to Alfred Marshall," *History of the Human Sciences* 11, no. 1 (1998): 30–35.

31. Geoffrey Alan Cranfield, *The Press and Society: From Caxton to Northcliff* (London: Longman, 1978), 119; T.R. Nevett, *Advertising in Britain: A History* (London: Heinemann, 1982), 40.

32. Margaret Beetham, *A Magazine of Her Own? Domesticity and Desire in the Women's Magazine, 1800–1914* (London: Routledge, 1996); Aled Jones, "The Press and the Printed Word," in *A Companion to Nineteenth Century Britain*, ed. Chris Williams (London: Blackwell, 2006), 376.

33. Lori Anne Loeb, *Consuming Angels: Advertising and Victorian Women* (Oxford: Oxford University Press, 1994), 7–9.

34. Early scholars of material culture including Beckow, Glassie, and Washburn saw objects as important markers of the social environment that

created them. The first discussions of material culture were heavily influenced by questions of written versus object-centered history. See for example: Steven M. Beckow, "Culture, History and Artifact," in *Material Culture Studies in America*, ed. T.J. Schlereth (Nashville: American Association for State and Local History, 1982), 114–23; Henry Glassie, "Folk Art," in *Folklore and Folklife: An Introduction*, ed. Richard Dorson (Chicago: University of Chicago Press, 1972), 253–80; William B. Hesseltine, "The Challenge of the Artifact," in *Material Culture Studies in America*, ed. T.J. Schlereth (Nashville: American Association for State and Local History, 1982), 93–100; J.T. Schlebecker, "The Use of Objects in Historical Research," *Agricultural History* 51 (1977): 200–208; D. Reidel Kouwenhoven, "American Studies: Words or Things?," in *American Studies in Transition*, ed. William Marshall Finshwick (Boston: Houghton Mifflin, 1964), 15–35; Wilcomb E. Washburn, "Manuscripts and Manufacts," *American Archivist* 27, no. 2 (1964): 245–50.

35. Jules Prown, "Mind in Matter: An Introduction to Material Culture Theory and Method," *Winterthur Portfolio* 17 (1982): 1. By the 1980s the emerging field of material culture began to define the methodology of its discipline, which would become useful for future scholars in the area. See for example: Jean Claude Dupont, "The Meaning of Objects: The Poker," in *Living in a Material World: Canadian and American Approaches to Material Culture*, ed. Gerald L. Pocius (St. John's, Newfoundland: Institute of Social and Economic Research Memorial University of Newfoundland, 1991), 1–18; Gregg Finley, "The Gothic Revival and the Victorian Church in New Brunswick: Toward a Strategy of Material Culture Research," *Material Culture Bulletin* 32 (1990): 1–16; Prown, "Mind in Matter"; Betsy Cullan-Swan and Peter K. Manning, "What Is a T-Shirt? Codes, Chorontypes, and Everyday Objects," in *The Socialness of Things: Essays on the Social-Semiotics of Objects*, ed. Stephen Harold Riggins (New York: Nouton de Gruyer, 1994), 415–33; E. McClung Fleming, "Artifact Study: A Proposed Model," *Winterthur Portfolio* 9 (1974): 153–73; Charles F. Montgomery, "The Connoisseurship of Artifacts," in *Material Culture Studies in America*, ed. Thomas J. Schlereth (Nashville: American Association for State and Local History, 1982), 143–52; Craig Gilbon, "Pop Pedagogy: Looking at the Coke Bottle," in *Material Culture Studies in America*, ed. Thomas J. Schlereth (Nashville: American Association for State and Local History, 1982), 183–91; John Dixon Hunt, "The Sign of the Object," in *History from Things: Essays on Material Culture*, ed. Steven Lubar and Kingery W. David (Washington, DC: Smithsonian Institution Press, 1993), 293–98; Perce F. Lewis, "Axioms of Reading the Landscape: Some Guides to the American Scene," in *Material Culture Studies in America*, ed. Thomas J. Schlereth (Nashville: American Association for State and Local History, 1982), 174–82; Ronald T. Marchese, "Material Culture and

Artifact Classification," in *American Material Culture: The Shape of Things around Us*, ed. Edith Mayo (Bowling Green, OH: Bowling Green State University Popular Press, 1984), 11–23; Jacques Marquet, "Objects as Instruments, Objects as Signs," in *History from Things: Essays on Material Culture*, ed. Steven Lubar and Kingery W. David (Washington, DC: Smithsonian Institution Press, 1993), 30–40.

36. Valerie Steele, *Fashion and Eroticism: Ideals of Feminine Beauty from the Victorian Era to the Jazz Age* (New York: Oxford University Press, 1985). For a thorough discussion of clothing as culturally defined see also: Valerie Steele, "Appearance and Identity," in *Men and Women: Dressing the Part*, ed. Claudia Brush Kindwell and Valerie Steele (Washington, DC: Smithsonian Institution Press, 1989), 6–21. I was also influenced by other material culture studies of the Victorian period, especially Kenneth Ames's study of hall furnishings in Victorian America and Katherine Grier's work on parlors. Kenneth L. Ames, "Meaning in Artifacts: Hall Furnishings in Victorian America," *Journal of Interdisciplinary History* 9, no. 1 (1978): 19–46; Katherine C. Grier, *Culture and Comfort: People, Parlors, and Upholstery 1850–1930* (Rochester: University of Massachusetts Press, 1988).

37. Anne McClintock, *Imperial Leather: Race, Gender and Sexuality in Colonial Conquest* (New York: Routledge, 1995), 5.

38. Judith Butler, *Bodies That Matter: On the Discursive Limits of Sex* (New York: Routledge, 1993); Judith Butler, *Gender Trouble: Feminism and the Subversion of Identity* (New York: Routledge, 1990); Judith Butler, "Performative Acts and Gender Constitution: An Essay in Phenomenology and Feminist Theory," in *Performing Feminisms: Feminist Critical Theory and Theatre*, ed. Sue Ellen Case (Baltimore: Johns Hopkins University Press, 1990), 270–82.

39. Butler, "Performative Acts and Gender Constitution," 274.

40. Veblen, *The Theory of the Leisure Class*.

41. Davidoff and Hall, *Family Fortunes*.

42. Pamela Horn, *The Rise and Fall of the Victorian Servant* (Dublin: Gill and Macmillan, 1975), 17. There is some controversy as to whether or not the lower rungs of the middle class would have been able to afford to employ a full-time domestic servant, or a maid-of-all-work. Hobsbawm, Harrison, and McBride believe that the middle class employed manual labor in the form of servants to define themselves as nonlaboring and middle class. However, Branca states that "there is no guarantee that every household in [the middle class] afforded a servant at all." Banks demonstrates that it was only at the end of the century that authors began tentatively to suggest to middle-class housewives that they could do without a maid-of-all-work. But what all of these authors indicate is that *most* middle-class families could afford and most likely did employ at

least one servant. John Fletcher Clews Harrison, *Early Victorians 1832–1851* (London: Weidenfeld and Nicolson, 1971), 110; Eric Hobsbawm, *Industry and Empire: From 1750 to the Present Day* (New York: Penguin Books, 1999), 63; Banks, *Prosperity and Parenthood*, 71; Branca, *Silent Sisterhood*, 55; McBride, *The Domestic Revolution*, 18.

43. The anxieties surrounding women's work and leisure are examined in Chapter 1 of this book: "The Beauty of Her Hands": The Glove and the Making of Middle-Class Womanhood." For information on how middle-class women felt pressure to present themselves as leisured women see: Veblen, *The Theory of the Leisure Class*; Davidoff and Hall, *Family Fortunes*. Looking at the question of women's housework, historians Anne McClintock and Patricia Branca suggest that women did not cease to work once the domestic ideology took hold, instead their work was denied by the culture at large. This situation—the need to show that one is leisured while still participating in manual labor—meant that women needed to perform their status as leisured. McClintock, *Imperial Leather*, 216; John Tosh, "New Men? Bourgeois Cult of Home," in *Victorian Values: Personalities and Perspectives in Nineteenth-Century Society*, ed. Gordon Marsden (London: Longman, 1998), 80; Patricia Branca, "Image and Reality: The Myth of the Ideal Victorian Woman," in *Clio's Consciousness Raised: New Perspectives on the History of Women*, ed. Mary S. Hartman (New York: Octagon Books, 1976), 179–90.

44. For secondary sources that explain how race and class were conflated categories see: Judith R. Walkowitz, *City of Dreadful Delight: Narratives of Sexual Danger in Late-Victorian London*, Women in Culture and Society (Chicago: University of Chicago Press, 1992); Alastair Bonnett, "How the British Working Class Became White: The Symbolic (Re)Formation of Racialized Capitalism," *Journal of Historical Sociology* 11, no. 3 (1998): 316–40; McClintock, *Imperial Leather*, 132–80.

45. Class takes on a racial component in various nineteenth-century journalistic reports. See for examples: Jack London, *The People of the Abyss* (London: Pluto Press, 1998 [1903]); Henry Mayhew, *London Labour and the London Poor* (New York: Dover Publications, 1968 [1851]); Andrew Mearns, *The Bitter Cry of Outcast London* (New York: Humanities Press, 1970 [1883]); Judith R. Walkowitz, "The Indian Women, the Flower Girl, and the Jew: Photojournalism in Edwardian London," *Victorian Studies* 42, no. 1 (1998): 3–46; Beatrice Webb, "The Diary of Beatrice Webb: 1873–1892," ed. Norman MacKenzie and Jeanne MacKenzie, Vol. 1 (Cambridge: Belknap, 1982).

46. Mayhew, *London Labour and the London Poor*, 348. For a discussion of the origin of the term *vagabond savage* see: Adam Hansen, "Exhibiting Vagrancy, 1851: Victorian London and the 'Vagabond Savage,'" in *A Mighty*

Mass of Brick and Smoke: Victorian and Edwardian Representations of London, ed. Laurence Phillips (New York: Rodopi, 2007), 61.

47. Mayhew, *London Labour and the London Poor*, 1. Often the terms *vagabond*, *wanderer*, and *nomad* are used to describe Romani people. In Mayhew's case, however, I believe he is describing the poor more broadly but at some points he does address the Romani directly. Mayhew describes the London poor thus: "The nomadic races of England are of many distinct kinds—from the habitual vagrant—half beggar, half thief—sleeping in barns, tents, and casual wards—to the mechanic on the tramp, obtaining his bed and supper from the trade societies in different towns, on his way to seek work. Between these two extremes there are several mediate varieties—consisting of peddlers, showmen, harvest-men, and all that large class who live by either selling, showing, or doing something through the country."

48. Mayhew, *London Labour and the London Poor*, 348.

49. London, *The People of the Abyss*, Chapter 24.

50. Anon., *Etiquette for the Ladies: Eighty Maxims on Dress, Manners and Accomplishments* (London: Charles Tilt, 1837), 51–52.

51. The men and women who were directly involved in empire building represented a small fraction of the British population. India, Britain's most prized colony, was an example of the small number of Anglo Saxons in the colonies at end of the century. By the time of the 1891 *Census of India*, the European community (mostly English) in India was little more than 165,000 in comparison to a total population of 287 million for the British Indian Empire as a whole (making Europeans 0.06% of the population). The occupational breakdown of Europeans was dominated by the military, which exceeded 85,000 (including 67,800 troops, 5,080 officers, and over 11,000 wives and children). Civil state employees and their families totaled about 10,500, while the railway community was approximately 6,100, leaving well over 65,000 men, women, and children supported by the professions, trade, commerce, planting, missionary work, and many other nonofficial positions. These men and women came from all levels of the British social strata: colonial officers and the upper echelons of the Indian government tended to be the younger sons of aristocrats; other state employees, professionals, and those involved in trade and commerce were typically of the upper middle class; some government officials were solidly middle class; missionaries were typically of the lower middle class; and soldiers and sailors from the working class. Elizabeth Buettner, *Empire Families: Britons and Late Imperial India* (Oxford: Oxford University Press, 2004), 8. H. G. Keene, *History of India: From the Earliest Times to the End of the Nineteenth Century, Volume II* (Edinburgh: Grant, 1915), 344. For information on the social status of missionaries see:

Catherine Hall, "William Knibb and the Constitution of the New Black Subject," in *Empire and Others: British Encounters with Indigenous Peoples, 1600–1850*, ed. Martin Daunton and Rick Halpern (Philadelphia: University of Pennsylvania Press, 2000). For information on the working class in the empire see: Linda Colley, *Captives: Britain, Empire and the World, 1600–1850* (London: Jonathan Cape, 2002), 241–68.

52. John Hitchcock, "GenDocs: Geneological History of England and Wales," http://homepage.ntlworld.com/hitch/gendocs/pop.html (accessed October 25, 2007).

53. For nineteenth-century examples of British middle-class women as representatives of the nation see: Eliza Lynn Linton, *The Girl of the Period and Other Social Essays*, 2 vols., vol. 1 (London: Richard Bentley & Son, 1883), 1–9; Noble, *Every Woman's Toilet Book*, 63. For a discussion of fashionable women as representatives of the nation see: Kristin Hoganson, "The Fashionable World: Imagined Communities of Dress," in *After the Imperial Turn: Thinking with and through the Nation*, ed. Antoinette Burton (Durham, NC: Duke University Press, 2003), 216; McClintock, *Imperial Leather*.

54. Bernard Porter, *The Absent-Minded Imperialists: Empire, Society, and Culture in Britain* (Oxford: Oxford University Press, 2004), vii. The difference in my findings and those of Porter may be a question of who was buying the consumable objects. While men might not notice the everyday colonialism in their lives we must take into consideration that the primary consumers, women, had a different sense of what they were buying and why. While the average man might not notice the imperially suggestive images to do with a bar of soap, the woman who had an intimate connection with that product through purchase and use likely did.

55. Edward Said argues that there was a culture of imperialism in the West dating back to the late eighteenth century and that cultural forms such as the novel produced, mediated, and interpreted imperialism for the West. John MacKenzie shows that from the 1880s onward ideas of empire were expressed in the education system, in youth movements such as the Boy Scouts, and in public entertainments such as music halls and exhibitions. And Felix Driver and David Gilbert's edited volume shows that Europeans cities were shaped by imperialism. Public buildings such as the Bank of England, for example, were reconstructed using Roman architecture to demonstrate the ancient roots of English imperialism, exhibitions like the Crystal Palace helped to bring the empire into the metropolis, and suburban gardens were filled with exotic plants providing the scenery of the far-off places of the world. Edward Said, *Culture and Imperialism* (London: Chatto & Windus, 1993); John M. MacKenzie, *Propaganda and Empire: The Manipulation of British Public Opinion, 1880–*

1960 (Manchester: Manchester University Press, 1984), 3; Felix Driver and David Gilbert, eds., *Imperial Cities: Landscape, Display and Identity* (Manchester: Manchester University Press, 1999). For other sources on European metropoles and colonial styles see: Patrick Conner, *Oriental Architecture in the West* (London: Thames and Hudson, 1979); Raymond Head, *The Indian Style* (London: George Allen & Unwin, 1986).

56. Antoinette Burton, *Burdens of History: British Feminists, Indian Women, and Imperial Culture, 1865–1915* (Chapel Hill: University of North Carolina Press, 1994).

57. For examples of etiquette manuals see: Anon., *Complete Etiquette for Ladies and Gentlemen: A Guide to the Rules and Observances of Good Society* (London: Ward, Lock and Co., 1900); Anon., *Etiquette for All; or, Rules of Conduct for Every Circumstance in Life: With the Laws, Rules, Precepts, and Practices of Good Society* (Glasgow: George Watson, 1861); Anon., *Etiquette for Ladies and Gentlemen* (London: Frederick, Warne and Co., 1876); Anon., *Etiquette for the Ladies*; Anon., *The Ladies' Hand-Book of the Toilet*; Anon., *The Science of Dress for Ladies and Gentlemen* (London: Groombridge and Sons, 1857); Anon., *The Woman of the Future* (London: J. G. Berger, 1869); Ada S. Ballin, *The Science of Dress in Theory and Practice* (London: Sampson Low, Marston, Searle, & Rivington, 1885); Lady Colin Campbell, *Etiquette of Good Society* (London: Cassell and Company, 1893); Maud Cooke, *Twentieth Century Hand-Book of Etiquette* (Philadelphia: Co-Operative Publishing, 1899); Maud C. Cooke, *Social Etiquette; or, Manners and Customs of Polite Society: Containing Rules of Etiquette for All Occasions* (London: McDermid & Logan, 1896); Noble, *Every Woman's Toilet Book*; Florence B. Jack and Rita Strauss, *The Woman's Book: Contains Everything a Woman Ought to Know* (London: T. C. & E. C. Jack, 1911); Sylvia, *How to Dress Well on a Shilling a Day: Ladies' Guide to Home Dressmaking and Millinery* (London: Ward, Lock & Tyler, 1876).

58. Women's magazines used for this project include: *The Illustrated London News, The Ladies' Monthly Museum, Myra's Journal of Dress and Fashion, Cosmopolitan, Beauty and Fashion: A Weekly Illustrated Journal for Women, Household Words: A Weekly Journal, Woman's Art-Journal*, and *Ladies' Magazine of Fashion*.

59. Fashion plates were seen at the John Johnson Collection of Printed Ephemera as well as in the following women's magazines: *The Queen: The Lady's Newspaper, The London and Paris Ladies' Magazine, Townsend's Monthly Selection of Paris Costumes, The Ladies' Cabinet of Fashion, Music and Romance, Ladies' Magazine of Fashion*, and *Le Journal des Demoiselles*.

60. *The Brush Journal* 1–5 (1895–1899).

61. *The Bag, Portmanteau and Umbrella Trader* (1907–1910).

62. For information on the United Society of Brush Makers see: United Society of Brush Makers, *Balance Sheets and Report with Names and Amounts Paid to Receivers to End of March 1894* (London: F. W. Worthy, Trade Union Printer, 1894); United Society of Brush Makers, *List of Fair Employers* (London: Issued by the Society, 1892, 1893); James Greenwood, Hohn Birchall, Walter Marshaman, Eli Norton, Thomas Stonehouse, George Stonehouse, Henry Earnshaw, and George Hulme, "A Collection of Leaflets etc., Issued by the Society" (Manchester: United Society of Brush Makers, 1894); John K. Boyd, Thomas Elliott, Joseph Willis, and A. J. Cockburn, "United Society of Brush Makers, 43 Stanhope Street, Newcastle-on-Tyne" (Newcastle-on-Tyne: United Society of Brush Makers, 1894); William Kiddier, *The Brushmaker and the Secrets of His Craft: His Romance* (London: Sir Isaac Pitman & Sons, 1928); United Society of Brush Makers, *General Trade Rules of the United Society of Brush Makers* (London: Printed by F. W. Worthy, Trade Union Printer, 1894).

63. Celluloid Committee, *Report of the Departmental Committee on Celluloid Presented to Both Houses of Parliament by Command of His Majesty* (London: His Majesty's Stationary Office by Eyre and Spottiswoode, 1913); Fann-makers, "The Case of the Fann-Makers Who Have Petitioned the Honorable House of Commons, against the Importation of Fanns from the East-Indies," in *Early English Books, 1641–1700; 1664: 5* (1695).

64. British Xylonite Company, *Catalogue of Articles Manufactured from Xylonite and Other Plastics* (Hasell: Watson and Viney, 1936); British Xylonite Company, *Halex 1950* (London: The British Xylonite Company, 1950); British Xylonite Co., *Halex Catalogue* (London: The British Xylonite Company, 1950); British Xylonite Company, *Halex Catalogue* (London: The British Xylonite Company, 1954); British Xylonite Company, *Halex: Export Price List* (London: Haleford Press, 1949); British Xylonite Company, *Catalogue of Xylonite Articles* (London: Gale and Polden, 1931); Halex Limited, *Catalogue of Articles Manufactured from Plastics and Other Materials by Halex Limited* (London: Halex Limited, 1939); British Xylonite Company, *Catalogue of Xylonite Articles* (London: Gale and Polden, 1931).

65. B. Harraden, "A Study about the Umbrella-Mender," *Blackwood's Edinburgh Magazine* 146 (1889): 122–31.

66. W. S. Gilbert, *The Mikado; or, The Town of Titipu* (Studio City, CA: Players Press, 1997).

67. George Arthurs, Harry Gifford, and Fred E. Cliffe, "Rotten Cotton Gloves," (London: Montgomery & Co., 1928).

68. Mary Hoskin, "The Little Green Glove," in *The Little Green Glove and Other Stories*, ed. Mary Hoskin (Toronto: Extension Print, 1920), 1–90.

69. For examples of the history of the fan see: Anon., "Fans in Past and Present Times," *The Queen* 72 (1882); Max von Boehn, *Modes and Man-*

ners: Ornaments; Lace, Fans, Gloves, Walking-Sticks, Parasols, Jewelry and Trinkets (London: J.M. Dent & Sons, 1929); Liberty & Co., Fans: A Brief Sketch of Their Origin and Use (London: Liberty & Co., 1896); M.A. Flory, A Book about Fans: The History of Fans and Fan-Painting (New York: Macmillan and Co., 1895); Arthur Robinson Wright, "Fans," in A Collection of Newspaper Cuttings on Walking Sticks, Umbrellas, Parasols, Fans and Gloves (London: Author, 1932), unpaginated. For examples of the history of the umbrella see: Anon., "The Evolution of the Umbrella," Chambers's Journal of Popular Literature, Science and Arts 67 (1890): 394–96; Anon., "Pagodas, Aurioles, and Umbrellas: Umbrellas, Ancient and Modern Part II," The English Illustrated Magazine 5 (1888): 654–67; Anon., "The Religious Character of Umbrellas," The Saturday Review 55 (1883): 497–98; Anon., "The Story of the Umbrella," Person's Magazine 6 (1898): 37–42; Anon., "Umbrella Evolution: The Umbrella and Parasol in History," The Bag, Portmanteau and Umbrella Trader 2, no. 35 (1909): 36–38; Anon., "Umbrellas in the East," The Penny Magazine of the Society for the Diffusion of Useful Knowledge 4, no. 235 (1835): 479–80; Clyde Black, Umbrellas and Their History (New York: Riverside Press, 1864); Octave Uzanne, The Sunshade, the Glove, the Muff (London: J.C. Nimmo and Bain, 1883).

70. For examples of the history of the glove see: William Beck, "The Romance of Gloves," Cosmopolitan XIII (1892): 450–57; von Boehn, Modes and Manners; Dent, Allcroft & Co., A Brief Description of the Manufacture, History and Associations of Gloves: With Illustrations from Dent, Allcroft & Co.'s Manufactory, Worcester (Worcester: Baylis, Lewis & Co., 189?); James William Norton-Kyshe, The Law and Customs Relating to Gloves, Being an Exposition Historically Viewed of Ancient Laws, Customs, and Uses in Respect of Gloves, and of the Symbolism of the Hand and Glove in Judicial Proceedings (London: Stevens and Haynes, 1901); Willard M. Smith, Gloves Past and Present (New York: Sherwood Press, 1917).

–1–

"The Beauty of her Hands":
The Glove and the Making
of Middle-Class Womanhood

In her 1908 etiquette guide, *Every Woman's Toilet Book*, Mrs. Noble offered her commentary on the place of hands in the overall perception of a British woman. "One of woman's greatest charms," Noble claimed, "is in the beauty of her hands, members which are truly adorable when their smallness is combined with other indications of fine breeding; but," she insisted, "even if they are large they may still be beautiful if they are shapely, finely made, and white, with blue veins, taper fingers, and rosy nails, slightly arched."[1] Noble's observations suggest that there was more at stake in the perfect hand than simple physical traits; hands were a manifestation of class and gender written on the body. In the Victorian and Edwardian periods, the ideal hand was thought to be particular to the middle class and was often cited in opposition to working-class hands, which were "large and strong and coarse,"[2] and aristocratic hands, which were "long and sometimes too thin."[3] Throughout the nineteenth century delicate white hands were considered a primary indicator of women's "fine breeding" as well as a corporal expression of minimal manual labor. Mrs. Noble's observations, then, were a reflection and a reaffirmation of the bodily identity that came to distinguish the middle-class women's physique from that of other social classes.

In the Victorian and Edwardian periods women used gloves not only to cover their skin as a protection from the elements but also as a defense from the gaze of women like Mrs. Noble who prided themselves on the ability to read class status upon the hand. What lay beneath the glove, in the case of the middle and working classes, was the hand of someone who labored—more often than not these women dusted, gardened, scrubbed, shook, painted, and handled large objects. In other words, the glove hid the hands of women who exposed their bodies to the elements and got dirty. The glove was an open secret—it was a well-known way to hide one's labor, and to level the hierarchy of classes in Britain. To put on a glove was to participate in an act that likened the middle class to the aristocracy and the working class to the middle class. To adorn one's self in this accessory was a way to both prevent and achieve class slippage. As the practice of wearing gloves became standardized, however, people found new ways of distinguishing the minutiae of class hierarchy; they looked to the glove itself, reading class through fit, fabric, cleanliness, repair, and color. This chapter will show that small pieces of fabric could become a focal point for women's anxieties surrounding class.

In this chapter, I draw on the work of Michel Foucault who asserts that "one of the primordial forms of class consciousness is the affirmation of the body."[4] In this instance, it is a specific part of the body—the hands—that confirm the woman's status as part of the middle class. Following upon Foucault's insight, Michael T. Gilmore and Wai Chee Dimock suggest that classes "become 'real'—become solid, integral, and perhaps even acquirable—to the point where they appear entirely objective and self-evident," once the characteristics of the class are inscribed on the body.[5]

Along the same lines, Judith Butler argues that besides class, gender is an attainable state. Butler suggests that femininity is an identity constructed through a series of gestures and movements that come to represent "womanhood."[6] In Butler's work the female body "becomes its gender through a series of acts which are renewed, revised and consolidated through time."[7] I respond to Butler's call for scholars to "describe the mundane manner in which [gender] constructs are produced, reproduced, and maintained within the field of bodies."[8] The glove was involved in the fabrication of Victorian femininity as various hand shapes were thought to represent different types of women. It was the tight, well-fitted, and easily moldable glove that helped women to create the hand shape required to be a proper middle-class lady. I use prescriptive literature, etiquette manuals, advertisements, women's magazines, fashion plates, *cartes de visite*, and dance-hall music to find instances of how the middle-class female body was "made-real."[9]

All of the sources I use encouraged women to pay more attention to their physical self, actively critiquing their bodies. This literature was likely to have created self-criticism and a sense of lack that could be fixed partly through diet, exercise, and posture, but also by buying commodities such as gloves and creams. Erika Rappaport suggests that etiquette literature, in particular, "contributed to a tendency to look at one's body as a commodity and visual spectacle."[10] The critique of one's body, was, and still is, a necessary mechanism of the consumer society.

Apprehension surrounding social rank was pervasive among the middle class. They were anxious that if they failed to represent their status correctly, they would not only be seen as working class, they would also be seen as having a characteristic of a different race: a darkened complexion. Class, race, and nation were embedded into the practice of wearing gloves, which protected white skin. During the period under study, Britain was at the height of its empire. Imperialism encouraged middle- and upper-class Britons to invent racial categories, placing themselves at the top of the racial hierarchy. The discussion of middle-class whiteness, thus, implicitly engaged women in the colonial discourses of the day; women were encouraged to maintain their skin as white, the standard skin color that all other races were measured against. As we will see, whiteness became central not only to the self-definition of middle-class women but it also helped define the working class as the racial "other" within English borders.

In a more immediate way, though, women's concern for their skin had to do with upholding the tenets of the perfect middle-class family. Historians Leonore Davidoff and Catherine Hall's study, *Family Fortunes*, demonstrates that the ideal middle-class Victorian household had a working husband and a domestic wife.[11] Men were supposed to make money to provide their family with a suitable home. Women were to be proficient household managers; they had to keep account books, plan meals, supervise home and garden cleaning, send for groceries and household supplies, sew or commission clothing for the family, hire and manage servants, look after child care and education, and maintain an active social circle by organizing morning visiting, children's parties, and formal dinners. All of this was done to create a caring and happy domestic space, a haven from the public world of economics and politics. A typical middle-class family had between one and three servants, but the upper middle class could have considerably more household employees. Lower-middle-class wives tended to have one maid-of-all-work who did household chores such as laundry, cooking, cleaning, and gardening alongside her mistress while the wealthier wife managed the servants by delegating tasks to cooks, gardeners, maids, and governesses.[12] Women of the middle class were often prized for their fragility and the religious doctrine of the early Victorian period suggested that physical suffering, as well as cloistering in the home, refined a woman's character making her the strong moral center of the family. Both the images of the invalid mother and the upper-middle-class wife give the impression that middle-class women were not overly engaged in manual labor. Despite these tropes necessity dictated that many middle-class women, but especially those from the lower middle class, had to do housework and gardening to keep their homes looking suitable.[13] But this did not stop women from wanting to appear as if they had enough help to delegate all the household chores to servants. As an etiquette manual from 1850 attests: "So much care is now bestowed upon the hands by some persons, that it would seem as if it was not supposed they were made to be used."[14] One way in which women demonstrated their household's affluence was by maintaining soft white hands despite the labor in which most wives engaged.

This story ends in the 1920s when sunny vacations and tanned skin reduce the need for gloves, and it begins in the 1830s when various phenomena coalesced to provide the pressure and the means to compel middle-class women to take special care of their hands.[15] In the 1830s etiquette manuals made a transition from conduct-oriented to consumption-oriented, women's magazines began to proliferate indicating the type of gloves preferable for the middle class, and the glove industry started to standardize its wares, increasing production and ensuring a snug fit. These factors, all examples of the expanding consumer culture, worked together to create an unsettled sense of self that surrounded the middle-class hand.

We begin this book with a chapter about gloves because as an article of dress they were knowingly used to give a certain impression of character. When women put on gloves they were attempting to create a certain perception of self; they were participating in what historian Stephen Greenblatt has identified as "self-fashioning."[16] Texts from the Renaissance period onward were alive to the idea that one could create an impression of an inner personality through one's outward looks and behavior. Conduct manuals embodied the tension between natural inner beauty and acquired attraction. That is, conduct manuals may say that beauty is an inner quality, but their very existence is predicated on the idea that manners can be learned (by reading the text) and that the reader can change his or her demeanor. Until the late eighteenth century, however, these texts were directed toward the wealthy. By the nineteenth century etiquette manuals were written for the middle classes, some even for the lower middle class. Their main focus moved away from how to act toward what could be bought to create a good outward impression. The Victorian American writer Mark Twain summed up the change in attitude in his quip: "Clothes make the man. Naked people have little or no influence in society."[17] A chapter about gloves is an important starting point for the work because these accessories helped destabilize conceptions of class and gender (if they were ever stable to begin with) and helped to define the self as something that might be purchased rather than enacted. In the upcoming chapters about fans, parasols, and vanity sets, we will see how race and empire were added to the mix becoming things that could be consumed to indicate status and identity.

"THE GLOVE IS A TYRANT OF WHICH THE HAND IS A SLAVE": CONSTRUCTING THE MIDDLE-CLASS HAND

Victorians considered it improper for a woman to appear in public without her gloves and women of the middle and upper classes were encouraged to put on their gloves before crossing the threshold into the street. Women wore gloves in church, at the theater, on promenade, to dances, while shopping, and even to dinner parties hosted in other people's homes.[18] It was seen as a mark of intimacy between a man and woman for the woman to take off her gloves while in a semipublic space like a garden or at a seaside resort. And a great deal was made in songs and novels about the bare, lily-white hand of a lady accepting a marriage proposal.[19] When signing a legal document, swearing an oath, and as a bride at a wedding a woman removed her gloves to demonstrate that she was sincere in her commitment (figure 1.1).[20] This is

Figure 1.1 A woman signs the register after her wedding with gloveless hands symbolizing that her intentions of marriage are sincere. Circa 1880. 10028031, Mary Evans Picture Library.

perhaps an extension of the practice of knights taking off their gloves while addressing royalty to show that they were not hiding anything and they had honest intentions.[21] While in one's own home bare hands were the norm, therefore husbands would be well aware of the state of their wife's hands. It was also common for a woman's social circle to see her hands; when dining or having tea in another's domestic space gloves were removed (figure 1.2). This was something that potter Josiah Wedgwood took into account when designing black basalt tea sets, writing to a business associate in the late eighteenth century, "I hope *white hands* will continue in fashion, and then we may continue to make *black Teapots*."[22] The black basalt design continued to be popular into the nineteenth century allowing Victorian ladies to show off their pristine hands with help of the backdrop of their black china. By the 1890s as women became more active, they often sported naked hands in the country while sailing or rowing boats, playing lawn tennis or croquet (figure 1.3).[23] While the glove acted as a protective measure from the gaze of strangers, the gloveless hand indicated the special intimacy of lovers, family, and close friends. The hand itself, therefore, had to be washed and covered in creams, primped, and protected for the benefit of a woman's social circle. For Victorians gloves were items of clothing that women had to wear in order to

Figure 1.2   Afternoon tea was a time when women revealed their hands to an intimate circle of friends. 1892. 10000818, Mary Evans Picture Library.

be considered proper ladies. Gloves were a covering that indicated a lack of familiarity as they hid a personal part of the body. But gloves also bound, as did corsets, so that the shape of the hand became distorted from its original form. Finally, there was the idea of honesty and the gloveless hand; in putting on gloves, women were wearing masks that hid their true identity, if, as the Victorians believed, identity could be read on the palm of the hand.

Victorian and Edwardian men's etiquette surrounding gloves was much the same as for women, though men were more likely to reveal their hands to a wider circle of people. When meeting a friend, men were expected to extend a gloveless hand, which meant that many wore gloves only on their left hand when expecting to encounter gentlemen they knew.[24] When calling on a lady, however, men were never to take off their hats or gloves.[25] Much was made of the man's handshake and if it was limp or the palm sweaty this was seen as a defect of character.[26] Wealthy men changed their gloves up to six times a day depending on the occasion.[27] For middle-class men "in good taste" new, clean gloves had to be worn on every occasion: they were to wear gloves of subdued colors when walking, in church, and at public places of amusement and white gloves with formal dress.[28] There was some concern that men's glove wearing could become effeminate if they wore gloves that came too far past the wrist, or if they wore their gloves too tightly, as was the custom for ladies.[29] When engaging in sport, men were instructed to buy gloves that were

Figure 1.3 The "awful effects of too much lawn-tennis by the sea" is experienced by women once they return to Society events in the city. Robarts Library, University of Toronto, *Punch; or, The London Charivari,* October 20, 1883.

at least one size too big because "the ordinary glove is made for the hand at rest, and, when you grip the reins or the handle bar with such a [tight] glove, it splits at the seams."[30]

Prescriptive literature provides insight into the time and energy that was spent on the creation and preservation of delicate white hands. This literature encouraged women to present a standardized body that came to be understood as specifically middle class. In an etiquette manual written in 1893, Lady Colin Campbell reassured middle-class women, who used their hands in labor, that they might achieve respectable-looking hands: "it is supposed that one must have descended from a stock that has enjoyed five centuries of leisure to possess a perfectly elegant and aristocratic hand. I know not whether the recipe is infallible; it is certainly not within the reach of all." That included Campbell herself, a dark-eyed, pale-skinned beauty, whose birth family had owned estates for only four hundred years, a century less than the prescribed time it would take to achieve the perfect hand. Lady Campbell had gained a title when she married (and later attempted to divorce) Lord Campbell in 1881. Nonetheless she reassured her readers that, "it is something to have a white and delicate hand, to begin with, even if it be not perfectly modeled; and this is quite possible even if we work, occupy ourselves with our households, and even do gardening: on condition, let it be understood, that we take some pains and trouble."[31] Twenty years later *The Woman's Book* made a similar claim, suggesting that women's work could be hidden by cleansing their hands: "with little care the busy housewife can keep her hands in as good condition as the lady of leisure."[32] In other words, with constant tending appropriate middle-class hands could be achieved. But what kind of care did women take with their hands?

For Victorians, the glove was a conforming and contorting device, similar to the corset. However, the hand was a more crucial site than the waist; while the corset cinched the midriff and suggested fertility by pronouncing hips and bosom, the glove hid women's well-worn hands and protected them from class slippage. Before placing their hands into gloves for an evening out, women were known to actively shape hands into forms they did not take on naturally. Mrs. Noble explained that when women's fingers did not meet the right standards, they could be coaxed into the resemblance of a point with a few simple exercises. "In addition to capping the fingers at bedtime," she suggests, "the woman whose bump of vanity is abnormally developed can materially improve the appearance of her hands when a dinner or bridge-party is contained in the evening's program, by wearing her black velvet 'strait-jackets' for a couple of hours previously, and molded tips preserving their acquired shape in a satisfactory manner throughout the evening."[33] The "bump of vanity" referred to was a phrenological condition, where a bump in the skull indicated that a woman might be vain or have ambitions beyond her station.[34] If women's "fingers are square or wide at the ends," Lady Campbell suggested an alternative way of creating pointed fingers: "by pinching and squeezing the tips. Needless to say," she cautioned, "you will not obtain the taper fingers you desire all at once, but in time you will become aware of a notable and pleasant change."[35] In both of these examples, women were encouraged to critique their hands; if they did not meet the correct standard, they were told to obsessively pinch their fingers to shape their appendages so that they fit the standards of the day.

Along with the active shaping of the fingertips, women were encouraged to protect their hands from calluses and dirt by wearing gloves. Jane C. Loudon, the wife of herbologist John C. Loudon who composed a plethora of works on gardening for experts in the field, wrote the first books on introductory botany in the early Victorian period. These volumes became immensely popular, bringing Loudon to fame for her work that taught average woman how to create elaborate flower gardens.[36] Loudon revolutionized clothing worn while gardening, encouraging women who were likely to stain, roughen, or redden hands to wear "a pair of stiff thick leathern gloves, or gauntlets, to protect her hands, not only from the handle of the spade, but from the stones, weeds, &c., which she may turn over with the earth."[37] For the rest of the century, etiquette guides urged women gardeners to use old gloves too loose for wear while gardening.[38]

Women also used old gloves at night; they were filled with cream and worn while sleeping in order to ensure that hands remained pristine. "On retiring to rest," John H. Young explained in a section of his manual titled "To Make the Hands White and Delicate," "rub them well over with some palm oil and put on a pair of woolen gloves."[39] Women filled their gloves with various skin-improving recipes that were extolled in fashion magazines, advice manuals, and encyclopedias as both preventative measures and remedies for freckled, tanned, or burned skin. These creams were concocted from ingredients readily available in the household and were typically some combination of soap, buttermilk, lemon juice, vinegar, rainwater, rosewater, glycerin, horseradish, and oatmeal.[40] As well as domestic remedies, commercially made beauty recipes were also advertised in women's magazines. One such complexion bath was "Bridal Bouquet Bloom," advertised as a "lovely milky and hygienic liquid." Commercial cosmetics and creams were promoted as healthy and wholesome, but in reality, they contained such unsafe chemicals as lead and arsenic.[41] Advertising copy for "Bridal Bouquet Bloom" claimed that it "imparts exquisite Beauty to the Face, Neck, Arms and Hands. . . . It never fails to remove Freckles, Sunburn, and prevents all Roughness and Wrinkles" (figure 1.4).[42] This cure-all medicine was advertised both as a way to uphold the exquisite beauty of

Figure 1.4 Bridal Bouquet Bloom was advertised as a hygienic liquid; however, many of these mail-order beauty products contained dangerous ingredients like lead or arsenic. 1892. Bodleian Library, University of Oxford: John Johnson Collection: Beauty Parlour 1 (56).

the white skin, and as a remedy for women whose skin was rough or sun-damaged for "redness in the hands and arms [was] a certain antidote to everything like beauty."[43]

Since the hand is a continuation of the arm, much attention was placed on the treatment of the arm and how that affected the hand. "If your hands are rather fat," women were warned, "do not wear tight sleeves. The pressure and discomfort to the arm will only make the hand swell."[44] The respectable upright pose of middle-class women had practical consequences for the middle-class arm as well: by avoiding leaning, women could circumvent rough elbows. For Victorians, the ideal arm was smooth with dimples in the place of the elbow.[45] Women whose elbows were "coarse and scaly" were chastised in women's magazines for "leaning the elbows upon desk or table."[46] This sort of behavior was considered slovenly and more typical of the working class. Middle-class ladies were supposed to keep their postures straight with elbows free from contact.

The middle-class body was not only cultivated by a series of postures but also by eating habits. Plump, well-fed women tended to exhibit dimpled knuckles and elbows; the layer of fat under a lady's skin helped to generate the perfect hand and arm.[47] In fact, in the latter half of the nineteenth century, French actress Sarah Bernhardt popularized long gloves that reached past the elbow (called opera gloves or evening gloves), because she was ashamed of her thin arms. Throughout history there has been a strong association between wealth and weight. Dimpled knuckles were a direct reflection of the foods that women ate, as well as the wealth of her husband's household. Plump women were viewed as child-bearing women who could uphold the tenets of domestic motherhood and would reproduce the British race. Victorians often placed these women in opposition to the image of the emaciated, infertile working-class spinster or the thin aristocratic woman with long, slim fingers. Dimpled knuckles, therefore, were not only associated with middle-class leisure, but also with the role of the woman as mother prescribed by the separate-sphere doctrine (figure 1.5).

The upright posture suggested in the articles of women's magazines and prescriptive literature was visually represented in popular fashion plates. The primary purpose of fashion plates was to disseminate knowledge about the latest couture quickly in weekly and monthly periodicals.[48] These drawings consistently showed stylized female bodies with extremely small waists, hands, and feet. The bodies in fashion plates were models displaying the approved gestures, skin color, and posture that were held up as ideals to be emulated by the middle-class woman. Though the dress and female silhouette of fashion plates were ever-changing, the hand gestures and arm movements of the women in these images remained remarkably constant for the hundred years that they were in circulation.[49] The hands in fashion

P. NADAR

PARIS

Figure 1.5 Actress Sarah Bernhardt brought opera gloves back into fashion because she was embarrassed to show her thin arms. 1887. Philip H. Ward Collection of Theatrical Images, Rare Book and Manuscript Library, University of Pennsylvania.

plates had a set amount of gestures, all of which were inactive. Arms and hands were arrested in mid-motion: gently reaching for objects, calmly gesturing toward items of interest, and holding accessories insecurely within their gloved hands. As can be seen in the fashion plate from *The Queen, The Ladies Newspaper* (1880), women's small hands hold books and fans at the end of their tapered fingertips (figure 1.6). In fashion plates none of the objects are grasped firmly; in fact, most accessories depicted in women's hands are barely held at all. The fans are not being waved, nor are the parasols positioned directly over heads or leaned on for support. These images helped demonstrate to women that they must not use their hands for work, or even for holding objects of women's apparel too firmly, if they were to have the perfect hand. The limp hand gestures reminded onlookers of the female passivity and weakness apparently engaged in by noble women. The Countess de Soissons, mistress of Louis XIV, is said to never have closed her hands "for fear of hardening the joints." Other great ladies "made their servants open all the doors for them, for fear of widening their hands by

Figure 1.6   Fashion plates throughout the nineteenth century demonstrate passive hand gestures meant to be emulated by middle-class women. Robarts Library, University of Toronto, "Dress and Fashion," *The Queen, The Lady's Newspaper,* January 3, 1880, 21.

turning the handles and pushing back the bolts."[50] Though there was an element of envy and awe in these descriptions, prescriptive literature more often suggested aristocratic women's hands were long and too thin.[51] In comparison, middle-class women prefered a middle ground between working-class and aristocratic hands; they wanted to be able to use their hands but not so much that they did not remain lovely, tapered, and small. Middle-class fingers were ideally shorter and less slim than aristocratic women's. Fashion plates showed an extreme version of female passivity and leisure seen mainly as aristocratic; these images were an ideal to be emulated by middle-class women, but not to the extent that they might acquire a noble-woman's hands.

A study of middle-class portraiture shows that the conventional poses of fashion plates were reproduced in photographs of real men and women (figure 1.7). The semi-bent arm of the wife holding gloves and little girls with lax hands holding baskets of flowers are replicated over and over again in professional photographs. This demonstrates that, at least in a formalized

Figure 1.7 In this 1897 family photo, lax hands imitate the fashion plates of the day. 10126577, Mary Evans Picture Library.

setting, photographers encouraged average women to emulate the poses and gestures of fashion plates. The constant and consistent repetition of movements depicted in fashion plates, photographs, and etiquette manuals worked in unison to create the conventional poses that helped to produce a collective middle-class body.[52]

But the shape of a woman's hand was not all she had to be concerned about; women were cautioned that they must wear clean, well-fitted, kid gloves if they were to be considered middle class. The author of *Etiquette for Ladies and Gentlemen* (1876) warns against wearing "soiled or ripped gloves" when attending a public event: "With regard to dress itself, the first things a lady ought to think about are her gloves and shoes; for soiled or ripped gloves, or shabby boots, will destroy the effect of the most elegant gown ever worn."[53] Another example appears in *Etiquette of Modern Society*, "How often do we see a dress exquisite in all its parts, utterly ruined by the wearer . . . by the adoption of vulgar gloves!"[54] For nineteenth-century writers, *vulgar* was a derogatory term that served to separate those who had "good taste" from the ill-bred, uncultured, and socially mobile.[55] In these quotes Victorian authors demonstrated that class was made visible not only by a woman's primary covering, which indicates wealth, but also through the accessories worn with the dress. These warnings suggest that if a woman was unaware of, or could not afford, the right accessories she would not be considered a proper lady.

Leather gloves made from young goats ("kids," hence "kid gloves") were considered best for hiding imperfect hands while in public. It was thought that cotton and silk conformed to a woman's hand too readily, making them a real "test of shapely knuckles and tapering finger tips."[56] Only women with well-styled hands could wear silk gloves. In comparison to other fabrics, the soft leather of kid was more likely to preserve its shape than cotton or silk, and could even be manipulated to emulate tapered fingertips using glove stretchers—scissor-like devices that taper to a point used to recreate the shape of the finger after gloves had been washed (figure 1.8). Fabrics other than kid were considered tasteless and could be used as a way to recognize the lower classes.[57] In the comedic song "Rotten Cotton Gloves," a would-be lady sports a pair of cotton gloves that are described as misshapen, dirty, old, torn, and seam-stripped (figure 1.9):[58]

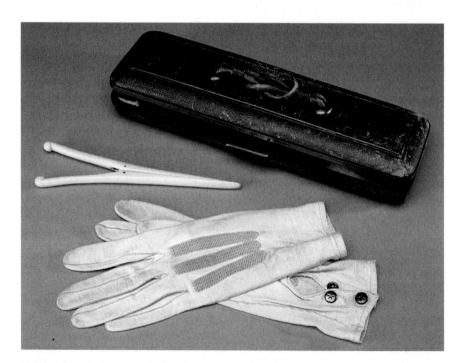

Figure 1.8   The glove stretcher's pointed tips (center object) helped keep the fingers of gloves tapered. This device allowed women to emulate the perfect Victorian hand when they wore gloves. Circa 1900. M979.34.1.1–3, Gift of Mrs. Justice G. Miller Hyde, McCord Museum.

Gloves always add a finish,
And they make you look a don,
I think these gloves were finished
Long before I put them on,
There's an openwork arrangement
Round the finger tips,
It comes in ve'ry handy
When you're eating fish and chips . . .

I'm wearing rotten cotton gloves;
Can't afford fur ones got no quids,
Can't afford a pair of "kids."

The British music halls, in which this song was performed, typically had audiences of young aristocratic men and the working class. Beginning in the

THE GALLERY OF THE "VIC."

Figure 1.9 Working-class women, possibly actresses, solicit wealthy gentlemen at the Victoria Theatre, a popular music hall of the 1870s. 10104032, Mary Evans Picture Library.

1860s, working-class women entertained in these ornately decorated theaters that plied their guests with alcohol. The would-be lady that sings this particular song was likely to have been from the working class. The song can be seen as an ironic performance as many actresses were known to marry well-off members of the audience.[59] The rotten cotton glove could also have been seen as an object of mockery by the gentlemen in the audience who knew the signs of poverty as displayed in gloves and shoes, or by the working-class audience who resented working-class upstarts.

Gloves were often stand-ins for the hands that middle-class women coveted. Women who could afford it made sure that their gloves were of high quality. Women were advised to change their gloves numerous times a day in order to avoid worn or loose gloves and to retain the well-shaped appearance of their hands. Women also purchased gloves that were too small to create the appearance of tiny hands.[60] The backs of gloves were generally decorated with three lines of "pointing," which was a technique of stitching creating a raised design on the back of the hand. The pointing may have acted as a reminder of the ideal hand underneath, emphasizing the blue veins that were essential elements of the perfect Victorian hand.[61] Similarly, white or pale-colored gloves were favored, perhaps emulating the "the colour of the inner leaves of a moss rose," which was the ideal complexion for women's naked palms and fingertips.[62]

During the early nineteenth century the glove industry began to mechanize, assuring middle-class women that their hands would be hidden in gloves that acted like a second, more perfect, skin. Mechanization meant that more gloves were made, better-fitting gloves were available, and kid gloves were affordable, making them more accessible to the middle class. Before the mechanization of the industry, kid gloves were either made-to-order for wealthy women or the sizing was decided at random by the glove cutters working on ready-made gloves for the middle class. Without using a pattern the latter type of glove rarely fit well.[63] Various inventions of the early and mid-nineteenth century helped improve gloves. In the 1830s, Xavier Jouvin, a Frenchman from the glovemaking town of Grenoble, had a profound effect on the glove industry. He went into the local hospital, measured the hands of patients and determined that hands could be classified into 320 shapes and sizes. In 1838 Jouvin patented a series of tempered-steel blades in the shape of thirty-two standardized hand sizes.[64] This allowed glove cutters to punch gloves with more precision and to cut up to six gloves at a time. Jouvin and his successors held the patent in France until 1849 and brought the glovemaking town out of a recession that had reached its lowest point in 1807. Jouvin's gloves became important for the English market because in 1826 the English government lifted the prohibition on French gloves and slowly reduced the tariffs on them. By 1850 England received more than one million of the almost five million pairs of gloves produced, just below 28% of the gloves made, and by 1865, 60% of the gloves prepared were sent to the United Kingdom. By 1863 Jouvin had a glove store in London, giving him control over each phase from production to consumption. Jouvin's invention made less obvious inroads into England as well: his patent only applied in France, so English glovemakers were able to use the glove punch with impunity[65] (figure 1.10). Other inventions that improved the snugness of gloves included elasticized wrists, glove fasteners, and the "looper" that enabled the entire glove to be machine-stitched including the fingertips.[66] The revolution in the glove trade was so thorough that middle-class women could afford a luxury that had previously only been known to the rich: well-fitting gloves. This consumer object was so popular, in fact, that the goat population in France could not keep up with women's demand for kid gloves, forcing glovemakers to import kid from Italy. Changes in glove production allowed women to buy respectability, and the look of fresh, clean hands, without having to give up their day-to-day work.

This section has explored the ways that middle-class women's hands—and by extension middle-class women's bodies—were created, enacted, and maintained. By wearing well-fitted kid gloves, hands were immobilized into their perfect state; by pinching their fingers, women created the semblance of tapered fingertips; by using whitening creams, women erased the dirt and

Figure 1.10 Male glovemakers at work in Grenoble, France. Late nineteenth century. Fonds documentaire du Musée du Gant de Grenoble.

roughness after a day's toils; by keeping an upright posture, they preserved perfectly dimpled elbows proving they did not hunch or lean in labor; and by keeping a proper diet, they ensured that their arms and hands were plump enough to generate the coveted dimpled elbows and knuckles. Through these everyday practices, women coaxed their bodies into culturally ordained shapes that they did not take on naturally, creating a formalized middle-class body. By keeping their hands in a state of soft whiteness, middle-class women were able to show that they had leisure time, something that was sorely lacking for most working-class women. By taking the time to make their hands tapered and white, middle-class women quelled their anxieties about class slippage, and gave themselves the sense that they were firmly part of the middle class. It was partially by maintaining a perfect-looking gloved hand, then, that middle-class women convinced themselves that they were distinct from the working class whose hands were large, rough, and red due to labor.

DIFFERENTIATING THE MIDDLE-CLASS BODY: THE "LARGE AND RED" HANDS OF THE WORKING CLASS

Class boundaries were not as firm as etiquette manuals and popular songs would have us believe. Working-class maids, who dressed like middle-class women on Sundays or when shopping for their mistresses during the week, were warned that they must "dress their station" and were sometimes fired for their cross-dressing.[67] The middle-class lady's concern surrounding the appearance of her social inferiors reveals that, at some level, she understood that class was a performance and the boundaries of class were permeable. Middle-class women found themselves in a bind: they insisted that their "snowy white" complexion was natural but revealed that their anxieties were well founded by insisting their servants not attempt to have white skin themselves. Middle-class women's primary concern was that they could be visually differentiated from working-class servants, factory workers, and shop girls not only through different consumption practices but also through a series of clues that appeared on their physical bodies. The Victorian period advice literature encouraged women to look for actual changes in the body like skin color and hand size as indications of who was middle class and who was working class.

The hand was such an important site for the production of class identity that the laborer was referred to as the "hand."[68] The *Oxford English Dictionary* indicates that the meaning of *hand* as a person employed by another in manual labor first appeared in 1657. By 1721 manufacturers are said to employ "hands."[69] In the Victorian period the word *hand* was fully entrenched as a synonym for the word *worker*; underlying the term were issues of power, control, and class hierarchy. If a person worked with his or her hands in a factory, farm, or domestic service, that person was considered working class; if a person owned or managed a business or home, that person worked with his or her mind and was considered to be middle class. Working-class hands made the lifestyle of the middle class possible, enabling middle-class persons to show little to no effect of this labor upon their bodies.[70]

The Victorian vocabulary that equated workers and hands had a visual component that associated large hands with laboring hands. The best and most elaborate examples of this type of thinking are contained within the diaries of Arthur Munby, an eccentric Victorian gentleman. A minor poet and civil servant, Munby had a fascination with working-class women. His diaries reveal the secret life of a voyeur who got a sexual thrill out of watching women get dirty and do physical work.[71] Though his obsession with dirt and working-class women's bodies may be atypical of the era, Munby's fixation with women's hands spoke to prevalent concerns of the time. Munby's diaries are littered with descriptions connecting women's large, red, raw hands with their working-class status. The extraordinary strength of Munby's obsession is apparent in an entry from August 21, 1860: "I passed a tallish young woman, evidently a servant, who was noticeable for the size of her gloveless hands. . . . I looked at her hands, and spoke my opinion of them." As a result, a dialogue took place between the two: "How can you like them?" she said, "they are so large and red, I'm ashamed of them." "They are just the hands for a servant," responded Munby: "They show you are hardworking, and you ought to be proud of them. You wouldn't wish them to be like a lady's?" The servant girl responded bitterly: "Yes I should! And I should like to be a lady, and I wish my hands were like yours!" Munby recollected that "she looked enviously at my hand, which was quite white and small by the side of hers. I could not then understand her vehemence: but remembering the difference between my fist and those small taper lady hands one sees in drawing rooms, it did seem pathetic that this poor wench should envy my hands, and fancy that if her own were like them, she would have reached a ladylike pitch of refinement."[72] This chance encounter between a gentleman and a servant played upon fears of gendered cross-dressing and class impersonation that both concerned and thrilled the Victorians. In Munby's insistence on praising the working-woman's hands, he reversed their gender roles, placing the servant as manly worker and himself as lady of leisure. Though he clearly had a desire to speak with laboring women, as can be seen by the repeated encounters he recorded in his diary, he also put them down suggesting they were "poor wenches" that did not truly understand what it took to be a lady. At the same time, the maid, who wished her hands were like Munby's, expressed her desire to be part of a class other than her own. The concept that class and gender were performative acts, made real by how one's hands were used, and through the comparison of one hand to another, generated a considerable amount of anxiety in the Victorian period. Fetishists like Munby took parts of the body that a culture deemed problematic sites of difference between men and women and sexualized them. In a culture where class and gender were such important factors, hands as a body part became sites of obsession (figure 1.11).

Albeit without the thrill of the clandestine encounter, the fixation with hands appeared in more pervasive and mundane publications like etiquette manuals. Isabella Mary Beeton, the best-selling author of household management books in the Victorian period, says in her *Manners of Polite Society* (1875) that "hand shape depends, of course, in a great measure, upon physical conformation, though doubtlessly, exertion early in life, such as continued musical practice, may disturb its symmetry. We refer more especially to the harp, which makes the fingers crooked and renders their tips hard and thick. This may also apply to many kinds of mechanical employment and manual labour."[73] Almost thirty years later, the advice remained consistent. *Every Woman's Toilet Book* (1908) suggested that hands could become enlarged with too much physical labor: "You may lead an active, energetic life, or rather, you should lead such a life," suggests the author, "and yet not enlarge your hand; but even in domestic duties or exercise you can take certain care. For instance, try never to stretch wide your hand by carrying more than you

Figure 1.11 Hanna Cullwick, maid-of-all-work and wife of Arthur Munby, showing off her large working hands and bicep. 1867. Master and Fellows of Trinity College Cambridge.

conveniently can, or doing man's carpentering, or lifting heavy weights. Of course, often we are powerless to avoid such work, but when possible think of your hands." She goes on to suggest that, "Our grandmothers would not row, golf was unheard of, and fine ladies would not even carry their prayer-books to church for fear of ruining their hands."[74] Manuals such as these warned that if a lady neglected to sustain the proper appearance of her hands by avoiding strenuous labor and repetitive movement, they would physically change— eventually becoming enlarged to the point where they looked like the hands of a laborer rather than the hands of a proper lady.

The idea that one's daily routines became physically apparent was part of nineteenth-century understanding of the self. Again and again etiquette manuals reinforced the concept that a woman's character—her inner thoughts, her private daily routines, even her soul—was manifested physically upon her body.[75] Mrs. H. R. Haweis suggested that clothing was but a gauze covering a person's essence, "dress, that tissue which man's soul wears as its outmost wrappage, . . . wherein his whole self lives, moves and has its being."[76] The author of *Etiquette for All* indicated similarly that "we cannot help forming some opinions of a man's sense and character from his dress." And John H. Young further addressed the connection between a woman's character and her appearance: "Indifference and inattention to dress is a defect of character . . . and often denotes indolence and slovenliness."[77] In all of these examples, beauty was internal and a reflection of a person's soul or character. What was on the inside was reflected on the outside; therefore, a woman's looks could be read as an indication of her morality.

Because hands were such a site of uncertainty and friction for Victorians, they permeated the culture in all sorts of ways, even having an effect on the most objective discipline: science. Authors of etiquette manuals shared with practitioners of phrenology the belief that a person's temperament was "depicted in legible characters upon the external countenance."[78] Phrenology was a science invented by Franz Joseph Gall, an eccentric Viennese physician, in 1796. His idea was that the brain was the primary organ of the mind and that one could read the bumps and divots of the skull to decipher a patient's personality. Gall proposed that there were twenty-seven different places on the head that could show a person's temperament and character. These twenty-seven areas corresponded to things as diverse as memory for words, love of offspring, and tendency toward vanity and ambition. Gall's book, *The Anatomy and Physiology of the Nervous System in General, and of the Brain in Particular, with Observations upon the Possibility of Ascertaining the Several Intellectual and Moral Dispositions of Man and Animal, by the Configuration of Their Heads*, was translated into English in 1835. The dissemination of phrenological ideas in the United Kingdom was facilitated by Gall's wayward student, Johann Kaspar Spurzheim, who coined the term *phrenology* in his 1815 book, *The Physiognomical System of Drs. Gall and Spurzheim*.[79] From this point on, phrenology increasingly gained a presence in the minds of upper- and middle-class Victorians. The Edinburgh Phrenological Society was established in 1820 and by 1830 one-third of the members had no medical background, hailing instead from the ranks of the government, artists, and liberal professionals.[80] By 1851 George Combe's textbook, *The Constitution of Man* (first published in 1828), that explained the science of phrenology for the general interest reader, had sold 90,000 copies. According to Victorian social theorist Harriet Martineau this volume became so well read that it was surpassed only by the Bible, *Pilgrim's Progress*, and *Robinson Crusoe*.[81] Most literate Victorians would have been aware of phrenological ideas as they appeared in the periodical press and newspapers of the day as well as popular novels such as *Jane Eyre* (1847) and *Great Expectations* (1860).[82] When Charles Darwin's *On the Origin of Species* appeared in 1859 it partially owed its popularity to phrenology, which introduced the British population to natural laws.[83] Though many scientists of the nineteenth century thought of phrenology as a pseudo-science, and ordinary Victorians engaged in debates about the validity of the science, it had an ongoing resonance throughout Victoria's long reign.

Phrenologists such as J.C. Lavater posited that along with the head, the hands could be studied to understand a person's intellectual and moral character.[84] In *The Psychonomy of the Hand; or, The Hand: An Index of Mental Development* (1865), Richard Beamish indicated that a woman's hands could tell onlookers what sort of wife and mother she might be: "The square fingers represent more delicacy, symmetry, arrangement, punctuality, and deference to precedent and authority than the spatulous" (or spread-out fingers). Beamish further proposed: "Where the thumb is small, there is the index of gentleness and love; where large, of precedent and legality, and a tendency to social and domestic harshness and despotism"[85] (figure 1.12). Recall also the "bump of vanity" that Mrs. Noble described that might cause women to bind the tips of their fingers. Using the scientific method of "impartial" observation, then, a woman's inner character appeared on the palm of her hand.

Using the hand as an index, etiquette books suggested that a woman's disposition became apparent through her hands: "Character, again, is largely to be determined by the hands," explained Noble. "You hear people say she is neat-handed, or has such strong, kind capable hands, or the sensitive hand of an artist . . . No woman should ever allow hands to get rough, even in the coldest and most severe weather, it is always a sign of carelessness."[86] This passage reads as a phrenological explanation of women's natures: artistic women have sensitive hands and careless women have rough hands. There are obvious class biases in this statement. As we have seen, rough hands tended to be working-class hands; and the quoted passage ignores the necessity of work and instead suggests that working-class women are careless rather than responsible and hardworking. The use of the science of body shapes in etiquette manuals, with their focus on the appearance of hands, helped

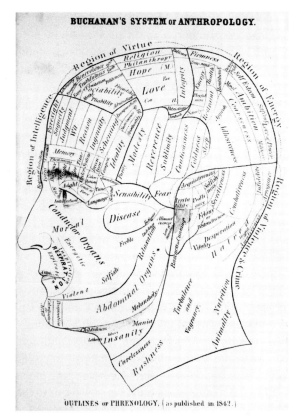

Figure 1.12 Victorians believed that a person's temperament could be read by observing certain aspects of their skulls and hands as demonstrated on this phrenological drawing of a head. Robarts Library, University of Toronto, Joseph R. Buchanan, M.D., *Outlines of Lectures on the Neurological System of Anthropology as Uncovered, Demonstrated and Taught in 1841 and 1843* (Cincinnati: *Buchanan's Journal of Man*, 1854), i, frontispiece.

women to identify the class of those around them. However, such advice also reaffirmed that middle-class women must uphold the tenets of the domestic sphere—they must remain kind and sensitive in order to appear as such. Alternatively, if a woman acted inappropriately for her station—if she worked, exercised, or carried too much—this would be represented physically through the increased breadth of her hands. The discourse of phrenology was used by etiquette manuals as a scare tactic that ensured that middle-class women experienced the sense that their bodies needed improvement.

From the 1830s until just after the turn of the nineteenth century, women took great pains to preserve their hands in a state of small, soft whiteness.

Fashion plates and etiquette manuals stressed the importance of the perfect hand to middle-class consumers, who, in turn, purchased such objects as gloves, creams, and washes. Together, these elements constitute what Judith Butler has identified as "the mundane way in which social agents *constitute* social reality through language, gesture, and all manner of symbolic social sign." The hand gestures depicted in fashion plates, the erect posture encouraged by etiquette manuals, and the exercises used to create tapered fingertips can all be considered mundane everyday practices. Put together with the maintenance of the skin through the use of gloves and creams, one can see that the obsession with perfect hands created a regimented daily routine focused on the management of the body. Through these daily rituals, women styled their bodies into a femininity that was particular to the middle class. Once this performance was accomplished, white middle-class women used their constructed identity as the norm against which to judge all other classes and femininities. Aristocratic women's overindulgent leisure, for example, was represented in their fingers that were considered "too thin," presumably because of their total lack of engagement with the physical environment. At the other end of the spectrum working-class women's need to labor was considered unladylike and was reflected in hands that had "nothing feminine about [them] in form or texture."[87] The literature, images, and corrective devices intended to distinguish the middle-class hand helped to produce a particular kind of body, which was associated with a middle-class identity in the nineteenth century. From the middle-class hand we now move to the fan, an object that many Victorian women maneuvered skillfully in their attempts to flirt their way into marriage. While the glove was a secretive device that helped hide the work of middle-class women in public, the fan was an object that supposedly revealed the inner thoughts and emotions of any woman who fluttered it.

NOTES

Excerpted by permission of the Publishers from "'The Beauty of her Hands': The Glove and the Making of Middle-Class Body," in *Material Women, 1750–1950*, ed. Maureen Daly Goggin and Beth Fowkes Tobin (Farnham: Ashgate, 2009), 167–84. Copyright © 2009.

1. Mrs. Robert Noble, *Every Woman's Toilet Book* (London: George Newnes, 1908), 56.
2. Arthur Munby, "Munby Diary," in *Munby, Man of Two Worlds: The Life and Diaries of Arthur J. Munby, 1812–1910*, ed. Derek Hudson (London: J. Murray, 1972), 72.
3. Noble, *Every Woman's Toilet Book*, 56.
4. Michel Foucault, *The History of Sexuality: An Introduction* (New York: Pantheon Books, 1978), 126.

5. Michael T. Gilmore and Wai Chee Dimock, *Rethinking Class: Literary Studies and Social Formations* (New York: Columbia University Press, 1994), 3.
6. Margaret Beetham, *A Magazine of Her Own? Domesticity and Desire in the Women's Magazine, 1800–1914* (London: Routledge, 1996), ix; Judith Butler, *Bodies That Matter: On the Discursive Limits of Sex* (New York: Routledge, 1993); Judith Butler, *Gender Trouble: Feminism and the Subversion of Identity* (New York: Routledge, 1990); Judith Butler, "Performative Acts and Gender Constitution: An Essay in Phenomenology and Feminist Theory," in *Performing Feminisms: Feminist Critical Theory and Theatre*, ed. Sue Ellen Case (Baltimore: John Hopkins University Press, 1990), 270–82. For a sociological perspective on gender performance, see Candace West and Don H. Zimmerman, "Doing Gender," *Gender and Society* 1, no. 2 (1987): 125–51.
7. Butler, "Performative Acts and Gender Constitution," 274.
8. Butler, "Performative Acts and Gender Constitution," 276.
9. Jules Prown, "Mind in Matter: An Introduction to Material Culture Theory and Method," *Winterthur Portfolio* 17 (1982): 1–12.
10. Erika Rappaport, "Introduction: Shopping as Women's Pleasure and Women's Work," *Defining Gender, 1450–1910*, http://www.gender.amdigital.co.uk/essays/content/rappaport.aspx (accessed June 29, 2010).
11. Leonore Davidoff and Catherine Hall, *Family Fortunes: Men and Women of the English Middle Class, 1780–1850*, Women in Culture and Society (Chicago: University of Chicago Press, 1987). The idea of separate spheres has been contested by many. Historians of consumerism such as Erika Rappaport, Thomas Richards, and Bill Lancaster have challenged the separate sphere doctrine by demonstrating how department store managers, women shoppers, and advertisements created a home away from home in nineteenth-century shopping centers. The department store effectively turned the separate sphere doctrine onto itself, granting women a place in the public sphere by equipping it with domestic necessities. Historians of feminism such as Lisa Tickner, Barbara Caine, and Linda Colley show how women manipulated the domestic ideology to gain access to the public sphere by presenting themselves as respectable women who were concerned with issues that were traditionally part of the woman's sphere of influence. Historians have also shown how female philanthropists accessed the public sphere by negotiating the boundaries of public and private to their own ends. See, for instance, William Lancaster, *The Department Store: A Social History* (London: Leicester University Press, 1995); Erika Diane Rappaport, *Shopping for Pleasure: Women in the Making of London's West End* (Princeton, NJ: Princeton University Press, 2000); Thomas Richards, *The Commodity Culture of Victorian England: Advertising and Spectacle, 1851–1914* (Stanford, CA: Stanford University Press, 1990); Barbara Caine, *Victorian Feminists* (Oxford: Oxford Univer-

sity Press, 1992); Linda Colley, *Britons: Forging the Nation, 1707–1837* (New Haven, CT: Yale University Press, 1992); Lisa Tickner, *The Spectacle of Women: Imagery of the Suffrage Campaign, 1907–14* (London: Chatto & Windus, 1987); Gareth Stedman Jones, *Outcast London: A Study in the Relationship between Classes in Victorian Society* (London: Penguin Books, 1992); Ellen Ross, *Love and Toil: Motherhood in Outcast London, 1870–1918* (New York: Oxford University Press, 1993); Judith R. Walkowitz, *City of Dreadful Delight: Narratives of Sexual Danger in Late-Victorian London*, Women in Culture and Society (Chicago: University of Chicago Press, 1992), 52–58; Amanda Vickery, "Golden Age to Separate Spheres? A Review of the Categories and Chronology of English Women's History," *The Historical Journal* 36, no. 2 (1993): 383–414.

12. Claudia Nelson, *Family Ties in Victorian England* (Westport, CT: Praeger, 2007), 23.

13. Looking at the question of women's housework, historians Anne McClintock and Patricia Branca suggest that women did not cease to work once the domestic ideology took hold; instead their work was denied by the culture at large. Anne McClintock, *Imperial Leather: Race, Gender and Sexuality in Colonial Conquest* (New York: Routledge), 216; John Tosh, "New Men? Bourgeois Cult of Home," in *Victorian Values: Personalities and Perspectives in Nineteenth-Century Society*, ed. Gordon Marsden (London: Longman, 1998), 80; Patricia Branca, "Image and Reality: The Myth of the Ideal Victorian Woman," in *Clio's Consciousness Raised: New Perspectives on the History of Women*, ed. Mary S. Hartman (New York: Octagon Books, 1976), 179–90.

14. Anon., *The Lady's Pocket Companion and Indispensable Friend Comprising the Whole Art of True Politeness, Dressing, the Toilette, Evening Amusements, Games, the Ball Room, Needle Work, Crochet and Netting, Knitting etc. Also Hints on Courtship and Marriage* (New York: Leaville and Allen, circa 1850), 38.

15. Glove wearing did not end entirely in the 1920s but it was greatly reduced after this period. Victorian anxieties surrounding hands are found well into the twentieth century; "dishpan hands" continued to be criticized into the 1950s and white gloves were required in public in the southern United States into the 1960s. In England until the 1960s women continued to wear gloves especially on Sundays, but this was considered a conservative religious trend, in many ways a throwback to Victorian values.

16. Stephen Greenblatt, *Renaissance Self-Fashioning: From More to Shakespeare* (Chicago: University of Chicago Press, 2005).

17. Louis J. Budd, ed., *Mark Twain: Collected Tales, Sketches, Speeches and Essays, 1891–1910* (New York: Literary Classics of the United States, 1992), 942.

18. Anon., *Etiquette for All; or, Rules of Conduct for Every Circumstance in Life: With the Laws, Rules, Precepts, and Practices of Good Society* (Glasgow: George Watson, 1861), 8.
19. Mary Hoskin, *The Little Green Glove and Other Stories*, ed. Mary Hoskin (Toronto: Extension Print, 1920); F.E. Weatherly and Charlotte Helen, "The Glove" (London: Enoch and Sons, 1873); Samuel Lover, "The Hand and the Glove Song" (London: Duff & Hodgson, 1843).
20. James William Norton-Kyshe, *The Law and Customs Relating to Gloves, Being an Exposition Historically Viewed of Ancient Laws, Customs, and Uses in Respect of Gloves, and of the Symbolism of the Hand and Glove in Judicial Proceedings* (London: Steven and Haynes, 1901), 82; Octave Uzanne, *The Sunshade, the Glove, the Muff* (London: J.C. Nimmo and Bain, 1883), 93.
21. Norton-Kyshe, *The Law and Customs Relating to Gloves*, 83.
22. Regina Lee Blaszczyk, *Imagining Consumers: Design and Innovation from Wedgwood to Corning* (Baltimore: John Hopkins University Press, 2002), 8.
23. Anon., *Etiquette for Ladies: A Guide to the Observances of Good Society* (London: Ward, Lock and Co., n.d.), 33.
24. Captain L.H. Saunders, "The Outer Man," *The Modern Man*, June 11, 1910, 24.
25. G.A. Gaskell, *Gaskell's Compendium of Forms, Educational, Social, Legal and Commercial* (Chicago: Fairbanks, Palmer & Co., 1881), 407.
26. One of Dickens's most famous villains, Uriah Heep, had sweaty hands: Charles Dickens, *David Copperfield* (New York: Sheldon and Co., 1863).
27. Cecil B. Hartley, *The Gentlemen's Book of Etiquette and Manual of Politeness* (Boston: DeWolfe, Fiske & Co., 1875), 119.
28. DeB. Randolph Keim, *Hand Book of Official and Social Etiquette and Public Ceremonials at Washington* (Washington, DC: DeB. Randolph Keim, 1886), 149.
29. Saunders, "The Outer Man," 24.
30. Captain L.H. Saunders, "The Outer Man," *The Modern Man*, December 26, 1908, 24.
31. Lady Colin Campbell, *The Lady's Dressing Room* (London: Cassells and Co., 1893), 184–85.
32. Florence B. Jack and Rita Strauss, *The Woman's Book: Contains Everything a Woman Ought to Know* (London: T. C. & E. C. Jack, 1911), 461.
33. Noble, *Every Woman's Toilet Book*, 65.
34. *Bump of vanity* is a fairly common phrase used by people of the nineteenth century to indicate the vanity of such men of note as Napoleon and Gladstone, ambitious women (especially writers), and occasionally beautiful birds and flowers. One of the original 27 "brain organs" identified by Franz Joseph Gall, founder of phrenology, was vanity. The term

bump of vanity is clearly phrenological in its origins as indicated in these two texts: Adlolphus Slade, Esq., Lieut. RN, *Records of Travels in Turkey, Greece, &c. and of a Cruise in the Black Sea, with the Captain Pasha, in the Years 1829, 1830 and 1831*, Vol. II, 2nd ed. (London: Saunders and Otley, 1833), 307; M. de Bourrienne, *Memoirs of Napoleon Bonaparte* (London: Crosby Lockwood and Son, 1888), 349.

35. Campbell, *The Lady's Dressing Room*, 196.

36. Bea Howe, *Lady with Green Fingers: The Life of Jane Loudon* (London: Country Life, 1960).

37. Jane Loudon, *Gardening for Ladies* (London: John Murray, 1840), 11.

38. Anon., *Etiquette for Ladies and Gentlemen* (London: Frederick, Warne and Co., 1876), 11; Campbell, *The Lady's Dressing Room*, 187.

39. John H. Young, *Our Deportment; or, The Manners, Conduct and Dress of the Most Refined Society* (Harrisburg, PA: F. B. Dickenson and Co., 1882), 365.

40. Noble, *Every Woman's Toilet Book*, 52, 53, 58, 61; Jack and Strauss, *The Woman's Book*, 450.

41. Valerie Steele, *Fashion and Eroticism: Ideals of Feminine Beauty from the Victorian Era to the Jazz Age* (New York: Oxford University Press, 1985), 126; James C. Whorton, *The Arsenic Century: How Victorian Britain Was Poisoned at Home, Work, and Play* (Oxford: Oxford University Press, 2010), 306; Elizabeth Carolyn Miller, *Framed: The New Woman Criminal in British Culture at the Fin de Siècle* (Ann Arbor: University of Michigan Press, 2008), 97.

42. Bridal Bouquet Bloom, "Bridal Bouquet Bloom," in *Beauty Parlour Box 1, Advertisements Beauty Parlour-Hair-dressers' Advertisements*, ed. John Johnson Collection (1892).

43. Anon., *Etiquette for the Ladies: Eighty Maxims on Dress, Manners and Accomplishments* (London: Charles Tilt, 1837), 35.

44. Campbell, *The Lady's Dressing Room*, 196.

45. Noble, *Every Woman's Toilet Book*, 49.

46. Jack and Strauss, *The Woman's Book*, 450.

47. Anne Hollander, *Seeing through Clothes* (New York: Penguin Books, 1988); Susan Bordo, *Unbearable Weight: Feminism, Western Culture, and the Body* (Berkeley: University of California Press, 2003); John Crowley, *The Invention of Comfort: Sensibilities and Design in Early Modern Britain and Early America* (Baltimore: Johns Hopkins University Press, 2001).

48. Vanda Foster, *A Visual History of Costume in the Nineteenth Century* (London: B.T. Batsford, 1984), 16; Vivian Holland, "On Collecting Fashion Plates," *The Book-Collector's Quarterly* 2 (1951): 13–18; Shanon Marcus, "Reflections on Victorian Fashion Plates," *Differences: A Journal of Feminist Cultural Studies* 14, no. 3 (2005): 10–11; Doris Langley Moore,

Fashion through Fashion Plates, 1771–1970 (New York: Clarkson N. Potter, 1971), 13–19.

49. The magazines that were consulted are *Townsden's Monthly Selection of Paris Fashions* (1832–1852), *Ladies' Cabinet* (1832–1852), *Ladies' Magazine* (1828–1869), *The Queen* (1847–1900), *Le Journal des Demoiselles* (1880–1890), *The Tailor and Cutter* (1870–1890).

50. Campbell, *The Lady's Dressing Room*, 185–86.

51. The literature that addresses aristocratic hands tends to focus on overindulgent leisure. There is a silence in this particular area about the other stereotype of aristocratic women being degenerate.

52. For a similar interpretation of pose, see: Richard L. Bushman, *The Refinement of America: Persons, Houses, Cities* (New York: Random House, 1993), 63–69; Andrea Volpe, *The Middling Sorts: Explorations in the History of the American Middle Class* (New York: Routledge, 2001), 159.

53. Anon., *Etiquette for Ladies and Gentlemen*, 12.

54. Anon., *The Etiquette of Modern Society: A Guide to Good Manners in Every Possible Situation* (London: Ward, Lock and Co., n.d.), 13.

55. Susan David Bernstein and Else B. Michie, eds., *Victorian Vulgarity: Taste in Verbal and Visual Culture* (Aldershot: Ashgate, 2009).

56. Willard M. Smith, *Gloves Past and Present* (New York: Sherwood Press, 1917), 106.

57. Valerie Cumming, *Gloves*, ed. Aileen Ribeiro, The Costume Accessories Series (London: B.T. Batsford, 1982), 19; Smith, *Gloves Past and Present*, 108.

58. Harry Gifford, Fred E. Cliffe, and George Arthurs, "Rotten Cotton Gloves" (London: Montgomery & Co., 1928).

59. For a list of peers or their heirs who have married actresses, dancers, or singers, see vol. xii, Appendix C of George Edward Cokayne, *The Complete Peerage of England, Scotland, Ireland, Great Britain and the United Kingdom* (London: St. Catherine Press, 1929).

60. Cumming, *Gloves*, 60.

61. For a description of the perfect hand emphasizing blue veins, see Noble, *Every Woman's Toilet Book*, 56.

62. Mrs. Beeton, *Manners of Polite Society: Complete Etiquette for Ladies, Gentlemen and Families* (London: Ward, Lock and Tyler, 1875), 328; Anon., *The Lady's Pocket Companion*, 18.

63. Vital Chomel, *Historie de Grenoble* (Toulouse: Edouard Privat, 1979), 257.

64. Xavier Jouvin won medals at French, English, and American exhibitions for his invention. B. Eldred Ellis, *Gloves and the Glove Trade* (London: Sir Isaac Pitman & Sons, 1921), 66; Jouvin's Glove Manufactory, "Jouvin's Glove Manufactory," in *Women's Clothes and Millinery Box 3; Advertisements-gloves*, ed. John Johnson Collection (Paris: Jouvin's

Glove Manufactory, 1862); Smith, *Gloves Past and Present*, 72; Cumming, *Gloves*, 17.

65. Chomel, *Historie de Grenoble*, 257–60. In 1850 400,000 dozens of pairs of gloves were made in France and 110,000 dozens of pairs were exported to England.

66. Cumming, *Gloves*, 62; Ada Heather-Bigg, "Women and the Glove Trade," *Nineteenth Century* XXX, no. 178 (1891): 941; Smith, *Gloves Past and Present*, 77.

67. The phrase *cross-dressing* is used by Anne McClintock to specify the substitution of one woman's garments for another woman's garments across class lines. Although typically cross-dressing refers to transgressing gender barriers, here it is not about gender so much as it is about class.

68. Janet Zandy, *Hands: Physical Labor, Class, and Cultural Work* (New Brunswick, NJ: Rutgers University Press, 2004), xii. For a popular Victorian novel that plays upon the connection between hands and workers, see Charles Dickens, *Hard Times* (New York: Pearson Longman, 2004).

69. "hand, n.1." *OED Online*, June 2011, Oxford University Press. http://oed.com/view/Entry/83801?rskey=A7O8QM&result=1&isAdvanced=false, 8a (accessed September 7, 2011).

70. Leonore Davidoff, "Class and Gender in Victorian England: The Diaries of Arthur J. Munby and Hannah Cullwick," *Feminist Studies* 5, no. 1 (1979): 89.

71. For further information on Arthur Munby's life see: Diane Atkinson, *Love and Dirt: The Marriage of Arthur Munby and Hannah Cullwick* (London: Macmillan, 2003); Davidoff, "Class and Gender in Victorian England"; Arthur Munby, "Munby Diary," in *Munby, Man of Two Worlds: The Life and Diaries of Arthur J. Munby, 1812–1910*, ed. Derek Hudson (London: J. Murray, 1972); McClintock, *Imperial Leather*; Barry Reay, *Watching Hannah: Sexuality, Horror and Bodily De-Formation in Victorian England* (London: Reaktion Books, 2002).

72. Munby, "Munby Diary," 71.

73. Beeton, *Manners of Polite Society*, 327.

74. Noble, *Every Woman's Toilet Book*, 59.

75. The anonymous author of *The Ladies' Hand-Book of the Toilet* reassured women that they could improve their external beauty by simply cultivating good character. For similar examples see: Anon., *The Ladies' Hand-Book of the Toilet*, vii; Noble, *Every Woman's Toilet Book*, 80; Michael Curtin, *Propriety and Position: A Study of Victorian Manners* (New York: Garland, 1987); Nancy W. Ellenberger, "The Transformation of London 'Society' at the End of Victoria's Reign: Evidence from the Court Presentation Records," *Albion* 22 (1990): 633–53; Marjorie Morgan, *Manners, Morals and Class in England, 1774–1858* (Houndmills: Macmillan, 1994). For an example of American women also believing that inner character is

reflected on the physical body, see Kathy Peiss, *Hope in a Jar: The Making of America's Beauty Culture* (New York: Metropolitan Books, 1998).

76. Mrs. H.R. Haweis, *The Art of Dress* (London: Chatto and Windus, 1879), 14.

77. Anon., *Etiquette for All; or, Rules of Conduct for Every Circumstance in Life*, 40; Young, *Our Deportment; or, The Manners, Conduct and Dress of the Most Refined Society*, 322.

78. Anon., *The Ladies' Hand-Book of the Toilet*, vii.

79. B.R. Hergenhahn, *An Introduction to the History of Psychology* (Belmont: Wadsworth Cengage Learning, 2009), 245.

80. Jan Verplaetse, *Localising the Moral Brain: Neuroscience and the Search for the Cerebral Seat of Morality, 1800–1930* (London: Springer, 2009), 28.

81. Sally Shuttleworth, *Charlotte Brontë and Victorian Psychology* (Cambridge: Cambridge University Press, 1996), 63.

82. John van Wyhe, *The History of Phrenology on the Web*, http://www. historyofphrenology.org.uk/literature.html (accessed June 29, 2010).

83. John van Wyhe, *Phrenology and the Origins of Victorian Scientific Naturalism* (Burlington: Ashgate, 2004), 21.

84. Joanne Finkelstein, *The Fashioned Self* (Cambridge: Polity Press, 1991), 18; John Casper Lavater, *Essays on Physiognomy: Designed to Promote the Knowledge and the Love of Mankind*, trans. Thomas Holcroft, 12th ed. (London: William Tegg, 1862), 180; Paolo Mantegazza, *Physiognomy and Expression* (London: Walter Scott, 1890), 257.

85. Richard Beamish, *The Psychonomy of the Hand; or, The Hand: An Index of Mental Development* (London: Frederick Pitman, 1865), 85.

86. Noble, *Every Woman's Toilet Book*, 58.

87. Munby, "Munby Diary," 72; Noble, *Every Woman's Toilet Book*, 56.

–2–

"The Language of the Fan": Pushing the Boundaries of Middle-Class Womanhood

In 1823 *The British Essayists* published a fictitious story that would reso-
nate for the Victorians and be republished in the nineteenth century time
and again. "Delamira Resigns Her Fan" is the story of a beautiful, confident,
fashionable young lady who, upon choosing a husband, was asked by a close
friend to divulge the secret of her success. Delamira responds that: "All she
had above the rest of her sex and contemporary beauties was wholly owing
to a fan, (that was left her by her mother, and had been long in the family)
which," she reveals "whoever had it in possession, and used with skill, would
command the hearts of all her beholders; and since, she said smiling, I have
no more to do with extending my conquests or triumphs, I will make you a
present of this inestimable rarity . . . I wish you heartily as much success in
the management of it as I have had."[1] This conversation shared between two
intimate friends sarcastically suggests that any man caught in the flutter of
Delamira's fan would be hopelessly attracted to her with a lack of free will.
Average Victorian women were likely not as sure of their fans as Delamira.
There is little doubt, however, that women used fans to their advantage as
performative accessories that opened up social possibilities; the color and
design of fans that were expertly deployed could attract the interest of those
around them.

The story of Delamira begins to develop the idea of flirting as a modern
middle-class behavior. Through cultural codes of flirtation, the fan offered single women a mechanism for attracting mates without compromising their social status through overt displays of public sexuality. The study of this open
yet illicit sexuality has been termed *parasexuality*. The word is suggestive of
a sexuality that is both engaged and limited; parasexuality is a carefully channeled and managed form, in historian Peter Bailey's words it is "everything
but."[2] This chapter suggests that flirtation *permeated* the cultural games of
the middle class, but that it is less visible because it is not part of a class
stereotype, as is the case with the aristocratic coquette, or as a transgression
of cross-class flirtation between the barmaid or shop girl and the middle-class
male customer.[3] As a colorful and rather large extension of the hand, the fan
can be opened, closed, and fluttered in a way that attracts attention and can

be used to emphasize a look, an emotion, or convey a point. By studying the fan, an object that takes on meaning because of social relationships that go on around it, middle-class flirtations are revealed. The phenomenon of flirtation within this class helps to challenge the separate sphere doctrine in which women are seen as asexual and passive.

Another phenomenon that created a debate about women and their place in society was the Census of 1851. For the first time in this census figures were released concerning the age, sex, and marital status of men and women in Britain.[4] This brought into focus what Britons of the time perceived as a demographic crisis: a surplus of unmarried middle-class women. Census numbers revealed that over half of the adult female population was unmarried. This quickly became part of a national debate, waged within newspapers, in pamphlets, and at public lectures, that came to be termed "the surplus women question."[5] After the Census of 1881 journalists identified that the surplus of women had been exaggerated, or at least misinterpreted. According to an 1889 article "Excess of Widows over Widowers" published in *Westminster Review*: "It is not the spinsters who constitute the surplus female population and by whom the labour market is flooded, but the widows."[6] Young widows would have had less social pressure to marry and might have chosen not to remarry, pursuing other options like paid employment. As early as the 1850s advocates for women's education, employment, higher wages, and fairer laws had used census data about surplus women to bolster their arguments for women's rights.[7] I will show that the fan was embroiled in two aspects of the surplus women question. First, it acted as a tool of the middle-class flirt who used it to attract a husband and thereby escape the social stigma of spinster or widowhood. And second, it offered respectable employment: fan design was an occupation acceptable for middle-class women. While Delamira's flirtatious fanning was one way of utilizing this accessory to escape the problems of redundancy, women's employment in fan design offered another.

Adding fuel to the fiery question of women's place in the world of work was the English fear that France was eclipsing Britain as the fashionable capital of Europe. The Great Exhibition of 1851 held in London's Hyde Park was promoted by Prince Albert "for the purposes of exhibition, of competition and of encouragement." Victoria's consort believed that such an exhibition "would afford a true test of the point of development at which the whole of mankind has arrived in this great task, and a new starting point from which all nations would be able to direct their further exertions."[8] All of the objects displayed at the Exhibition were under competition for prizes. England did not submit any fans for competition (though some of her colonies did) leaving France to win the gold medal for fan manufacture. Heeding Albert's suggestion that the competition would create new directions for industry and design, the British government honed in on the fan as an accessory that could prove the nation's artistic merit.[9] During the second half of the century, the government established such institutions as schools of design, the Victoria and Albert Museum, and the Department of Practical Art. It also supported national and international exhibitions to develop an English aesthetic. Springing from these efforts, fans became the object that sustained England's concept of itself as a fashionable nation.

The increased role of women within the public sphere worried some Victorians who became nostalgic for a mythical past when British women stayed in the home as submissive wives and attentive mothers. Many looked to East Asia, the birthplace of the fan, as the idealized British past in which gender roles were well defined.[10] Lisa Lowe, a scholar of comparative literature, suggests that the fetishized preoccupation with oriental women was really a reflection of a range of British national concerns including changing sexual roles in a time of rapid industrialization.[11] During the last third of the nineteenth century, after Japan had been opened to the West, the British created a stereotype of the innocent and submissive maid from Japan who forever hid her loveliness behind a fan.[12] In British writing, Japanese women were depicted as having submissive behaviors, and the fan's flirtatious potential was downplayed so that the Japanese woman appeared to be the idealized middle-class woman of the British past.

MANUFACTURING THE FAN: IMPLICATIONS FOR FASHION AND "THE SURPLUS WOMEN QUESTION"

In the nineteenth century the British tried to revive the art of fanmaking in part in order to address what Victorians had come to call the "surplus women question." This debate, which centered around definitions of what type of woman a middle-class lady should be and what her place should be within society, came to the fore because of statistics revealed by the 1851 Census. Victorians exaggerated the census data in order to emphasize the seriousness of having a population of women who had no place in society because of their inability to find a husband. In a lecture, "Sisters of Charity: Abroad and at Home," feminist Anna Jameson stated "that in the last census of 1851, there appears an excess of the female over the male population of Great Britain of more than half a million."[13] Relying on this same census another feminist of the mid-nineteenth century, Barbara Leigh-Smith, wrote, "of women at the age of 20 and upwards, 43 out of 100 in England and Wales are unmarried."[14] Leading journalist W. R. Greg wrote in his article "Why Are Women Redundant?": "there is an enormous and increasing number of single women in the nation, a number quite disproportionate and quite abnormal; a number which, positively and relatively, is indicative of an unwholesome social state."[15] Historian Martha Vicinus shows that these claims were exaggerated, and that about seven of every eight women could expect to marry.[16] But for

Victorians "the surplus women question" was a real problem that deserved their attention. Conservative thinkers on the subject could not see past women's domestic role. They suggested solutions such as emigration to a better marriage market, and encouraging men and women to marry at an earlier age, as well as recommending that men end their bachelorhood. Another group, however, considered "the surplus women question" an opportunity to carve out new roles for middle-class women in society where they might still maintain their femininity but be able to engage in well-paid work informed by a technical education. It was this latter group of liberal thinkers with whom we are concerned here.

To understand the movement to engage middle-class women in the manufacture of fans, it is helpful to provide some background on the history and structure of this industry. Originally fans were not manufactured in England; they were a foreign import. No solid historical work has been done about the worldwide history of the fan; nonetheless authors from the nineteenth century as well as modern writers about fan collection suggest that they came from Japan to England through Europe in the early 1500s.[17] Some historians credit the Italian-born French queen, Catherine De Medici, for bringing the folding fan from her native country and making it a popular accessory in France.[18] The story of De Medici's introduction of the fan helps to explain why fan manufacture took off in France with the result that it became the premier fanmaking and fan-exporting country of Europe from the last quarter of the fifteenth century well into the early twentieth century.[19] During the 1600s the fan became fashionable in England as well. Nineteenth-century authors suggest that the fan took longer to gain popularity in England because "the sturdy ladies of this island [never] thought of any special manufactured appliance to protect themselves from the mild heat of a summer consisting of three days and a thunderstorm."[20] Yet by the beginning of the eighteenth century, the growing British interest in fans was reflected by the increased cultural recognition they were receiving. In 1709 the Worshipful Company of Fan Makers was established (acquiring 266 members in one short year), and *The Tatler* and *The Spectator* wrote popular satirical articles about women's fan use in England.[21]

The making of the folding fan was a complex process that required precision at every stage.[22] When assembled in a factory a single fan was handled by between fifteen and twenty different workers. First there were those who made the guards and the ribs of the fan: they began by cutting rough shapes out of materials such as ivory, tortoise shell, mother of pearl, bone, bamboo, or wood, and then using scrapers to thin the material down. These were then passed on to the piercers and inlayers who made designs in the material. This was men's work that was done by hand until a machine to cut and pierce sticks was invented in 1859 by Alphonse Baude of Oise, France.

The image on the fan leaf, which was made of lace, thin paper, or paper lined with silk, calico, parchment, lamb or chicken skin, required the expertise of a designer and painter, or printer. Such famous artists as Francois Boucher, Antoine Watteau, and Camille Roqueplan designed fans in their workshops that were later copied by working-class women in fanmaking factories. As we will see, a higher class of British women artists aspired to add their names to these French masters. Once the leaf was painted the fan was pleated with the help of a mold made of walnut, which was invented in 1760 by the Petit family of France.[23] To insert the sticks into the leaf a tool similar to a paper knife was probed between the two layers of the fan leaf and the sticks were inserted and secured with glue. Adding the finishing touches like the tassels, loops, and ribbons was traditionally working-class women's work.

While the popularity of fans increased in Britain into the 1800s, the British fanmaking industry did not grow at the same pace. Britain was simply not able to compete with the French manufacturers despite efforts by both the British government and the Worshipful Company at various times to bolster the English fanmaking trade. They imposed tariffs and prohibitions on imports, seized and burned foreign fans, established a newspaper and handbill campaign imploring women to buy British, and invited French fanmakers to establish themselves in England.[24] By 1822 there were only nine London fanmaking establishments and by 1839 the number had dwindled to two. By comparison, in 1827, the number of French manufacturers was 15 and this increased to 122 by 1847.[25] At the Great Exhibition of 1851 Britain did not submit a single item for the fanmaking competition, leaving all the prizes to be won by the French.

During this same year, the British Census was published, the response to which led to the public preoccupation with the "surplus women question." Louisa Avant & Co. (a London fan manufacturer), the Female School of Design, and the Worshipful Company all saw a solution in this convergence of events: why not revive the British fanmaking industry and provide work for middle-class women at the same time?

"The fan is so essentially feminine," suggested an article from *The Lady* in 1890, "and is so delicate and pretty in every stage of its creation, that women should be responsible for its manufacture from beginning to end."[26] While working-class women had been involved in certain aspects of fan manufacture from the beginning, in the middle of the nineteenth century, some began to suggest that fanmaking would be an excellent pursuit for the "dainty grace" of middle-class women.[27] Since fanmaking required a varied expertise that no one person was expected to possess, unmarried women in need of employment were encouraged to concentrate on a particular aspect of the fan trade, traditionally reserved for skilled craftsmen: fan painting and design (figure 2.1). Given that there were very few fanmaking establishments in mid-nineteenth-century England, these women were welcomed as artists that might revive a lost London trade. There is evidence that some women were successfully employed in this way. The Working Ladies' Guild established in

THE FAN PAINTER.

Figure 2.1 A young woman paints a fan. This was thought of as a proper middle-class pastime. Bodleian Library, *Beauty and Fashion*, February 28, 1891, 177.

1877 "to aid Gentlewomen requiring assistance" had a depot where handi-work done by ladies could be viewed and orders could be taken. As part of the guild a special Fan Department was created to ensure that women's fan painting could be shown, bought, and distributed.[28] For example, Charlotte James, a graduate of the Female School of Design (that was established to help train and find employment for redundant middle-class women) was em-ployed as a fan designer.[29] In 1909 the Women Workers' Directory advertised that two places were taking fan painting pupils.[30] And finally, *Ladies at Work: Papers on Paid Employment for Ladies* suggested in 1893 that women artists would not make much money as painters in their early careers but that they might supplement their income by "designing Christmas cards and booklets; painting panels, screens and fans, drawing costumes, etc." Women were as-sured that if they did a variety of delicate painting jobs "it is not very difficult to make an income of one or perhaps two hundred pounds in a year, if one is willing to do anything."[31]

The Warehouse and Manufactory of Louisa Avant & Co. in London was more dedicated than most to generating employment for ladies in need.[32] An 1889 article, "Finding Employment for Women," explained that "All employed here are women, and the energetic ladies who have originated and who carry on the business may be called public benefactors" for their part in providing a solution to the "surplus women question."[33] Engaged at the firm were five hundred "lady workers" in the form of artists, apprentices, and needlewomen who "busy as bees" made a variety of fancy articles, including fans.[34] In what were reassuringly described as "airy and spacious workrooms" women made fans by applying "appliqué on net; scrolls of brocade . . . on grounds of chicken skin or kid; bouquets and wreathes and festoons of flowers exquisitely painted on gauze; and finally, lace in its richest of textures and its grandest forms of arrangement."[35] These "subtleties of ordinance, arrangement, and contrast," thought the author of an article in *The Daily Telegraph*, "are employments peculiarly adapted to the capacity of the female sex."[36] A speaker "On Civic Art" went one step further arguing that the company helped "emancipate" women by "increasing their facilities for studying art." Before this company opened, suggested Mr. Sala, "not 5 percent—not 2.5 percent—of the fans used were made in England," a situation that was thought to be rectified by this single company.[37] Adding to Sala's praise, the Worshipful Company of Fan Makers granted Louisa Avant and her business partner the Freedom of the City of London for the steps they had taken "to bring English girls into the trade."[38] Neither did the firm stop at creating expertise in fan design and fan painting, the company brought experts from Paris and Venice to teach fan mounting and began to offer two- and three-year apprenticeships with a guarantee of employment in the firm "if the pupil be a good worker."[39] This expertise would come in handy, when the lady workers of Louisa Avant & Co. were commissioned to mount fans designed and painted for the fanmaking exhibition of 1890.[40]

Another institution that was dedicated to answering the surplus women question in the form of training and employing women was the Female School of Design.[41] According to an 1860 article from *Macmillan's Magazine* an objective of the school was to "enable young women of the middle class to obtain an honourable and profitable employment."[42] During the first ten years of its existence the Council of the School of Design encouraged "redundant" women to apply to its institution by asking for a small tuition fee, appropriate for lower-middle-class ladies.[43] At this point the school was meant only for middle-class women in search of respectable employment in lieu of marriage to the exclusion of such other groups as working-class women, and leisured women of the aristocracy and the middle class.[44] By the 1870s the school was teaching fan design as a strategy to help middle-class women become self-sufficient.

The school delighted in explaining the successes of those pupils who had gone through sad circumstances. When the schools of design were under review by a Select Committee in 1849 the Female School's superintendent, Fanny Mclan, was asked what type of students attended her school. She responded that, "They are highly respectable, the whole of them; we have had most distressing and painful cases of the daughters of professional men, whose fathers have died prematurely; the young women have been brought up in great comfort," Mclan explains, "but from their fathers leaving no provisions for them they are entirely dependent upon their own exertions. There is one who is receiving a guinea and a half for lithography whose father has just died . . . but for the School she must have gone out as a servant in some other way."[45] In another instance it was said that seventy-seven of one hundred students in 1860 "are studying with the view of ultimately maintaining themselves. Some of them, daughters of Clergymen and medical men, unexpectedly compelled, by a variety of causes, to gain their own livelihood, and even to support others besides themselves, have through the instruction and assistance received here, obtained good appointments in Schools, or are enabled to live independently by means of private teaching."[46]

In seeking an answer to "the surplus women question," the school had to offer feminine job opportunities for graduating middle-class pupils. To this end Mclan established formal connections between her school and industry to ensure a smooth transition for the women who graduated from her program. In 1845, for example, Mclan acquainted herself with every porcelain manufacturer of note in England. She reported in *The Athenaeum* that women designers would be welcome in the industry: "I have been assured by the chief artists of one of the principal porcelain establishments in Staffordshire, that if, in the Female School of Somerset House, a class were formed for studying the art of painting porcelain in a superior manner, the more skilful pupils might readily obtain from the manufacturers transmissions of work to be executed *at home*; so that," she notes, bringing a class element into the discussion, "without any injurious interference with the uneducated female artists, or rather artisans, in the potteries, a constant and beneficial employment might be procured."[47]

The school would go on to have other successes in connecting women and industry. By 1850, *The Art-Journal* reported that women from the Female School of Design had successfully sold designs for a variety of items including chintz, table-covers, muslin, paper hangings, mosaic-tables, carpets, and print dresses.[48] By 1860 students found work in an increasing variety of areas including linen, carpet, and papier-mâché designing. Queen Victoria supported the pupils by buying lace designs to be worn by three of her daughters as part of their wedding dresses, and another student was commissioned to paint portraits of the royal dogs.[49] Some were even employed full-time, six students "gained their living for several years, by Designing and Painting Japanned Articles, in Wolverhampton; one was for several years a Designer in Damask Manufactory in Scotland; and another supports herself by Lithography; and three are employed in a Glass Factory; where they draw and paint figures and ornamental subjects for glass windows." The promise was that female designers could work in all of these industries "without necessarily taking them out of their proper sphere."[50]

Around the 1870s the Female School of Design turned its attention to fan painting and design. In 1869 "as a means of stimulating a new branch of industry specifically available to women" a prize for fan design was established by the Department of Science and Art for government-affiliated art schools. In 1873 the Queen's Scholarship (valued at £30) was awarded to Alice Blanche Ellis for a design of flowers in watercolor to be printed on a silk fan. Ellis's fan was also purchased locally for £3.3s. by Dr. John Braxton Hicks, the doctor who specialized in obstetrics famous for "discovering" the Braxton Hicks contractions.[51] More than thirty years later, the famed historical and portrait painter Jonn Seymour Loucas encouraged women of the school to continue with this artistic endeavor saying "fan painting . . . is very beautiful work."[52]

Some believed that the potential of women to reignite the English fan industry was so great that a special school for fan design should be established. In 1878 Mr. E. Barrington Nash began to raise money for a school of artistic fan painting. "The object of this school," explained Nash, "is to provide profitable employment for the gentlewomen of artistic ability, and to retain some portion of the 100,000 pounds, which enormous figure represents the value of the annual import of fans of an artistic character in England."[53]

Women from technical schools became increasingly interested in fanmaking as a trade due to the variety of fanmaking competitions that appeared in the last quarter of the nineteenth century. The Department of Science and Art hosted a series of annual fan exhibitions from 1868 to 1871.[54] It encouraged entries from the female schools of design by establishing monetary prizes for women who would take up the craft as a form of employment. For the International Exhibition of 1871 Queen Victoria offered a prize of £40 "for the best fan exhibited . . . executed by a lady artist or artists."[55]

In 1877, however, The Worshipful Company of Fan Makers was languishing; fanmaking was not an important trade in London, leaving the company with a lack of purpose and a lack of fanmaking members. But when a solicitor by the name of Sir Homewood Crawford became the Master of the Company his "untiring efforts" to revive the fan trade took the form of three increasingly successful exhibitions.[56] As well as highlighting Britain's design abilities, these exhibitions also were said to give "elegant and artistic employment to . . . gentlewomen" and received much attention from technical schools, some of whom bought special equipment to ensure their female students had a good chance of coming away with a prize.[57]

Crawford's main vision for these exhibitions was patriotic: "In the hope of reviving the trade of fan making in Great Britain."[58] But the exhibitions had a secondary mission to "induce many English ladies to paint and push the sale of fans in this country."[59] The first exhibition, held at the Drapers' Hall in July 1878, was successful on both these counts. It had more than one hundred exhibitors, including manufacturers, amateurs, collectors and dealers, contributing £15,000 worth of fans into five categories ranging from Ancient European Fans to Modern Fans of British Manufacture.[60] Prizes were granted for the purpose of highlighting British manufacture on the basis of taste, excellence of workmanship, and originality of design for "fan-leaves painted or embroidered on silk, satin, cloth or any other material, and of fan-leaves made of lace of various sorts."[61] Modern fans "completely made in Great Britain or Ireland by British subjects" received the Freedom of the Company Gold, Silver, and Bronze medals, and monetary prizes ranging from five to twenty-five guineas.[62]

Helping to prove that employment in fanmaking might be a solution for "surplus women," five out of six of the prizes for mounted and unmounted fans went to unmarried women. And London's mayor, speaking at the prize ceremony, announced, "I am pleased to find an Irish lady [Miss Elizabeth Laird] in the proud position of first winner."[63] Schools of design also benefited from the exhibition: "so that technical education might be encouraged," the show was open for two nights at a reduced cost and the large attendance on these nights added to the 12,000 total visitors at the exhibition.[64] Furthermore Mr. Wallis, one of the judges, "having noted the great excellence of the workmanship of some of the fans, . . . recommended that they should be purchased by the Science and Art Department at South Kensington," which had a mandate to circulate objects of interest to schools of design helping to create further interest in fanmaking.[65] Despite the overwhelming enthusiasm for the exhibition the Fan Makers found themselves at a deficit after this exhibition. It is perhaps for this reason that they did not run another exhibition for more than ten years.

In 1889 the Worshipful Company put on a second fan exhibition but this time it decided to focus entirely on modern British design and manufacture to the exclusion of other countries and historic fans.[66] Since the first exhibition, the company seems to have become increasingly active in the design community and it now attracted prize donors such as Lady Charlotte Schreiber, famous for her fan collection; Mr. George Wallis, of the South Kensington Museum; and Mr. Edward Joseph, art editor of *The Queen*. The exhibit attracted 100 original designs from England, Scotland, Wales, and Ireland. In terms of gender the prize distribution favored unmarried women: the metal prizes were won by two women and three men, and seven women and three men received mention for their Highly Recommended fans. However, the overall winner of the competition was Mr. Walter W. Morris.

By 1890 the Worshipful Company was well versed in how to put on a successful exhibition; for this final exhibition the company widened its expectations and pushed British fanmakers to become proficient in all aspects of their craft. No longer was it willing to accept unmounted fans: there had been criticism in the press suggesting that the fanmaking trade would never be successful if British manufactures kept sending their fans abroad to be mounted, driving up the costs of the British-made product.[67] It also created new categories for the competition to encourage certain aspects of the trade such as competition for stick and guard makers, a class for fans of entirely novel designs not found in France or Japan, and a class for designs of inexpensive fans of five shillings to three guineas.[68] Along the same lines, the organizers sought to encourage those already involved in the trade by including categories for apprentices, and for any person or firm who was carrying on a commercial retail business.[69] And they drew, once again, on their connections to the London design community, receiving donated prizes worth £275, which attracted 600 exhibits.[70]

The rhetoric surrounding this particular fan exhibition was especially geared toward employing the "brains and fingers" of unmarried ladies.[71] Early on in the preparations an article in *Echo* praises the Worshipful Company for "not forg[etting] their responsibilities towards what might be made a very remonstrative industry to women of artistic tastes."[72] Later the *St. James' Gazette* reported that the revival of fanmaking in the country would be "to the benefit of the regiments of educated and artistically minded women who are sighing for the means to a livelihood."[73] At a livery dinner of the fanmakers at the end of February, Mr. Bigwood "hoped" in his speech "that the forthcoming exhibition would be successful, and that they might induce many English ladies to take up fan-painting, whereby they might assist not only in developing a pleasing and interesting art, but also provide themselves with profitable employment."[74] At this same event Mr. Hume-Williams received cheers when he suggested that these fanmaking exhibitions "develop the artistic proclivities, especially of the womanhood of England, increasing their incomes in their homes, and cultivating a refined and gentle science."[75] Near the end of the exhibition *Whitehall Review* added that "a demand for good painted fans would be a great assistance to struggling women artists; and we may hope that the pretty examples" from the exhibition "will find their way afterwards into our shops," helping these women make a decent livelihood.[76] Nonetheless to the disappointment of the "lady correspondent" of the *Birmingham Daily Post* "though ladies were in the majority among the prize winners, the highest prizes of all were won by men."[77]

This being the third exhibition of the company it also received more concentrated criticism in the press than did the previous two exhibitions. A correspondent from the *Manchester Examiner* admitted that the exhibition "is decidedly better than last year's" but adds scathingly: "many of the competitors show ignorance of the first principles of decorative art, and send ambitious landscapes and figure groups where flowers, butterflies, or sprays are wanted. Moreover," suggests the author, "the figures are universally weak in drawing, as indeed one expects in nearly all English work."[78] An article from

The Queen agreed with this point adding that "many fan painters fail utterly in presenting pleasing faces."[79] In one article the *Daily Graphic* argues that the exhibition "demonstrates that the fan trade is still at a stage which needs fostering care, if it is to resume the position it enjoyed in the last century as a great national art craft."[80] In another article the newspaper praises the company for including prizes for "cheap fans" but criticizes the exhibitors in this category for submitting painted fans, which "at that price would simply mean starvation to the unfortunate woman artist employed to execute it."[81] The author further condemns the fan stick class, saying that it was "poor, and lacking in originality."[82] Reporters for *The Queen* who were great supporters of the exhibition, even donating prizes, said that while many exhibits were worthy of notice "many, too, [were] deserving of strong censure; indeed, it was a matter of wonder how the managers of the exhibition permitted the presence of several."[83]

Sir Polydore De Keyser, the former Lord Mayor of London, believed that the fan exhibitions "led to industry." In fact, he "felt convinced that in this particular instance they would find the trade of fan making would come back to this country."[84] This was not, however, to be the case. By the nineteenth century France had developed a fan industry with a strong exporting trade. In both Oise and Paris there were trained artists, designers, and artisans that came together to make fans from beginning to end. This differed from London fanmaking companies who routinely sent fan-leaves to the Continent, or to French fanmaking companies within London, where beautiful sticks were created and artisans were trained in fan-mounting.[85] Also the French industry had a variety of price ranges for its fans, allowing it to access more markets. Even France's most famous fan house, Maison Duvelleroy, exported fans for as little as 40s per dozen.[86] During the third exhibition of the Worshipful Company it was demonstrated that fan designers in the United Kingdom were much more interested in the expensive and artistic fan market than in developing cheap fans. The French also had the artistic cachet that attracted famous artists to paint on fans, unlike English designers who tended to be women with less prominence in the art world and were accused of being "weak in drawing." Around 1890 an English newspaper reported that "several of our large millinery and fancy firms spend from 2,000 to 6,000 a year" purchasing fans from the Continent.[87] In the final years of the nineteenth century, European fanmaking was decidedly centered in France not England.[88]

The practice of English fanmaking intersected with various cultural concerns: the unease with the French ascendancy in areas of fashion, art, and design; the fear of the loss of English industry to other nations; and the need to provide work for redundant middle-class women. In the end, the companies, design schools, and exhibitions that encouraged women to enter the fan trade generated more trained women than the British fan industry was likely to be able to absorb. Though fanmaking was not a viable option for middle-class women seeking work in industry, it became part of the way that people addressed "the surplus women question."

A second way in which the fan was implicated in "the surplus women question" was through flirtation. Women trying to survive in an overpopulated marriage market had two main options: to find work so that they would not become destitute, or to attract a man to marry. During the second half of the nineteenth century, as "the surplus women question" began to pick up steam, the fan became strongly associated with the husband-hunting coquette.

CONSUMING THE FAN: THE FAN AS AN ACCESSORY OF THE COQUETTE

As we have seen, after the Census of 1851 the media, along with women's rights groups, became increasingly vocal about what they thought was a bad marriage market for middle-class women due to the late age of marriage, male emigration to the colonies, and earlier male-to-female death rates.[89] In 1891, according to historian Martha Vicinus, there were 2,009,489 unmarried women between the ages of twenty and forty-four in England and Wales and 342,072 unmarried women of forty-five years and older.[90] Victorians themselves believed that the problem was even worse than modern historians have shown; in 1892 an article in *The Nineteenth Century* suggested that one in six women in England and Wales would likely become spinsters.[91] Though these claims were exaggerated, some women of the period must have believed in the hype and looked for advantages that would help them attract a husband. Conservative thinkers on the matter, like W. R. Greg, suggested that women act as courtesans, to attract a husband.[92] The fan was a known quantity in the battle for men's hearts. Middle-class women who learned to use their fans properly might have an advantage in what was thought to be a bad marriage market. However, to many a vicious poet, unsympathetic and unsupportive of women's plight, the flirt was drawn as a troubling social type as she was aware of the power she possessed through her sexuality. While flirtatious women were essentially "good women" who had taken the search for a husband into their own hands, the move away from domestic womanhood created anxiety for some Victorians who preferred to see women's true nature as passive and domestic.

Advice writers in the nineteenth century insisted that the things with which women surrounded themselves—clothing, accessories, home decor—were reflections of their inner characters. Ideally, the fan presented no exception to the notion that a woman's true nature was reflected in her interactions with her accessories. An article in *The Illustrated London News* suggested that women "not only" used fans to "move the air and cool themselves but also to express their sentiments."[93] Articles of this persuasion showed that the very materiality of the fan, as a light object held in the hand near the face, created an almost inevitable transfer of a woman's emotional state to her fashionable accessory. The fan was thus a direct reflection, or an "outering" of the woman's inner state. In 1864 an article in *The Queen* demonstrates this point: "I have seen a fan so very angry, that it would have been dangerous for the absent lover who provoked it to have come within the wind of it," suggests the author, "and at other times so very languishing, that I have been glad for the lady's sake the lover was at a sufficient distance from it. I need not add," the author went on, "that a fan is either a prude or coquette, according to the nature of the person who bears it."[94] At the prize ceremony for the 1878 exhibition put on by the Worshipful Company of Fan Makers, Mr. Sherif Beven's speech was greeted with laughter when he similarly explained "the sentimentality of fanship." He joked that "every form of emotion was produced in the flutter of a fan." For example, "There was the flutter of anger, of modesty, the merry flutter, and the amorous flutter. Show him the fan of a disciplined lady," boasted Beven, "and he would tell whether she would laugh, frown, or blush."[95] At the final exhibition put on by the Fan Makers, Crawford speaks similarly about his beloved British fan: "there is no mood it is not capable of representing . . . no passion almost which it cannot reflect."[96] These views of the fan continue into the Edwardian period; an article entitled "Weapons and Ornaments of Woman" from 1909 notes: "Whether the woman who wields it be inquisitive, nervous, capricious, indiscreet, ironic, spiteful, passionate or languid, caressing or sad, feline or haughty, the fan expresses her every state of mind, her anxieties, her vanities, her weaknesses."[97] These articles and speeches conceptualize the fan as a mirror for the inner emotions of its bearer, be she angry or sad, a proper Victorian lady or an insatiable flirt. This begs the question, does the fan always act as an extension of the body transparently reflecting women's emotions or can it be consciously used as a prop by women who are playing a game? In other words can fans be used to conceal emotions and sexual appearance or interest rather than simply acting as an object that is affected directly by a woman's character? Also what sorts of interpersonal relationships come out of a society that is increasingly invested in things like fans?

If a woman was aware that her fan was an accessory that might express her emotional state, she could also use it to conceal unwanted thoughts or as a device to be manipulated into demonstrating feelings that the woman wished she possessed. "Artful maneuverings are concealed behind those fluffy little tips," suggests an article in *Beauty and Fashion*, "which are useful for so many purposes, and serve to hide . . . various awkward habits of nature, such as a vivid blush or a tear that we would fain conceal from strangers' eyes."[98] Here the fan is used to cover up the feminine nature of a good woman who would prefer her embarrassing emotionality represented in a flushed or sad face to be hidden at public occasions. If, on the other hand, the vivid blush of innocence had been lost, the *Daily News* suggested ways in which women could feign innocence through the use of their fans: "It is the movement betwixt heart and lip which is so important. When a blush refuses to suffuse the snowy neck, then must be brought into play the modest flutter— a gentle wafting of a morsel of ivory and Watteau painted silk with a scarcely palpable trembling of the hand." And, to complete the illusion of innocence, "eyes must be cast downwards."[99] The passive asexual woman of the middle class is not depicted in this later example, which suggests instead the artful manipulation of the predominant gender norms.

The most explicit example of women using fans as performative accessories is what contemporaries called "the language of the fan."[100] Legend has it that Louis Duvelleroy, the illegitimate son of the founder of the House of Duvelleroy, brought the language of the fan to England in the mid-nineteenth century.[101] The Maison Duvelleroy in London included instructions for flirtation with each fan sold while similar directives appeared in advertisements for perfume and encyclopedias.[102] When fan motions became a set of instructions and communications, Victorians were lightheartedly acknowledging a frivolous but key element to heterosexual courtship. Consider, for example, these instructions that appeared in a pamphlet in 1899:

Open and shut—you are cruel.
Open wide—Wait for me.
Closing—I wish to speak to you.
Shut—You have changed.
Handle to lips—Kiss me.
Dropping—We will be friends.
Carrying in right hand—I wish to be acquainted.
Twirling in right hand—I love another.
Twirling in left hand—I wish to get rid of you.
Resting on right cheek—Yes.
Resting on left cheek—No.
Drawing across forehead—We are watched.
Drawing across eyes—I am sorry.
Drawing across cheek—I love you.[103]

According to these instructions particular turns of the fan could communicate interest, scold, and even invite closer physical contact. Though some men "never succeeded in solving the mystery of their witchery," the fan was an object that pronounced body language. It was not imperative that a male suitor understand the language explicitly; it was sufficient for him to know that he was being flirted with. As the Baronne de Chapt explains: "What a brilliant role is played by the fan when it is found at the end of an arm which gesticulates and salutes from the depth of a carriage or a garden. It says to him who understands it that she who holds it in her hand is in raptures at seeing him."[104] By helping to exaggerate flirtatious body language, the fan brought sexual feelings into the public sphere; it became a way of acknowledging and indicating heterosexuality without actually talking about sex directly.

Apart from the quip made by Addison that "I teach young gentlemen the whole Art of Gallanting a Fan," there is no evidence that "the language of the fan" was reproduced for a masculine audience.[105] However, it is not hard to imagine that women could convey simple signals with a hand-held accessory. Writing in 1906 Octave Uzanne shows how women communicated with their fans without using an explicit fan language: "She knows instinctively that all the intrigue of lover, all the finesse, all the graces of her 'yes' or 'no,' every inflection of her sigh, are hidden in the folds of her fan."[106] In his *Contarini Fleming: A Psychological Romance* author and once Prime Minister Benjamin Disraeli illustrates how much men actually did pay attention to the fluttering of fans. Musing about a gathering in Spain Disraeli writes: "The fan is the most wonderful part of the whole scene." He goes on, explaining how the simple device can hold the attention of the men standing round. "Now she unfurls it with the slow pomp and conscious elegance of the bird of Juno; now she flutters it with all the languor of a listless beauty, now with all the liveliness of a vivacious one. Now, in the mist of a very tornado, she closes it with a whirr, which makes you start. In the midst of your confusion Delorous taps you on your elbow; you turn round to listen, and Catalina pokes you on your side. Magical instrument! In this land it speaks a particular language, and gallantry needs no other mode to express its most subtle conceits or its most unreasonable demands than this delicate machine."[107] Disraeli shows that even when the fan is not being used to speak directly, it conveys certain thoughts and feelings to male onlookers; a strike on the back, a poke in the side, and a change of movement depending on emphasis of speech and emotion would easily be deciphered by men of this era. The fan represented a reversal of predominant gender norms of the day, making the male observer a recipient of the woman's advances. Though the man could choose to respond, the female fan holder possessed the instrument of communication and therefore the power to converse with or ignore interested parties (figure 2.2).

While the language of the fan gave women an active role in the process of finding a lover and potential husband, the iconography of the fan still dichotomized women along the lines of the good asexual woman and the flirtatious coquette. Fashion plates of the day reinforced the iconography of passive womanhood. The vast majority of folding fans in these images remained closed. The woman of the fashion plate was a proper British lady: asexual and passive. Therefore, fans remained folded: hung from clasps on the waist, held nonchalantly at the side, or positioned to draw attention to tiny torsos (figure 2.3). Perhaps the closed fan guards, which held leaves in place and hid the flowers that often decorated folding fans, could represent the woman's closed legs and her impenetrable chastity.

Figure 2.2 A pretty young woman surrounded by six male admirers uses her fan to communicate her chosen companion for the last waltz. Circa 1875. 10128323, Mary Evans Picture Library.

On the rare occasion that fashion plates incorporated unfolded fans, the posturing of the device and the passivity of the gaze negated any coquettish implications that the object might have conveyed. In the conservative fashion plate iconography, women only held unfolded fans below their face and neck or at their sides with glances focused away from the viewer toward nothing in particular, rather than looking toward the man she intended to seduce (figure 2.4). In fashion plates, the potential for flirtation was stopped by the way women's eyes were cast; the gaze remained passive when the fan was open, or the fan was kept resolutely closed. In these cases the iconography of the fan reinforced the Victorian ideals of female passivity and asexuality that were all-important for maintaining the separate sphere ideology explored in the pervious chapter.[108]

Images from song sheets tended to emphasize the second, more dangerous, model of womanhood: the flirtatious female. These images almost

No. 2. DINNER BODICE.

Dark terra-cotta satin, trimmed with a band of a deeper shade, studded with pearls. Bouillonné plastron of cream Indian muslin, with under sleeves to correspond. The square opening has a frill of the muslin. The bodice is laced at the back. Peasant cap with field flowers. Bodice, 2s. 7d.

Figure 2.3 The vast majority of the fashion plates picture women with their fans closed and their gazes passive, giving the onlooker the impression that these are proper Victorian wives and mothers rather than flirtatious coquettes. Robarts Library, University of Toronto, "Dress and Fashion," *The Queen, The Lady's Newspaper*, July 9, 1881, 46.

exclusively illustrate fashionable middle-class women as coquettes who used their fans to attract male attention. In these images the iconography is sexual and almost aggressive: women hold fans over their noses to emphasize "the language of the eye," which is directed toward potential lovers; "the flirt" brings her open fan at her breast allowing an "innocent" blush to be seen on her cheeks while deliberately toying with three male suitors; and the "belle of the ball" is so practiced at fan flirtation that she need not open her weapon but rather holds it closed, up to her chin with a perceptive nod and half grin (figure 2.5).[109] In all of these images the women demonstrate knowledge of their powers as seductresses. The passive, unfocused gazes of fashion plates are replaced with fleeting, purposeful glances over fan leaves: these women were aggressively hunting for husbands rather than passively waiting for a proposal.

Middle-class women who actively sought out husbands were trafficking in coquettery. In the eighteenth century the meaning of the coquette was split between the positive figure of the Grand Dame of the French salon known for

Figure 2.4 The open fan of fashion plates is never the fan of a coquette. This woman does not use the fan to accentuate her eyes nor does she look out at the viewer with knowledge of her sexual power. Robarts Library, University of Toronto, "Dress and Fashion," *The Queen, The Lady's Newspaper*, July 24, 1880, 78.

her conversational talent and social performance, and an unsettling social type engaged in "wicked erotic gamesmanship" that threatened the stability of the emerging middle-class morality.[110] In either case the coquette was a woman who teased men arousing their passions while refusing their sexual advances. By the nineteenth century the aristocratic coquette was joined in this game by young working-class service workers, such as shop girls and bar maids, who flirted with their middle-class male customers. Historian Peter Bailey suggests that this type of cross-class flirting was "open yet illicit," representing a sexuality that was "developed but contained, carefully channeled rather than fully discharged; in vulgar terms it might be represented as 'everything but.'"[111] Bailey contends that this form of sexuality emerged because of the newly established leisure industry that took place across class boundaries. Sexuality appears in managed ways also *within* the middle class. The

Figure 2.5 Three images of women flirting their way into men's hearts. When the fan is depicted in conjunction with music, its flirtatious potential becomes evident. 1857, 1882, 1858. Bodleian Library, University of Oxford: John Johnson Collection: *Music Titles 5, Music Titles 5, Music Titles 9.*

flirtatious socialite became a parallel to the passive domestic woman. The coquette was acknowledged within the middle class, but some felt unsure about this middle-class form of femininity.

In novels of the nineteenth century, the coquette was a middle-class character who knowingly walked the line between sexual actor and innocent flirt.[112] The game of the flirt was to entice a lover to become a husband without becoming sexual and therefore fallen. However, some saw the flirt as a dangerous type both because of her potential to "fall," and because of the power that she held over men. In the novel *Dangers of Coquetry* written in 1790 by Amelia Alderson Opie, Lord Bertie explains: "I do not say that she is actually guilty but the woman who is not startled at indulging the adultery of the mind, is not far removed from yielding to that of the body; and the former, I am sure, she is not far from."[113] The utterings of Lord Bertie suggest that the flirt is involved in a dangerous practice that may lead from thought to action. In the mid-nineteenth century ambiguous feelings about coquetry continued to appear. A manual about *Etiquette; or, Love, Courtship and Marriage* (1847) expresses similar sentiments to Lord Bertie: "a lady must be very much degraded indeed before she can practice the art of coquetry. She must possess much levity of character, and be sadly deficient in moral principle."[114] The author goes on to tell the story of a lady who practiced coquetry breaking off many engagements with young handsome men. One day after "sinking into middle life" she promised to marry a man with whom she had once been betrothed, only to suffer the same fate as she had put countless men through when her lover refused to marry her.[115]

Despite these tales of caution, most middle-class Victorians were willing to ignore the occasional flirtation if only because its evidence consisted of glances and coded utterings behind a fan. After all, flirtation left no physical evidence and relied on conversational ambiguities, creating a situation that could lend itself to subsequent denial. As "The Fan," a poem by J. Mew tells us:

> Better the fan to write and speak
> Than the mouth, or pen with its ink tear
> For it writes—and spelling is not to seek
> And it speaks, what none, save one, may hear (figure 2.6).[116]

Along the same lines, Victorians noted that the fan "in turn discloses all that is apparently hidden, conceals all that is apparently exposed."[117] Writing in 1911 the German sociologist Georg Simmel reinforced the Victorian perception that flirtation was somewhat ephemeral. He defined flirtation as "the alternation or simultaneity of accommodation and denial." He goes on to propose that "In the behavior of the flirt, the man feels the proximity and interpenetration of the ability and the inability to acquire something."[118] For Simmel, as for the Victorians, flirtation existed in the nebula between consent and refusal—it was a game of hide and seek. As such the true woman behind the fan rarely became apparent. In a 1904 novel *The Woman with the Fan* a beautiful and coquettish wife who nonetheless has a good heart uses her fan to attract, first her husband, then a second man once her husband's affections had turned to another. "Throw away your fan," her friend told her, knowing the goodness of her soul, "it's the fan he cares for." But the lady refused to relinquish the coquettish object "which is her outer beauty, her act of herself, her ability to attract men." Years later when the lady's beauty had not only faded but her face was disfigured by a terrible accident her friend returns. Musing upon the changes this lady had gone through the friend said: "I see her now without the fan. With it she was a siren, perhaps but without it she is . . . eternal woman. Ah, how much better than the siren! . . . You taught her what she could be without the fan."[119] Victorians imagined that without the fan the woman was much easier to understand; she fitted much better into the category of "good" or "bad". However, with the fan her true essence was being hidden along with her true feelings.

Figure 2.6   Lovers communicate behind a fan. 1894. 10128470, Mary Evans Picture Library.

Some poets and short-story writers saw the fan as much more dangerous to the men around them than to the women who wielded them. These narratives portrayed fan-wielding women as practiced seductresses who ensnared men against their will. Writers of this ilk envisioned the fan as a dangerous weapon of female seduction that captured the hearts of the unwitting bachelors who happened to come within wind of it. In the Victorian period, many wrote about the fan not as a fashionable accessory, but as a "weapon in the armory of [women's] charms."[120] Victorians delighted in repeating the saying: "women are armed with Fans as Men with Swords, and sometimes do more Execution with them."[121] One author even quips that it has become an unfair fight because "men have given up wearing swords, but women still carry fans."[122] Tales of the dangerous seductive fan were written throughout the nineteenth century. Consider, for example, this poem, "The Fan," which appeared in *Pall Mall Magazine* in 1896:

Men a many its victims are
(Lords of creation as they surmise);
It draws them near, and it drives them far
Just like Japanese butterflies . . .

Men by dozens, like moths by night
Slaves of the lamp, in its glamour share;
The stubbornest male in his own despite
Moves when this magnet attracts his chair.[123]

Here the fan is portrayed as an all-powerful female weapon that exerts a pull on men who have a total lack of free will. The message conveyed is that while men believe they are in charge of heterosexual courtship, they are not. This poem is one of the more extreme conceptions of the power of the fan and female sexuality, and it was far from a reality for Victorian men and women who both had agency through the process of courtship. Going back to the types of women portrayed in stories and images with fans, the seductive woman of the fan represented an alternative type of femininity to the passive, asexual woman of the domestic sphere. The dynamics between men and women within these two contrasting forms of femininity represent divergent relations of power. The passive domestic woman who used her fan only as a fashion accessory was not a threat to male power. The seductress on the hunt for a husband, however, was critiqued by unwilling bachelors who were uncomfortable and unfamiliar with the power of women's sexuality.

Men's unease with the coquette had much to do with the changing status of women in Victorian society. Women's consumer agency as purchasers of fans (and a myriad of other items) helped to highlight their agency in the heterosexual marketplace, and showed previous models of domestic womanhood as unequal and outdated. The social type of the coquette allowed for a more complex and ambiguous notion of middle-class female behavior and it was based on the purchase of things. In the middle-class Victorian context, the flirt opened possibilities for alternative sexual expressions from those available to the respectable Victorian lady, demonstrating that the middle class was not as rigidly ideological as some would have us believe. This modern coquettish woman made some Britons nostalgic for a mythic past in which women were passive and asexual. In the next section we will see how these ideal features of the domestic British woman were displaced from the metropole and placed upon women of East Asia.

THE COLONIAL FAN: THE DOMESTIC WOMAN OF EAST ASIA

In response to "the surplus women question," feminists encouraged middle-class women to get jobs. Another suggested solution to the imagined problem of women's redundancy was for women to take a more active role in attracting husbands, giving rise to a new social type: the middle-class coquette. Amidst these uncomfortable shifts, some Victorians began to dream of a simpler time, an imaginary time in which middle-class women stayed in the domestic sphere and took on the role of the passive, yet supportive, wife and mother. This sense of loss led some to look toward Japan, the birthplace of the fan, as a civilized region that remained untouched by the modernization that forced British women out of their passive roles as domestic housewives. A trope that was frequently employed cast Japanese women as innocent and simple maids who submissively kept house and entertained their husbands after a long day's work. In this section we will explore the emerging perception of Japanese women as the ideal domestic women of England's past.

During the last half of the nineteenth century, Japan was seen as civilized yet exotic. East Asia was associated with leisure, pleasure, and beautifully decorated objects. The connection with leisure was solidified on British soil as porcelain, kimonos, and fans were displayed and sold in such holiday locations as world exhibitions, public gardens, department stores, and stately homes.[124] Generally Victorians saw Japan as an ancient culture, more civilized than other colonial nations, which were understood as lacking in the areas of sophistication and development (this theme will be taken up in the next chapter about parasols and umbrellas).

Victorians admired Japan because of developments within the country, during the last quarter of the century, that were thought of as progressive by the British.[125] But the relationship between Britain and Japan started out as quasi-imperialist; the Japanese semi-voluntarily traded with the West in 1853 after two centuries of self-imposed isolation. The 1858 British Treaty of Edo further subjugated the Japanese to Western trade under circumstances that likened their situation to "undeveloped" colonies. However, in the Meiji period (1868–1912) Japan pursued a vigorous modernizing program that included creating a Westernized government, military, and legal system. In 1905 Japan won the Russo-Japanese War putting the country on par with the other Western nations.

The civilization and culture of Japan were represented by English writers most clearly in the appearance, position, and demeanor of the country's women. Japanese women were given a particularly high ranking in the hierarchy of women of the world. They were praised for their "wonderful goodness and gentleness."[126] The purity and kindness of Japanese women were often emphasized in British writing about the country. In a volume first published in 1891 entitled *The Real Japan*, Japanese women were described as having all the essential female attributes known to Western women: "If you could take the light from the eyes of a Sister of Mercy at her gracious task, the smile of a maiden looking over the seas for her love, and the heart of an unspoiled child, and materialize them into a winsome and healthy little body, crowned with a mass of jet-black hair and dressed in bright rustling silks, you would have the typical Japanese woman."[127] While singular types of Western women in the form of the devoted nun, faithful wife, and innocent maiden are referred to in this passage, the Japanese woman is depicted as embodying all three of these types, seemingly making the Japanese woman the perfect Victorian lady.

Japanese women were also said to attend to domestic affairs in a way that rivaled middle-class English women. Writing in 1841, Dr. P. F. von Siebold, explains: "at home, the wife is mistress of the family . . . she is expected to please [her husband] by her accomplishments, and to cheer him with her lively conversations."[128] Another writer explains that Japanese women were also good housekeepers: "She is expected to wait on [her husband, and] brush and mend his clothes."[129] The Japanese husband, on the other hand, dealt with business affairs outside the home. Even the premarital education of Japanese women was described in similar terms as that required by middle-class English women: "Her education consists of reading and writing, the polite accomplishments of dancing and playing on the *samisen* and *koto*," the author reassures us that "the reading of the polite literature of poetry, the tea-ceremonial, *cha-no-yu*, and the flower-ceremonial [were] all very civilizing studies." These were peculiar representations of Japanese women that were based on what the British imagined middle-class or noble Japanese life to be like, as these were certainly not working women or peasants. The depiction of Japanese women attending to their husbands, maintaining clean households, and participating in genteel pastimes was an orientalist fantasy predicated on the assumption of the simplicity of Japanese society.

However, as travel writers were quick to point out, this enviable domestication came at a cost to women. Japan was said to be "a man's country"[130] and as such women were placed in a position of subservience and "treated rather as a toy for her husband's amusement."[131] While women were supposed to be helpmates for their husbands, they "never suffered to share his more serious thoughts, or to relieve by participation his anxieties and cares. "She is," Dr. P. F. von Siebold went on to say, "kept in profound ignorance of his business affairs."[132] Sir Henry Norman suggested that there was a dark side of Japanese husband and wife relations: "in many respectable households there is a concubine—perhaps two or even three—in addition to the wife," a practice that Norman considers "a miserable state of affairs, degrading, unhappy, and mediaeval."[133] Furthermore, a woman was subservient to her husband, a wife was "only to speak when she is spoken to, and [was expected to] always give *place aux hommes*."[134] When viewed through English eyes, Japanese marriages seemed unequal, even barbaric. In England companionate marriage, which was the basic concept behind the separate sphere ideology, allowed the husband to find his deepest solace in the home.[135] Within an ideal companionate marriage, a wife was a support to her husband as well as his confidant and intellectual equal. When Victorians considers this against the writings about Japan, gender interactions were seen as similar but slightly distorted. One gets the impression that Victorians thought the Japanese went too far in upholding the separate-sphere ideology.

It is perhaps the very tension between the differences and similarities of English and Japanese women that encouraged so many English writers to fetishize the latter. Japanese women were admired for their slight figures, small hands and feet, red lips, white skin, ebony hair, and simple, gentle smiles (figure 2.7).[136] The stereotype of Japanese women was sometimes placed in opposition to British women, who, according to some, were far too concerned with fashions that altered their bodies. One author suggested that Japanese women treated their bodies in a more civilized manner than their English counterparts: "The women of this country [Japan] never abbreviated the interval between themselves and savagery by boring holes in their ears to hang baubles there, by loading their fingers with rings, by encasing their breast in frames of steel and bone," or "by distorting their feet with high-heeled shoes."[137] Simple Japanese tastes did not stand up, in this author's view, to the overmediated British femininity. English writers, poets, and composers spilled much ink on the "belle in far Japan."[138] In the latter half of the nineteenth century she became a fantasy girl perpetuated in cultural stereotypes of the meek and demure lady hiding behind her fan. Confronted with real women at home who flirted with fans but also marched for the vote, the image of the coy Japanese woman, who would be a submissive wife and not meddle in public affairs, could be appealing.

The most famous example of Japanese fan-wielding women in British popular culture was, of course, Gilbert and Sullivan's *The Mikado; or, The Town of Titipu* that opened on March 14, 1885, in London. In this comedic musical, set in Japan, the "three little maids from school" made their first appearance flirting and giggling in ways that would soon attract husbands. The coy female flirtations continued when Yum Yum, one of the three maids, encountered her long-lost sweetheart Nanki-Poo. Though "to flirt is illegal," the two thwarted the law while singing about the impossibility of their love affair:

> *Nank*—If it were not for the law, we should now be sitting side by side, like that. *(Sits by her.)*
>
> *Yum*—Instead of being obliged to sit half a mile off, like that. *(Crosses and sits at the other side of stage.)*
>
> *Nank*—We should be gazing into each other's eyes, like that. *(Approaching and gazing at her sentimentally.)*
>
> *Yum*—Breathing vows of unutterable love—like that. *(Sighing and gazing lovingly at him.)*
>
> *Nank*—With our arms round each other's waists, like that. *(Embracing her.)*
>
> *Yum*—Yes, if it wasn't for the law.[139]

1900   OCTOBRE – II   Nº 44

LE THÉATRE

DIRECTION ET RÉDACTION :   PUBLICITÉ :   CONDITIONS DE L'ABONNEMENT :   ABONNEMENT ET VENTE :

THÉATRE LOIE FULLER (Rue de Paris). — Mᵐᵉ SADA YACCO. — Rôle de la Ghesha. — *LA GHESHA ET LE CHEVALIER*

ÉDITEURS : Manzi, Joyant & Cⁱᵉ, 24, Boulevard des Capucines, Paris. — PRIX NET : 2 fr. ; Étranger, 2 fr. 50

Figure 2.7   Sada Yacco was a Japanese actress who toured Europe and America in the late nineteenth and early twentieth centuries. She possessed the fetishized Japanese traits of white skin, red lips, jet black hair, and small hands. 10097045, Mary Evans Picture Library.

While embracing, Yum and Nank sang about the impossibility of their embrace; while gazing lovingly, they maintained physical separation. When acted on stage, this song perfectly embodied the fine line that couples tread between refusal and acceptance—a line that Simmel defined as the very essence of flirtation.

Though there was little mention of fans within the script, and no stage directions that incorporated fans within *The Mikado*, there is no question that the fan was an essential prop for the flirtatious little maids. Every visual representation of women in *The Mikado* shows women posing meekly behind their fans (figure 2.8).[140] On a song-sheet cover the three little maids pose coyly behind their fans. In case the viewer missed this reference to Japan's most popular accessory, the maids themselves were displayed upon a fan. A *carte de visite* from the 1886 Berlin production of *The Mikado* picture European women with fans adorning their hair and hands. One woman demurely held her pinkie

Figure 2.8 The three little maids from *The Mikado* pose coyly with their fans. 1885. Bodleian Library, University of Oxford: John Johnson Collection: *Music Titles 11* (7).

finger to her lips; the other two leaned over their fans as if to blow kisses at the onlooker (figure 2.9). In all of these cases, the fan was an important prop for the flirtatious play of the characters. Furthermore, the cast members of the first London production of *The Mikado* gave autographs upon fans. Fans were so strongly intertwined with the British perception of Japanese culture that they appeared as props over and over again in the play's production, promotional images, and as part of the audiences' interaction with the play.

Japanese flirtations were undertaken in a different marriage market from the one in England. In *The Mikado*, for example, Yum had a choice between two husbands. Furthermore, sources that equated Japanese women with flirtation did not take on the negative connotations of female power and male submission as it did in the English context. Instead, Japanese female flirts were viewed as participating in an innocent game that would result in their entrance into a submissive marital state. The contrasting reactions to Japanese and British flirts were probably due to the semi-imperial ranking of Japan. British men had nothing to fear from Japanese flirts both because they posed

Figure 2.9 *Carte de visite* for Berlin production of *The Mikado*. Actress from the first production of *The Mikado* in Germany poses in what purports to be the Japanese style. 1886. The Fan Museum, Greenwich, London.

no immediate threat, being thousands of miles off in a leisured dreamland, and because Britons felt some amount of superiority over ancient cultures that were yet to modernize in areas of government structure and gender relations.

The fan was at once a product and a consumer good. The fan as product was embroiled in questions of England's place in the wider world that were being played out at the international, national, and local exhibitions that proliferated in the nineteenth century. Throughout the Victorian period, British government officials asked themselves if a country known for being first to rationalize and industrialize could also maintain a stronghold in the realm of fashion and design? It was also as a product that the fan weighed in on one of the major social concerns of the period: what to do about the great number of unmarried middle-class women? Here journalists, business owners, guilds, and school directors scrambled to find areas in which redundant women could get employment while still maintaining their status as respectable ladies. As a consumer good, the fan intersected with social controversies about the overall position of middle-class women within the larger society. What rights to the public sphere would the middle-class woman be able to gain? Were there other types of women that could be acceptable counterparts to the domestic woman? Finally, the fan came to represent an escape for the controversial modern woman that emerged in part due to the industrial and colonial state that Britain had become. In the hands of a Japanese belle, the fan stood for the innocent, submissive lady of Britain's past. The fan evoked, as it was actually used or merely in the imagination, both apprehension and nostalgia. Whether it was a purposeful tool or merely an accessory, it was either forecasting the dreaded New Woman or reminding people of the Angel of the Hearth. Fans might well have been painted with portraits of Janus, the two-headed god with each face looking in the opposite direction, one into the future and the other to the past.

As both a product and a consumer good, the history of the fan reveals anxieties over questions of British taste, female redundancy, orientalism, and changing gender norms. The next chapter, about umbrellas and parasols, continues on the theme of orientalism. But instead of valorizing Japanese women, as was the case with the fan, British writtings about the parasol focused on Western superiority over undeveloped imperial nations.

NOTES

1. Reverend Lionel Thomas Berguer, "Delamira Resigns Her Fan," *The British Essayists; with Prefaces Biographical, Historical and Critical* 1 (1823): 97–100. The story of Delamira was also published in *The British Essayists* in 1803 and 1808. The story was further reproduced in Ernest Hart, *Fan Exhibition, 1894* (London: Liberty & Co., 1894), 10–11; Anon., *Thackerayana: Notes and Anecdotes Illustrated by Hundreds of Sketches* (New York: Hansell House, 1901), 240–41; Epharaim Chambers, "Fan," *Chambers's Encyclopedia and a Dictionary of Universal Knowledge for the People* IV (1862), 240–41 (this encyclopedia was republished with the same entry in 1868, 1874, and 1885); "Fan," *Library of Universal Knowledge* 5 (1880), 711. The original story dates back to 1709 when it was first published in *The Tatler*. Anon., "Delamira Resigns Her Fan," *The Tatler* 3, no. 52 (1814): 312–13. *The Tatler* was reproduced at least five times in the nineteenth century, in 1803, 1814, 1832, and 1898–1899. Victorians variably read Addison's interpretations of fan-wielding women as "not contain[ing] a line that gives occasion to controversy" or alternatively as strongly satirical. Newspaper clipping, *The Daily Telegraph*, Thursday June 13, 1889, Worshipful Company of Fan Makers Collection, MS 21435, Guildhall Library.
2. Peter Bailey, *Popular Culture and Performance in the Victorian City* (Cambridge: Cambridge University Press, 1998), 223.

3. Erika Diane Rappaport, *Shopping for Pleasure: Women in the Making of London's West End* (Princeton, NJ: Princeton University Press, 2000).

4. Judith Worsnop, "A Reevaluation of 'The Problem of Surplus Women' in Nineteenth-Century England: The Case of the 1851 Census," *Women's Studies International Forum* 13, nos. 1/2 (1990): 21–31.

5. Claudia Nelson, *Family Ties in Victorian England* (Westport, CT: Praeger, 2007), 15. According to the 1851 Census there were 1.7 million spinsters and 800,000 widows in Britain.

6. Anon., "Excess of Widows over Widowers," *Westminster Review* 131 (1889): 501. See also Anon., "Women and Work," *Westminster Review* 131 (1889): 270–79.

7. Worsnop, "A Reevaluation of 'The Problem of Surplus Women' in 19th-Century England."

8. Malcolm Tait and Edward Parker, *London's Royal Parks* (London: Think Publishing, 2006), 66.

9. The Department of Science and Art hosted a series of fan exhibitions every year from 1868 to 1871.

10. Douglas Sladen, *Queer Things about Japan* (London: Anthony Treherne & Co., 1904), 25; Sheila K. Johnson, *The Japanese through American Eyes* (Stanford, CA: Stanford University Press, 1988), 77–79; Henry Norman, *The Real Japan: Studies of Contemporary Japanese Manners, Morals, Administrations, and Politics*, 5th ed. (London: T. Fisher Unwin, 1908), 178.

11. L. Lowe, *Critical Terrains: French and British Orientalisms* (Ithaca, NY: Cornell University Press, 1991), 8.

12. For histories of Japan from the British point of view see: Olive Checkland, *Britain's Encounter with Meiji Japan, 1868–1912* (Houndmills: Macmillan, 1989); Olive Checkland, *Japan and Britain after 1859: Creating Cultural Bridges* (New York: Routledge, 2003); Toshio Yokoyama, *Japan in the Victorian Mind: A Study of Stereotyped Images of a Nation 1850–80* (Houndmills: Macmillan, 1987).

13. Mrs. Jameson, *Sisters of Charity: Abroad and at Home* (London: Longman, Grown, Green & Longmans, 1855), 56.

14. Barbara Leigh-Smith, "Women and Work (1857)," in *What Is a Woman to Do? A Reader on Women, Work and Art, c. 1830–1890*, ed. Kyriaki Hadji-afxendi and Patricia Zekreski (Bern: Peter Lang, 2011), 43.

15. W.R. Greg, *Why Are Women Redundant?* (London: N. Trubner & Co., 1869), 5.

16. Martha Vicinus, *Independent Women: Work and Community for Single Women, 1850–1920* (Chicago: University of Chicago Press, 1985), 26.

17. The exact date and route of migration that the fan took from Asia into Europe is under dispute by fan experts. Alexander argues, for example, that the folding fan first appeared in Venice and Ferrara around 1500 before it disseminated throughout Europe. An anonymous history of the

fan presented in *The Illustrated London News* argues that the folding fan came through Portugal in the fifteenth century. Flory suggests that the folding fan must have come into England from Italy via France in the mid-1500s. Cynthia Fendel suggests that the folding fan arrived in Europe much later, in the seventeenth century. Hélène Alexander, *Fans* (Cromwell House: Shire Publications, 2002), 9; Anon., "The Exhibition of Fans," *The Illustrated London News* LVII, no. 1602 (1870): 42; Cynthia Fendel, *Celluloid Hand Fans* (Dallas: Hand Fan Productions, 2001), 11; M. A. Flory, *A Book about Fans: The History of Fans and Fan-Painting* (New York: Macmillan, 1895).

18. Liberty & Co., *Fans: A Brief Sketch of Their Origin and Use* (London: Liberty & Co., 1896); Flory, *A Book about Fans*, 20.

19. In 1678 a French guild for fanmakers was established. Eleanor Johnson, *Ladies' Dress Accessories* (Cromwell House: Shire Publications, 2004), 50; Alexander, *Fans*, 10.

20. Newspaper clipping, *Newcastle Chronicle* 18.5.90 (continued), Worshipful Company of Fan Makers Collection, MS 21435, Guildhall Library.

21. "Delamira Resigns Her Fan" was first published in *The Tatler* in 1709, and the spoof on an academy for fan-wielding women was first published by *The Spectator* in 1711. Anon., "Fans," *The Perruquier* 1, no. 3 (1878); Bernard Ross Collins, *A Short Account of the Worshipful Company of Fan Makers* (London: Favil Press, 1950), 4, 27; Anon., "Delamira Resigns Her Fan," *The Tatler*; Joseph Addison, "Mr Spectator," *The Spectator* 1 (1826): 134–35.

22. There were two types of fans, the fixed fan and the folding fan, and it was the latter that we will concentrate on here because it was more popular with ladies in the nineteenth century. For detailed information on how the folding fan was made please see: Nancy Armstrong, *A Collector's History of Fans* (London: Cassell & Collier, 1974), 185–88; Bertha de Vere Green, *A Collector's Guide to Fans over the Ages* (London: Frederick Muller, 1975), 195–226; Bertha de Vere Green, *Fans over the Ages: A Collector's Guide* (Cranbury: A. S. Barnes and Co., 1975), 104–19; Charles Blanc, *Art in Ornament and Dress* (New York: Scribner Welford, and Armstrong, 1877), 193–94; John Tallis and Jacob George Strutt, *Tallis' History and Description of the Crystal Palace: And the Exhibition of the World's Industry in 1851*, Vol. 1, Part 2 (London: London Printing & Publishing Co., 1852), 216.

23. With the help of this mold about twenty grooves each an eighth of an inch thick were made by a worker who gently pushed the leaf over the surface of the mold making sure that none of the design was hidden by a fold. When the craftsman or woman was happy with the layout of the fan, pressure was applied to make the folds crisp.

24. The 1685 revocation of the Edict of Nantes drove Protestant fanmakers from France into England. Under Charles II and also in 1695 the House of

Commons approved a duty on imported fans from France and the East Indies. Under Charles II painted fans were prohibited from entering the country entirely. The Worshipful Company employed a Foreign Warden who was allowed to seize all foreign fans imported into the country contrary to the Law of the Realm. According to an article in *The Northern Whig* the charter of the Worshipful Company even "permits the Master and two liverymen to enter any shop devoted to the sale of fans and destroy all those of foreign manufacture." On July 1, 1779, there was a discussion with the Court of Assistants led by company member Robert Clarke who stated that the "importation of French and foreign fans daily increased" and suggested that a newspaper and handbill campaign against this trend be undertaken by the company. Collins, *A Short Account of the Worshipful Company of Fan Makers*, 4; Fann-makers, "The Case of the Fann-Makers Who Have Petitioned the Honorable House of Commons, against the Importation of Fanns from the East-Indies," in *Early English Books, 1641–1700; 1664: 5*, 1695; Sam Redgrave, *Fans of All Countries: A Series of Twenty Photographs of Spanish, French, German, Italian and English Fans under the Sanction of the Science and Art Department, for the Use of Schools of Art and Amateurs* (London: Arundel Society for Promoting the Knowledge of Art, 1871), 4. Newspaper clipping, *The Northern Whig* 29.1.90; Worshipful Company of Fan Makers Collection, MS 21435, Guildhall Library. The company minute book of 1775 has various notes that indicate the changing laws for importation; Collins, *A Short Account of the Worshipful Company of Fan Makers*, 29.

25. The trend in Paris, in comparison, was toward an increase in the fan industry. The number of fanmakers, or eventaillists, in 1827 was 15 and by 1847 there were 122 fanmakers who sold 110,000 livres' worth of fans a year. Even political and economic disturbance did not affect the industry for long. The Revolution of 1848 rocked the French fan industry reducing its workforce of 565 by over half, putting 315 people out of work. However, the export market kept the industry going and by the Paris Exhibition of 1867 M. Duvelleroy, a French fanmaker of high repute, reported in the *Rapports du Jury* that there were 4,000 fanmakers in Paris and Oise producing fans were worth ten million francs a year, three-quarters of which went to foreign markets. Armstrong, *A Collector's History of Fans*, 113; *Reports by the Juries of the Great Exhibition 1851* (London: William Clowes & Sons, 1852), 668; de Vere Green, *A Collector's Guide to Fans over the Ages*, 146; M. Duvelleroy, "Fabrication des Evantails," *Exposition Universelles. Paris 1867, Rapports du Jury International*, Vol. V, 325.

26. Newspaper clipping, *The Lady*, 1890, Worshipful Company of Fan Makers Collection, MS 21435, Guildhall Library.

27. Newspaper clipping, *The Lady*, 1890.

28. Anon., *Explanatory Report of the Working Ladies' Guild* (London: Hatchards Publishers, 1877), 5, 9.

29. F. Graeme Chalmers, *Women in the Nineteenth-Century Art World: Schools of Art and Design for Women in London and Philadelphia* (Westport, CT: Greenwood Press, 1998), 63.

30. Anon., *Women Workers' Directory* (London: John Bale, Sons and Danielsson, 1909), 12.

31. Lady Jeaune, *Ladies at Work: Papers on Paid Employment for Ladies by Experts in the Several Branches* (London: A. D. Innes & Co., 1893), 50.

32. Readers are reassured that the company "founders are two English ladies," though Avant is a French name and the manufactory based at 10 and 12 Moor Lane and Fore Street was in a traditionally Huguenot area east of the city where French silk weavers settled after the revocation of the Edict of Nantes. Newspaper clipping, *The Daily Telegraph*, Thursday June 13, 1889, Worshipful Company of Fan Makers Collection, MS 21435, Guildhall Library.

33. Anne Beale, "Finding Employment for Women," *The Quiver: An Illustrated London Magazine for General Reading* (1889): 115.

34. Beale, "Finding Employment for Women."

35. Newspaper clipping, *The Lady*, 1890; Newspaper clipping, *The Daily Telegraph*, Thursday June 13, 1889, Worshipful Company of Fan Makers Collection, MS 21435, Guildhall Library.

36. *The Daily Telegraph*, Thursday June 13, 1889.

37. Newspaper clipping, "Mr. Sala on Civic Art," *The Lady*, Worshipful Company of Fan Makers Collection, MS 21435, Guildhall Library.

38. Newspaper clipping, *The Lady*, 1890.

39. Newspaper clipping, *The Lady*, 1890.

40. Newspaper clipping, *City Press*, 15.2.90, Worshipful Company of Fan Makers Collection, MS 21435, Guildhall Library.

41. Paula Gillett, *The Victorian Painter's World* (Gloucester: Alan Sutton, 1990), 141.

42. Rev. F. D. Maurice, July 1860, "Female Schools of Art" [Extract from *Macmillan's Magazine*], Pressmark 97.P Box 0004, National Art Library, London.

43. F. Graeme Chalmers, "Fanny Mclan and London's Female School of Design, 1842–57: 'My Lords and Gentlemen, Your Obedient and Humble Servant'?," *Women's Art Journal* 16, no. 2 (1996): 3; Laurel Lampela, "Women's Art Education Institutions in Nineteenth Century England," *Art Education* 46, no. 1 (1993): 66.

44. From its inception in 1842 until about 1850, the Female School of Design fulfilled its original mandate of educating lower-middle-class women for gainful employment in areas of design. But in the early 1850s the policy of the school suddenly changed. Though many continued to speak about the Female School as a solution to "the surplus women question," the school began to admit leisured ladies who had no intention of

seeking employment once they graduated. The policy change began in 1852 when Henry Cole became the civil servant in charge of the Department of Practical Art. He sought to make the school more profitable by increasing class sizes, cutting in half the number of staff per student, and creating a graduated system of tuition in which leisured ladies would pay more than lower-middle-class women. Though the school continued petitioning for money on the basis of the help it gave to unmarried women in need of employment, the school gained increasing aristocratic and royal patronage that changed the tone of the education that was given. The fee-paying students used the institution as a finishing school allowing them to receive an education in art before they got married. These students also received special privileges; they were allowed to alert the superintendent if a busy social schedule would interfere with their classes, while nonfee-paying students were required to attend every day. Gillett, *The Victorian Painter's World*, 141–42.

45. Select Committee on the School of Design, "Report from the Select Committee on the School of Design: Together with Proceedings of the Committee, Minutes of Evidence, Appendix and Index" (London: House of Commons, 1849), 119; Charles Dickens, "The Female School of Design in the Capital of the World," *Household Words. A Weekly Journal. Conducted by Charles Dickens* 2, no. 51 (1851): 577–81. Ellen C. Clayton, *English Female Artists* (London: Tinsley Brothers, 1876), 148. After a visit to the Female School, Charles Dickens confirms Fanny Mclan's statement by writing: "Many of these young persons, though, are, no doubt, of highly respectable families, well educated, and who once had very different expectations; though now, for the purpose of making design, they are learning drawing, perhaps, to sell them." Ellen Clayton, author of *English Female Artists*, had a friend named Eliza Turck who was a former student of the Female School of Design. Clayton included some of Turck's story in her book, which again confirms the idea that middle-class women who had fallen on hard times were the main type of pupils at the school: "During the time spent here [Female School of Design] by Miss Turck occurred her father's failure in business, which naturally induced her to take an even more serious view than before of her favourite pursuit [art]. Although her family still continued somewhat to discountenance the idea of an artist's career for her, she herself never ceased from that period to regard painting as the occupation of her life."

46. Maurice, July 1860, "Female Schools of Art" [Extract from *Macmillan's Magazine*].

47. Fanny Mclan, "On Porcelain Painting," *The Athenaeum Journal of Literature, Science and the Fine Arts*, no. 906 (1845): 250.

48. Anon., "The Female School of Design," *The Art-Journal* X11 (1850): 130.

49. Chalmers, *Women in the Nineteenth-Century Art World*, 60–61.

50. Maurice, July 1860, "Female Schools of Art" [Extract from *Macmillan's Magazine*].

51. H.R.H. the Princess of Wales, March 26, 1873, Statement of the Proceedings at the Annual Meeting and Distribution of Medals and Prizes to the Students of the Female School of Art by HRH the Princess of Wales (Theater of the University of London: Burlington Gardens). Alice Blanche Ellis's experience in rendering natural plants would serve her well when she was commissioned to paint apples and pairs for the Woolhope Naturalists' Field Club after her schooling. And it was perhaps because of Dr. Braxton Hicks's interest in natural history (the good doctor had been a member of the Royal Society of London for Improving Natural Knowledge since 1862) that he chose to purchase a fan that depicted flowers.

52. Chalmers, *Women in the Nineteenth-Century Art World*, 56.

53. Armstrong, *A Collector's History of Fans*, 81.

54. Anon., "The Exhibition of Fans," 42; Armstrong, *A Collector's History of Fans* 79; Redgrave, *Fans of All Countries*, 5.

55. Anon., "Fan Making: An Employment for Women," *The Queen, The Lady's Newspaper* 48 (1870): 64.

56. Collins, *A Short Account of the Worshipful Company of Fan Makers*, 7.

57. Newspaper clipping, "Exhibition of Fans at Drapers' Hall," *City Press*, 21.5.90, Worshipful Company of Fan Makers Collection, MS 21435, Guildhall Library; Newspaper clipping, *Standard*, 24. 9. 90, Worshipful Company of Fan Makers Collection, MS 21435, Guildhall Library.

58. Newspaper clipping, Worshipful Company of Fan Makers, *Report of the Committee &c. Competitive Exhibition of Fans Held at Drapers' Hall*, London, July 1878, Worshipful Company of Fan Makers Collection, MS 21435, Guildhall Library, 2.

59. Newspaper clipping, Worshipful Company of Fan Makers, *Report of the Committee &c. Competitive Exhibition of Fans Held at Drapers' Hall*, 4; Newspaper clipping, "The Company of Fan Makers," *Standard*, 25.2.90, Worshipful Company of Fan Makers Collection, MS 21435, Guildhall Library.

60. The official categories were: I. Ancient European Fans, II. Modern Fans, III. Exotic Fans, IV. Modern Fans of British Manufacture, V. Fans Not Comprised in the Above Classes.

61. "Report of the Exhibition Sub-Committee to the Committee of the Whole Court of the Worshipful Company of Fan Makers," *Fan Makers Company's Competitive Exhibition, 1878*, Worshipful Company of Fan Makers Collection, MS 21435, Guildhall Library.

62. Newspaper clipping, Worshipful Company of Fan Makers, *Report of the Committee &c. Competitive Exhibition of Fans Held at Drapers' Hall*, 12.

63. Newspaper Report of Proceedings, 1878, Worshipful Company of Fan Makers Collection, MS 21435, Guildhall Library. In the category of

Modern Fans of British Manufacture Section I: Mounted Fans, first prize went to Miss Elizabeth Laird, second prize to Miss Charlotte Radford, third to Mr. L. J. Juchan. In Section II: Unmounted Fans, first prize went to Miss C. J. James, second to Miss Emma Radford, and third to Miss J. R. Pitman. In Section III: Sticks of Fans, Ivory Bone, Wood etc., the first two prizes went to Robert Gleeson.

64. Newspaper clipping, Worshipful Company of Fan Makers, *Report of the Committee &c. Competitive Exhibition of Fans Held at Drapers' Hall*, 3.

65. Newspaper Report of Proceedings, 1878, Worshipful Company of Fan Makers Collection, MS 21435, Guildhall Library.

66. Newspaper clipping, "Worshipful Company of Fan Makers," *Daily Telegraph*, May 8, 1889, Worshipful Company of Fan Makers Collection, MS 21435, Guildhall Library.

67. Newspaper clipping, "The Fan Exhibition," *The Draper*, Worshipful Company of Fan Makers Collection, MS 21435, Guildhall Library; Newspaper clipping, *Daily Chronicle*, 3.5.90, Worshipful Company of Fan Makers Collection, MS 21435, Guildhall Library; Newspaper clipping, "The Exhibition of Fans," *Sunday Times*, 18.5.90, Worshipful Company of Fan Makers Collection, MS 21435, Guildhall Library; Newspaper clipping, "Brocades and Fans," *Daily Graphic*, 19.5.90, Worshipful Company of Fan Makers Collection, MS 21435, Guildhall Library; Newspaper clipping, *Saturday Review*, 24.5.90, Worshipful Company of Fan Makers Collection, MS 21435, Guildhall Library; Newspaper clipping, *City Press* 28.5.90, Worshipful Company of Fan Makers Collection, MS 21435, Guildhall Library; Newspaper clipping, "English Fans and Fan-Painters," Worshipful Company of Fan Makers Collection, MS 21435, Guildhall Library.

68. Newspaper clipping, *Citizen*, 2.5.90, Worshipful Company of Fan Makers Collection, MS 21435, Guildhall Library; Newspaper clipping, *Echo*, 30.1.90, Worshipful Company of Fan Makers Collection, MS 21435, Guildhall Library.

69. Newspaper clipping, "Competitive Fan Exhibition," *The Queen*, 7.2.90, Worshipful Company of Fan Makers Collection, MS 21435, Guildhall Library.

70. Newspaper clipping, *St. James' Gazette*, 17.5.90, Worshipful Company of Fan Makers Collection, MS 21435, Guildhall Library.

71. Newspaper clipping, *Daily Graphic*, 17.5.90, Worshipful Company of Fan Makers Collection, MS 21435, Guildhall Library.

72. Newspaper clipping, *Echo*, 30.1.90, Worshipful Company of Fan Makers Collection, MS 21435, Guildhall Library.

73. Newspaper clipping, *St. James' Gazette*, 17.5.90, Worshipful Company of Fan Makers Collection, MS 21435, Guildhall Library.

74. Newspaper clipping, *Morning Post*, 25.2.90, Worshipful Company of Fan Makers Collection, MS 21435, Guildhall Library.

75. Newspaper clipping, "Mr. Hume-Williams on the Third Exhibition on Fans," *City Press*, 26.2.90, Worshipful Company of Fan Makers Collection, MS 21435, Guildhall Library.

76. Newspaper clipping, *Whitehall Review*, 24.5.90, Worshipful Company of Fan Makers Collection, MS 21435, Guildhall Library.

77. Newspaper clipping, *Birmingham Daily Post*, 24.4.90, Worshipful Company of Fan Makers Collection, MS 21435, Guildhall Library.

78. Newspaper clipping, *Manchester Examiner*, 21.5.90, Worshipful Company of Fan Makers Collection, MS 21435, Guildhall Library.

79. Newspaper clipping, "Exhibition of Fans," *The Queen*, 23.5.90, Worshipful Company of Fan Makers Collection, MS 21435, Guildhall Library.

80. Newspaper clipping, "Broades and Fans," *Daily Graphic*, 19.5.90, Worshipful Company of Fan Makers Collection, MS 21435, Guildhall Library.

81. An article from the *Saturday Review* agrees with the assessment that exhibitors in the inexpensive fan category were too ambitious stating, "It is excellent work, however, though the price is suggestive of the most insignificant margin of profit to designer and retailer."

82. Newspaper clipping, *Daily Graphic*, 17.5.90, Worshipful Company of Fan Makers Collection, MS 21435, Guildhall Library.

83. Newspaper clipping, *The Queen*, 23.5.90, Worshipful Company of Fan Makers Collection, MS 21435, Guildhall Library.

84. Newspaper clipping, *Citizen*, 17.5.90, Worshipful Company of Fan Makers Collection, MS 21435, Guildhall Library.

85. Newspaper clipping, *Citizen*, 17.5.90, Worshipful Company of Fan Makers Collection, MS 21435, Guildhall Library; Newspaper clipping, "The Fan-makers' Exhibition," *Court Journal*, 27.9.90, Worshipful Company of Fan Makers Collection, MS 21435, Guildhall Library.

86. *Reports by the Juries of the Great Exhibition 1851*, 669.

87. Newspaper clipping, "English Fans and Fan-Painters," Worshipful Company of Fan Makers Collection, MS 21435, Guildhall Library.

88. Armstrong, *A Collector's History of Fans*, 81.

89. Lucy Bland, *Banishing the Beast: English Feminism and Sexual Morality, 1885–1914*, Penguin Women's Studies (London: Penguin, 1995), 162.

90. Vicinus, *Independent Women*, 294.

91. Clara Collet, "Prospects of Marriage for Women," *The Nineteenth Century* 31 (1892): 540.

92. Greg, *Why Are Women Redundant?*, 5.

93. Anon., "The Exhibition of Fans," 42.

94. This story was first published by Addison in 1711 and was repeated many times by the Victorians. Joseph Addison, "I Do Not Know Whether to Call the Following a Letter," *The Spectator* 2 (1897): 79. *The Spectator* was republished at least twice in the nineteenth century in 1800 and 1897. This article is well known to Victorians and was quoted from

extensively with and without reference to the original publication in the following articles: Anon., "Fan Making: An Employment for Women," 64; Liberty & Co., *Fans: A Brief Sketch of Their Origin and Use*; Flory, *A Book about Fans*, 4; Redgrave, *Fans of All Countries*, 10–14.

95. Newspaper Report of Proceedings, 1878, Worshipful Company of Fan Makers Collection, MS 21435, Guildhall Library.

96. Newspaper clipping, *Standard*, 24.9.90, Worshipful Company of Fan Makers Collection, MS 21435, Guildhall Library.

97. Octave Uzanne, "Weapons and Ornaments of Woman: Glories of the Fan," *Cosmopolitan Magazine* 41, no. 2 (1906): 168.

98. Anon., "Fancies in Fans," *Beauty and Fashion: A Weekly Illustrated Journal for Women* 1, no. 9 (1891): 179.

99. Arthur Robinson Wright, "Fans," in *A Collection of Newspaper Cuttings on Walking Sticks, Umbrellas, Parasols, Fans and Gloves* (London: Author, 1932). This clipping entitled "The Flutter of the Fan" is from *Daily News*, November 2, 1921.

100. Max von Boehn, *Modes and Manners: Ornaments; Lace, Fans, Gloves, Walking-Sticks, Parasols, Jewelry and Trinkets* (London: J. M. Dent & Sons, 1929), 62–63. Fans became explicitly designed to be communicative devices in 1795 when a French craftsman invented a "telegraph fan." This fan allowed its female owners to use an alphabet printed on the inner side of the device to spell out words to onlookers. This form of communication is said to have become popular in Italy, Spain, and England. In the eighteenth century a prominent London fan dealer, Robert Clarke, took out a patent that greatly improved on the language of the fan by attaching specific movements to certain communications.

101. de Vere Green, *Fans over the Ages*, 83–84; Hélène Alexander, *Duvelleroy King of Fans: Fan Maker to Kings* (London: Fan Museum, 1995), 5; Armstrong, *A Collector's History of the Fan* (London: Studio Vista, 1974), 183.

102. Armstrong, *A Collector's History of Fans*, 183; Murray and Lanman, "Florida Water," in Beauty Parlour Box 2, Perfumes, eau de Cologne, Waters, John Johnson Collection (1899); Liberty & Co., *Fans*, 9.

103. Murray and Lanman, "Florida Water," in Beauty Parlour Box 2, Perfumes, eau de Cologne, Waters, John Johnson Collection (1899).

104. Armstrong, *A Collector's History of Fans*, 183.

105. Nicholas Flood Davin, *Mr. Davin on "Fanning in Church," and Addison and Steele on the Use of the Fan* (Toronto: Globe, 1874), 7.

106. Uzanne, "Weapons and Ornaments of Woman," 173.

107. Benjamin Disraeli, *Contarini Fleming: A Psychological Romance* (New York: Elbron Classic Series, 2005 [1904]), 9.

108. This ideology suggested that men and women had naturally opposing gender characteristics: men were active and women passive, men were

rational and women moral, men were practical and women ornamental. As a result of these opposing gender characteristics, Victorian men and women were thought by the general populace to be best suited to life in separate spheres. Men, with their aggressive and rational sensibilities, were more suited to the world of work and politics. Conversely, women, with their passive and moral outlook, should be protected from the public male world by staying in the home. Because of the domestic woman's dissociation from the world of work she was not supposed to do any manual labor including housework or gardening. In this manifestation a woman's position was to be leisured and ornamental. Leonore Davidoff and Catherine Hall, *Family Fortunes: Men and Women of the English Middle Class, 1780–1850*, Women in Culture and Society (Chicago: University of Chicago Press, 1987), 180–92.

109. Charles Coote Jr., "Bell of the Ball," in *Music Titles Box 9*, John Johnson Collection; Charles Westall, "The Flirt," *Music Titles 5*, John Johnson Collection; J. Duff and C. Hodgson, "The Language of the Eye," *Music Titles 5*, John Johnson Collection.

110. The "coquette" as a type dates back to the late 1600s when it was associated with gossip and provocative sexuality in both genders. *The New World of Words; or, A Universal English Dictionary* (1696), for example, defines coquettery as "An affected Carriage to win the love of Men or Women; Tattle in Men, Gossipy in Women, tending to Amorous Intrigue." Edward Phillips, *The New World of Words; or, A Universal English Dictionary*, 5th ed. (London: Printed for R. Bently, J. Phillips, H. Rhodes, and J. Taylor, 1696). *Early English Books Online*, http://eebo.chadwyck.com; Richard A. Kaye, *The Flirt's Tragedy: Desire without End in Victorian and Edwardian Fiction* (Charlottesville: University Press of Virginia, 2002), 52; Shelly King and Yaël Schlick, *Refiguring the Coquette: Essays on Culture and Coquettery* (Cranbury: Rosemount, 2008).

111. Peter Bailey, "Parasexuality and Glamour: The Victorian Barmaid as Cultural Prototype," *Gender & History* 2, no. 2 (Summer 1990): 148.

112. Kaye, *The Flirt's Tragedy*, 53.

113. Amelia Alderson Opie, *Dangers of Coquetry* (Peterborough: Broadview Press, 2003 [1790]), 251.

114. Anon., *The Etiquette of Love, Courtship and Marriage* (London: Simpkia, Marshal & Co., 1847), 31.

115. Anon., *The Etiquette of Love, Courtship and Marriage*, 32–33.

116. J. Mew, "The Fan," *Pall Mall Magazine* IX, no. 40 (1896): 481–88.

117. Blanc, *Art in Ornament and Dress*, 194. For similar examples see: Flory, *A Book about Fans*, 54. Flory describes the fan as a device that "becomes the sceptre and shield of beauty." Blanc, *Art in Ornament and Dress*, 195–96. Blanc explains how fan maneuvering produces flirtation: "For a Spaniard, all the intrigues of love, all the manoeuvres of

flirtation, are hidden in the folds of her fan. The shy audacity of her looks, her venturous words, her hazardous avowals, half uttered, half dying on the lips, all are hidden by the fan, which appears to forbid while it encourages, to intercept whilst it conveys."

118. Georg Simmel, *On Women, Sexuality and Love*, trans. Guy Oakes (New Haven, CT: Yale University Press, 1984 [1911]), 134.

119. Robert Hichens, *The Woman with the Fan* (London: Methuen & Co., 1904), 167, 300.

120. In the early modern period, when this piece was written, women were considered to be disorderly forces ruled by their physical bodies, rather than their rational minds. They were thought to have special powers as seductive temptresses who possessed charms that no man could resist. Within this construction of femininity, women and their sexualities were considered powerful and dangerous counterparts to the self-composed, sexually restrained man. Wright, "Fans." This appeared in a clipping labeled "West. Gaz., Oct. 14, 1922" and was from an article entitled "Fashion and the Fan" by E. C. Davies. For other examples of nineteenth-century authors who describe the fan as a weapon see: Blanc, *Art in Ornament and Dress*, 194; Hart Ernest, "The Fans of the Far East," *The Queen* (1893): 58; Flory, *A Book about Fans*, 4.

121. This saying was first developed by Addison, "I Do Not Know Whether to Call the Following a Letter," 76, and was repeated throughout the nineteenth century as a quip when speaking about fans. See, for example, Caroline Matilda Kirkland and John Sartain, "Academy for Instruction in the Use of the Fan," *Sartain's Union Magazine of Literature and Art* 7 (July–December 1850): 104; Chambers, "Fan," *Chambers's Encyclopaedia*, 241; Louis Antoine Godey and Sarah Josepha Buell Hale, *Godey's Magazine* 44–45 (1852): 13.

122. Newspaper clipping, "Fans," *Manchester Courier*, 25.9.90,Worshipful Company of Fan Makers Collection, MS 21435, Guildhall Library.

123. Mew, "The Fan." For other examples of women's power over men expressed by the fan see: Anon., "Delamira Resigns Her Fan," 312; Lew Brown, B. G. DeSylva, Ray Henderson, and George White, "Beware of a Girl with a Fan" (New York: Harms, 1925); Louise De Lange and Billee Taylor, "The Legend of the Fan" (New York: M. Witmark & Sons, 1902).

124. Sarah Cheang, "Women, Pets and Imperialism: The British Pekingese Dog and Nostalgia for Old China," *Journal of British Studies* 45, no. 2 (2006): 361; Anna Jackson, "Imagining Japan: The Victorian Perception and Acquisition of Japanese Culture," *Journal of Design History* 5, no. 4 (1992): 246. For further information see: Dawn Jacobson, *Chinoiserie* (London: Phaidon Press, 1993); Toshio Watanabe, *High Victorian Japonisme* (Bern: P. Lang, 1991).

125. For histories of Japan and China from the British point of view see: Checkland, *Britain's Encounter with Meiji Japan, 1868–1912*; Checkland, *Japan and Britain after 1859*; Colin Mackerras, *Western Images of China* (Oxford: Oxford University Press, 1989); Yokoyama, *Japan in the Victorian Mind*.

126. Sladen, *Queer Things about Japan*, 25. See also: Johnson, *The Japanese through American Eyes*, 77–79.

127. Norman, *The Real Japan*, 178.

128. P. F. von Siebold, *Manners and Customs of the Japanese in the Nineteenth Century* (Rutland, VT: Charles E. Tuttle, 1973 [1841]), 123–24.

129. Sladen, *Queer Things about Japan*, 18.

130. Sladen, *Queer Things about Japan*, 23.

131. Von Siebold, *Manners and Customs of the Japanese in the Nineteenth Century*, 123.

132. Von Siebold, *Manners and Customs of the Japanese in the Nineteenth Century*, 124.

133. Norman, *The Real Japan*, 183.

134. Sladen, *Queer Things about Japan*, 18.

135. For sources developing the idea of companionate marriage see: Edmund Leites, "The Duty to Desire: Love, Friendship and Sexuality in Some Puritan Theories of Marriage," *Journal of Social History* 15 (1982): 383–408; Alan Macfarlane, *Marriage and Love in England: Modes of Reproduction 1300–1840* (London: Blackwell, 1986); Lawrence Stone, *The Family, Sex and Marriage in England, 1500–1800* (New York: Harper & Row, 1991); Arland Thornton, "The Developmental Paradigm, Reading History Sideways, and Family Change," *Demography* 38, no. 4 (2001): 449–56.

136. Edwin Arnold, "A Japanese Belle," *Punch; or, The London Charivari* 98 (1890): 180; O. Lange, "Japanese Fans" (London: W. Paxton & Co., 1934); Gordon Balch Nevin, "Painted on a Fan Song" (Philadelphia: T. Presser Co., 1915).

137. Norman, *The Real Japan*, 190–91.

138. Arnold, "A Japanese Belle," 180.

139. W. S. Gilbert, *The Mikado; or, The Town of Titipu* (Studio City, CA: Players Press, 1997), 19.

140. W. S. Gilbert and Arthur Sullivan, "The Mikado," in *Music Titles Box 5*, John Johnson Collection. The Berlin *cartes de visite* were collected by Mrs. Alexander and are housed at the Fan Museum in Greenwich, London.

"Underneath the Parasol": Umbrellas as Symbols of Imperialism, Race, Youth, Flirtation, and Masculinity

When the Prince of Wales undertook his famous 1877 voyage to India, he was warned not to appear in public without an umbrella over his head.[1] The British press, which reported on the visit, explained that large umbrellas held over the sovereign decorated with pearls, exotic feathers, and gold were the exclusive right of sultans—a privilege that was protected by sumptuary laws. This ornate accessory was necessary because without it, natives would view Prince Edward as an unimportant Western visitor rather than the future emperor of their nation. Accordingly, the display of royal position through umbrellas was superimposed on the future British sovereign during his visit to India. Thus, by preserving the established rituals of the East, Prince Edward usurped the symbol of the umbrella and used it for his own ends. The use of exotic symbols of hierarchy helped to reinforce the imperial structure so that natives could understand the importance of their new ruler.

The imperial visit to India is one example of a more generalized Victorian trend that used umbrellas as the focal point in tales that differentiated the East from the West. Narratives about umbrellas proliferated between 1830 and 1900 in British popular sources. These narratives depict parasols and umbrellas as symbols not only of imperial rule, but also of feminine power, and British masculinity. In a surprising variety of areas, the umbrella appeared as a symbol of the larger interests of the British culture. In this chapter, we will look at the meaning of the umbrella and the parasol for Britons within their own nation and as symbols of their power on the world stage.

In the nineteenth century Britons believed in a version of history that placed Victorian Britain at the pinnacle of all great civilizations. This idea was so pervasive that writers for the periodical press used it to describe the history of the umbrella. Narratives of British superiority emerged in two forms: (1) The umbrella became the focal point in a narrative that depicted Asian, Middle Eastern, and African countries as unchanging and uncivilized in order to justify British imperial rule. There is a tension in these histories about the developing use of the umbrella for rain in the West and its use in hot sunny countries. (2) Writers claimed an alternative Greek and Roman origin for European umbrellas, making connections with Athenian democracy and portraying themselves as inventive, progressive, and civilized counterparts to non-Western states.

My purpose is not to trace the real history of the parasol but rather to think about the mindset that created the mythologies around the umbrella. Victorian writers produced a pseudohistory of the sunshade. The authors were mostly anonymous (and likely women) writing fluff pieces quickly to fill spaces in magazines and to make a bit of money. The narratives were often repetitive and "borrowed" heavily from one another. Invariably authors used their societal beliefs to help give cohesion and form to their narrative.

Theorist Margaret R. Somers explains that stories like those that surround the umbrella were not simply interesting tidbits of information imparted to the British population for light reading, but rather they were examples of ideas that constitute Victorian social identities. Somers posits that "all of us come to *be* who we *are* (however ephemeral, multiple, and changing) by being located or locating ourselves (usually unconsciously) in social narratives *rarely of our own making*."[2] Stories about umbrellas become part of what Somers identifies as metanarratives: grand narratives that were encoded with the most important concepts of Victorian society. These included tales about progress, industrialization, and enlightenment. The metanarrative also incorporated such epic dramas of the time as barbarism/nature versus civility, the emergence of Western citizenship, and the triumph of liberty. Even through stories of the umbrella Victorians were urged to see themselves as imperial masters who had a mission to civilize, enlighten, and liberate the rest of the world from the tyranny of their despotic, traditional kings. This is a perfect example of how imperialism encouraged Britons to invent ethnic categories and place themselves at the top of the cultural hierarchy.

While the history of the umbrella enabled Britons to feel superior in the world context, umbrellas also played an important part in defining the racial characteristics of Britons themselves. In the second part of this chapter, I demonstrate how whiteness was physically represented and maintained on British women's bodies partly through the use of parasols. The whiteness of British women was carefully constructed as a way to emphasize racial difference and thereby reinforce the hierarchies stressed by the metanarratives explained in the first half of the chapter. Women were encouraged to maintain their skin as white, which was the standard skin color that all other races were measured against. Here I follow the work of scholars James R. Barrett and Matthew Frye Jacobson who seek to "denaturalize race" by unpacking the details of its formation in order to demonstrate that whiteness is a "cultural construct." In doing so I suggest that Britons were not only establishing false worldwide hierarchies of race, but they were also actively maintaining their status as a white race through middle-class women.[3] In the last two sections of the chapter the frame is narrowed to British women within their country.

The third section looks at particular domestic uses of the parasol, that is, how these articles were used by women as flirtatious props to attract husbands. The final section of the chapter looks at how the material makeup, general upkeep, and the fold of umbrellas were indicators of social class and emblems of masculinity within the male population.

IMAGINED HISTORIES OF THE UMBRELLA

Narratives are a way for human beings of the past and present to understand their experiences and guide their actions.[4] An important metanarrative of Victorian society was the advent of democracy and constitutional government. Every British school child of the nineteenth century knew the progressive narrative of the rise of parliamentary democracy beginning with the Magna Carta, passing through the "Glorious Revolution," and ending with the reform acts. According to this view of history, the tempering of royal authority and the advent of democracy changed the English system of government from an absolute monarchy to a constitutional government that served the wants and needs of the voting populace. John Stuart Mill, one of the leading thinkers of the day, believed that liberty was a marker of civilization but that societies had to go through various phases of despotic rule before they might limit royal power and achieve self-governance.[5] The idea that non-Western countries were on a path leading toward democracy was thus all-pervasive in Victorian society. And so it should be no surprise that these beliefs entered popular histories of the umbrella.

Nineteenth-century historians gleefully collected examples of umbrellas as markers of royal status among "backward" non-European peoples. According to these authors, the umbrella was such an important symbol of status that many non-Western countries used sumptuary laws to restrict the umbrella to royal use. In East Asia the umbrella was "universally adopted as a sign of the highest distinction by Oriental peoples, to be displayed over the head of the king."[6] In the Middle East the umbrella "was a mark of distinction."[7] And Persians had white female slaves hold large umbrellas over the heads of their kings.[8] In Africa, the umbrella figured as an indication of royalty for Ashanti, Moroccan, Ethiopian, and Dahomey kings (figure 3.1).[9] And the king of the Fiji islands jealously guarded his exclusive right to the shade of parasols, only granting the privilege of umbrella use to others as a royal favor.[10]

According to British writers who expounded upon the worldwide significance of the umbrella, in non-Western countries umbrellas represented the power held by the supreme ruler over both the sun and his people. Here the supreme authority of absolute rulers was brought to its terrible conclusion; with a motion of their umbrellas they could enslave or kill those around them. The anonymous author of an 1879 article entitled "The Umbrella" argued

THE KING OF ASHANTEE AND HIS EXECUTIONERS.

Figure 3.1   The King of Ashanti under his official umbrella surrounded by his retinue. Robarts Library, University of Toronto, "The Ashantee War: Plan of the Attack on Elmina," *The Illustrated London News* LXIII, no. 1769 (July 26, 1873): 87.

that the power to convert sun into shade represented total authority on earth: "From time immemorial, the contrivance of warding off the sun's rays and casting an artificial shade has been symbolical of the supreme human authority that can convert light to darkness, and in a trice," the author continued, "drive ordinary mortals from the brightness of life to the gloom of death. No fitter emblem of his awful power could be imagined for the potentate who, by a word or a nod, could extinguish towards any of his creatures the sun of earthly happiness, and banish them suddenly to the abodes of gloom and despair."[11] So long as the sun is generally understood to be a symbol of freedom, any object that obscures the sun's light and casts a shadow is indicative of imprisonment.[12] Along the same lines, Octave Uzanne tells us that umbrellas were presented to kings after a battle was won in their favor. This umbrella "symbolized . . . the power of life and death, vested in the savage conqueror over the unfortunate conquered, delivered up wholly to his mercy."[13]

According to another anonymous author for *The Penny Magazine* the awful power of the monarch could also work against the rulers of exotic states. In Morocco it was reported that as the emperor "went out of the palace gate, the violence of the wind broke his parasol which was interpreted as an omen of the approaching end of his reign."[14] Here not only is a real umbrella broken but

also broken is the symbolic power of the emperor over his citizens and ene-
mies. Such a detail might have been included in a Victorian publication to indicate that even despotic authority was tenuous and could be put into question
based on such simple occurrences as a heavy wind and a turned-out umbrella.

Another device used by the writers of umbrella histories was to rank countries according to their level of liberty and civilization. According to Victorian
authors those countries that allowed their people, irrespective of status, to
use umbrellas were more democratic than those that restricted their use to
royalty. Persia and India fared the worst in these narratives of civilization. In
1835 the parasol remained a "distinction confined to royalty" within Persia.[15]
Similarly in the outlying peninsulas of India the umbrella remained "strictly
confined to royalty itself."[16] In what authors claimed was the more advanced
neighboring state of Burma, the king retained exclusive rights to white umbrellas; but, in acknowledgment of the advice of his court, those officially
connected with him carried various colors according to their status.[17] In nineteenth-century China, according to authors, the diffusion of the umbrella was
spread wider. The anonymous author of "The Story of the Umbrella" explained
that in China the object had been abandoned to the people: "No matter to
what part of China one travels, umbrellas may be seen everywhere." In fact,
the object had been democratized. "They are born aloft by servants, over the
viceroys and mandarins; students and tradesmen carry them, and every temple has a dozen umbrellas made of bright yellow silk surrounding the altar of
the Joss."[18] However, Chinese usage differed from European umbrella usage
through restrictions placed on fabric and color, which allowed onlookers to distinguish the governmental rank of those carrying the umbrella (figure 3.2).[19]
Turkey held its own as the only non-Western state that used umbrellas in a
way the authors thought was practical (in sunny as well as rainy weather). One
author, however, attributes this peculiarity to the Europeans who brought the
innovation into Turkey when they established themselves in the suburbs of
Pera. "And," he suggests, "much opposition to innovation was not to be expected from the present reforming sultans."[20] All of the countries that were
shown to be backward in their umbrella-bearing practices were under British
influence in one way or another.[21] The metanarrative about the lack of democracy and liberty in the non-Western world also offered a justification for British
imperialism. The stories about the strange and superstitious use of umbrellas
in these countries helped create a sense that Britain should exert a civilizing
influence over them.

This is not to say that Britons could get away with ignoring the meaning
of umbrellas in non-Western countries especially when it came to diplomatic
relations. Max von Boehn explains that "the sunshade was for a long time a
purely feminine adjunct and it was a concession to the Oriental point of view
when Queen Victoria presented the Sultan with one worth 3000 pounds."[22]
Similarly when the wives of British merchants trading in India had an audience

Figure 3.2 Procession of state umbrellas at the emperor's marriage in Peking. Robarts Library, University of Toronto, Anon, "Pagodas, Aurioles, and Umbrellas: Umbrellas, Ancient and Modern Part II," *The English Illustrated Magazine* 5 (July 1888): 611.

with the King of Delhi, "the ladies who were of the company were ordered to dispense with their parasols, as being an infringement of the great Mongol's prerogative."[23] The British were not shy to use their understanding of umbrellas for non-Western peoples to their advantage.

During the colonial expansion of the nineteenth century, England became "the storehouse for . . . old Royal Umbrellas."[24] Telegraphs announcing the defeat of Burmese forces in the Third Anglo-Burmese War reported that the British acquired symbols of Burmese national heritage through "the capture of their flags, and of sundry umbrellas!"[25] As part of the takeover of the Burmese palace of Mandalay, which ended the war on November 28, 1885, a royal umbrella was taken and brought to England. A few years later it was joined by the State Umbrella of King Prempeh, of Ghana.[26] This umbrella was presented to Queen Victoria after the Ashanti Campaign (1873–1874) led by Field Marshal Garnet Joseph Wolseley (who was the very model for Gilbert and Sullivan's Modern Major General) with this note: "a humble tribute of dutiful respect and affection from her Majesty's military and naval forces that took part in the war."[27] The act of taking royal umbrellas as spoils of war to be stored in England both demonstrated the imperial power of the British and symbolized the lasting defeat of former kings (figure 3.3).[28]

King Prempeh's
umbrella, now at
Windsor Castle.

*From a Photograph
taken by gracious
permission of Her
Majesty the Queen.*

Figure 3.3 King Prempeh's royal umbrella from when he ruled Ashanti. 1873. Robarts Library, University of Toronto, Anon., "The Story of the Umbrella," *Pearson's Magazine* 6 (July 1898): 41.

British writers also reveled in stories of "backward" people who had not yet found Christianity. The anonymous author of "Umbrellas" claimed that Eastern cultures practiced sun worship as a remnant of the religious festivals surrounding the Greek god Bacchus, patron god of agriculture.[29] The author of "The Religious Character of Umbrellas" examined this idea in detail, suggesting that the umbrella took on significance because it reminded religious observers in Siam not to stare directly at the sun, an act that was considered disrespectful to the deity. "In order to protect themselves against such thoughtlessness, and moreover to avoid the danger of unseemly actions and possibly disrespectful gestures in full view of the God of Day, the umbrella was invented. Consequently," the author elaborates, "when the article first came into use, it was most generally used in fine weather, when the sun was high in the heavens, and thus was most liable to be offended. In rainy weather the danger was not so serious, for the great luminary covered up his face in clouds as with a veil, and it was not so necessary to guard against being rude to him. As a natural consequence, whenever it rained the primeval sun-shade inventors put down their umbrellas and were happy." Having explained the thinking behind these ancient beliefs, the author suggested that the modern Western use of the umbrella was a perversion: "In later days skeptical people who did not scruple to speak disrespectfully of the sun . . . found the parasol—in the etymological sense—convenient for keeping off the rain; and, when the pious-minded were lowering their umbrellas, the heretical weaklings unfurled theirs to shelter their sorry bodies."[30] Underlying many of the stories of the non-Western history of the umbrella was a feeling that people who used it only for the sun were odd and in need of education (figure 3.4).

More typical articles of the period sought to highlight the misconceptions of the non-Western world to demonstrate the unreasoned origins of their religious practice. An article in *Pearson's Magazine,* for example, claimed that the Santal Hill peoples of India had misconstrued the idea of the sun deity and "have actually raised the umbrella to the position of a god, and make it an object of adoration." In a description that would remind Victorians of the may-pole, the author described a spring ritual where they "place a rude umbrella

Figure 3.4 Image of first primitive parasol (that looks like a fan) to protect royalty from the sun in India. Late nineteenth century. 10028488, Mary Evans Picture Library.

upon a tall pole, adorn it with garlands of flowers and leaves, and pay divine honours to it, the men and women of the tribe performing a religious dance round the pole"[31] (figure 3.5). The author concluded that the natives of India had misunderstood Greek myth, transferring what was once sun worship, personified by the god Helios, to umbrella worship. This article was written with an authority that helped to highlight irrational Eastern practices and demonstrate how non-Christian tradition ruled the lives of non-Western people.

In another story a newly converted Chinese Christian misread the meaning of the word *cross* and became the butt of a joke for British readers. The story goes that "A Chinese convert . . . in reading his New Testament, came to the passage: 'Whosoever will come after Me, let him deny himself and take up his cross and follow Me.' But he was not clear as to the meaning of the phrase: 'Take up his cross.' After pondering for a long time, the man arrived at the conclusion that the passage must refer to that which he regarded as most

Figure 3.5 The umbrella worship of the Santal Hill peoples. Robarts Library, University of Toronto, Anon., "The Story of the Umbrella," *Pearson's Magazine* 6 (July 1898): 40.

valuable and most highly esteemed." Misunderstanding the passage he "read the text thus: 'Leave everything but your umbrella; take that and follow me.' The man accordingly set out from his own village to visit the nearest mission station . . . and in token of his subjection to the God of the Christians, took with him simply—an umbrella!"[32] We can understand this man's thinking because both the cross and the umbrella were symbols of deities. While Western Christians were just as superstitious about the symbol of the cross, the joke assumes that Western ways were the most authentic.

Authors of fluff pieces about umbrellas often drew an entirely different timeline for European umbrellas beginning with Greece and Rome. Umbrella bearers in democratic Athens were supposedly the predecessors of British gentlemen and their black gamps. However, Greek and Roman umbrellas were used primarily by women; therefore, Victorian authors found themselves in an analytical dilemma (figure 3.6). In Rome female slaves, called *umbrelliferae*, held umbrellas over the heads of their mistresses, and in Greece the umbrella was said to be "borne by her bondswoman over the head of the Athenian belle."[33] The history of the umbrella in Greece and Rome was so

Figure 3.6 A royal parasol as used by the Assyrians, compared with Jonas Hanway's umbrella of 1786. 10053447, Mary Evans Picture Library.

firmly associated with femininity that male use of the object was considered effeminate.[34] According to *The Gentlemen's Magazine*: "To carry an umbrella on his own behalf was to blazon forth his effeminate nature, but classic mashers who desired to rank themselves among the slaves and their mistresses considered it was as much a point of honour to hold up the sunshade of the beloved object as do their modern successors."[35]

According to the British authors, after the fall of the Greek and Roman empires the umbrella did not again appear in the West until 1675 but here again it was entrenched as a feminine accessory carried by French ladies at court.[36] The parasol is said to have arrived in England around the same time, but only became fashionable for ladies of the English court during the reign of Queen Anne (1702–1714) (figure 3.7).[37] In the early 1700s, authors report, the English umbrella was almost exclusively associated with women as was demonstrated by *Kersey's Dictionary* of 1708 and *Baily's Dictionary* of 1720, which described the umbrella as a feminine protection from the rain and sun.[38] This is a moment when we see the separation between non-Western countries where umbrellas were used for the sun and Western countries where they

Figure 3.7 A lady in court dress with her fashionable parasol. 1715. 10092775, Mary Evans Picture Library.

were used for the rain. The popular press of the time also coupled the sunshade and the umbrella with women rather than men, as is evidenced in this poem from the 1712 edition of *Trivia*:

> Good housewives all the winter's rage despise,
> Defended by the riding hood's disguise;
> Or underneath th' umbrella's oily shed,
> Safe through the wet in clinking patens tread.
> Let Persian dames th' umbrella's ribs display,
> To guard their beauties from the sunny ray;
> Or sweating slaves support their shady load,
> When Eastern monarchs show their state abroad;
> Britain in winter only knows its aid,
> To guard from chilling showers the walking maid.[39]

By the Victorian period the accessory had split into the umbrella for protection from the rain (primarily associated with men) and a parasol that shaded pale female faces from the sun.[40] But before this division of use and gender association took root any man who dared to bare a brolly underwent his share of public ridicule.

The first man to use the umbrella in London was Jonas Hanway who famously walked down Pall Mall on a rainy day in 1756 sporting a silk umbrella.[41] *Cassel's Family Magazine* describes Hanway's reasoning behind introducing the umbrella to the fashionable set of men in England: "He was a highly respectable citizen, and took a great pride in his appearance. He had, moreover, traveled a great deal, and during his journeys in the East had derived great comfort from the use of a protection from the sun. He had also lived in Paris, and noted how the 'machine' had been adopted there" by men. According to Hanway's biographer "he accommodated himself to the prevailing fashion. He usually wore dress clothes, with a large French bag (wig). . . . He was in short, just the person who would be likely to adopt so sensible an idea as an umbrella" (figure 3.8).[42] Despite the fact that Hanway is here described as a highly fashionable yet sensible Englishman, on this first rainy promenade, he was mobbed by those who sought to "witness the shocking effeminacy into which man had fallen."[43] Twenty years later a footman named John Macdonald endured much the same ridicule when sporting a fine silk umbrella he had procured from Spain. In this case it was the coachman who protested by yelling at him: "Frenchman! Why don't you get a coach?"[44] This man tried to shame Macdonald by highlighting his actions as French, and therefore fashionable and effeminate. As late as 1813 Duke Wellington, the manliest of men, forbade his soldiers from sporting umbrellas under his command stating that he "does not approve of the use of umbrellas by *soldiers*, and especially *under fire*, nor can he permit gentlemen's sons to make themselves ridiculous

Figure 3.8   Jonas Hanway pioneers the first umbrella in London. 1756. 10053448, Mary Evans Picture Library.

in the eyes of the army."[45] The association of the umbrella with effeminacy lasted into the nineteenth century, prompting periodical writers to reassure men that umbrellas were now "fashionable for both sexes."[46]

According to Peter N. Stearns, a historian of consumerism, the umbrella had passed into general use by 1770.[47] And by the end of the nineteenth century Uzanne confidently cast the device as a common object used by all Europeans: "The sunshade is found today in the hands of everyone, as it should be in this practical and utilitarian age."[48] As a result of industrial advances alongside demand for the article, the object became smaller, lighter, and less expensive. The umbrella of the eighteenth century had eight ribs and was suitable only for a single person.[49] In the nineteenth century the heavy whalebone frame increasingly gave way to such lighter and less expensive materials as cane and hollow steel.[50] Finally, the expensive silk coverings used by women of the court were replaced by cotton and alpaca, which were more affordable materials for the middle and working classes. With these modifications the prices of French umbrellas changed from 15 to 22 livres in 1650 to less than 3 livres in 1776[51] and were sold in England by street-hawkers for a few pence by 1889 (figure 3.9).[52]

Another way that the European umbrella became increasingly utilitarian was the use of the object not only as a protection from the sun, but also from the rain. The author of "Umbrellas in the East" explains: "Notwithstanding the more stately appearance of the umbrella, it is but the child of the parasol, or rather, the original and almost exclusive use of the umbrella is that to which the parasol is now appropriated—to afford shelter from the sun. The applicability of the same implement as a defense against rain was sufficiently obvious, but is scarcely known in the original countries of the umbrella except as introduced from Europe."[53] The "obvious" appropriation of the umbrella as a protection from the rain was apparently lost upon simple Eastern peoples.

Figure 3.9 As umbrellas became more common they were sold on the street by hawkers. 1823. 10042675, Mary Evans Picture Library.

It was left to the Europeans to discover this secondary use and develop the implementation.

One story told to highlight the democratic use of the umbrella in England was the tale of a working-class man who lent his umbrella to Queen Victoria and Prince Albert. The story first appeared as a report in the *Morning Post* in 1844, and the incident was of sufficient interest that it was later written into a verse entitled "The Royal Umbrella: A Ballad of the Isle of Wight." The newspaper tells of a dedicated old postman of East Cowes and Whippingham who happened upon a gentleman and lady who got caught in the rain when they were out for their afternoon walk. The old Englishman offered them his "gingham, but perfectly waterproof, umbrella," which was graciously accepted with an invitation for the postman to follow them back to Osborne House. "Little did the poor postman imagine," however, "that it was to his Sovereign he had the honour of affording such seasonable shelter."[54] Later that night when the postman excitedly returned home with this story for his wife, she scolded him for not recognizing his queen when he saw her every day on the stamps of the letters he delivers:

The Queen was dressed in black, good wife,
The little stamps are red;
They have one eye, while two bright orbs
Were shining from her head.

She bore the stamp of Majesty;
What stamp with that can vie?
They're no more like the real Queen,
Old dame, than you or I.[55]

Whether or not this is a true story it certainly highlights the contrast between the non-Western umbrella stories told of royal umbrellas decorated to the hilt and the plain, serviceable umbrellas that royalty in England were willing to use in a pinch.

When writing the history of the umbrella, Victorian historians were not transparently relating the story of an object to the public. Embedded in these histories were various metanarratives designed to help Britons understand their place in the world. Most of the historical background of the umbrella was immersed in tales that compared and contrasted Western and non-Western practices in a way that favored Western traditions. Historians saw the use of large, ornate umbrellas, that covered the heads of sultans, as marks of despotic rule in comparison to the democratic use of the article in Britain, that symbolized representative governments. They saw the singular use of the sunshade as a mark of tradition and simple-mindedness in comparison to the innovative and progressive West who used the article as a protection from the sun and rain. They even claimed that Western umbrella traditions originated in the great empires of Greece and Rome in order to place themselves as the culmination of the great empires of the West.

COMPLEXION, YOUTH, AND FLIRTATION: THE PARASOL AS A FEMININE ACCESSORY

Many young Victorian women feared they would fall into spinsterhood due to the lack of bachelors in Britain.[56] Maintaining a youthful complexion for as long as possible allowed women to entertain the prospect of attracting a suitable husband. Etiquette manuals, which span the Victorian period, reinforced the idea that beauty and youth were categories that might have little to do with the actual age of a woman.[57] In 1908 etiquette writer Mrs. Robert Noble warned young maids that although their complexion was naturally healthy, it might not stay that way if they spent too much time in the sun: "The fairest and most delicate complexion can be shriveled, and, unless remedies are used, spoilt beyond hope of redemption. . . . So many girls think it will all come right, it is only a temporary disfigurement of the skin. Now," she warns, "this is not so. If the skin be burnt up, tanned and scorched perpetually under fierce suns, it will harden and toughen, and crease and line. It will become prematurely coarse and old-looking."[58] Mrs. Noble goes on to encourage women to use parasols when out in the mid-day sun to protect their complexion, which was the ultimate marker of youth, beauty, and race (figure 3.10).[59]

While parasols could be used as a protective shield for the complexion, they could also make women look older or younger depending on the color of the accessory. In the Oxford periodical entitled *The Parasol*, a young woman at a boat race appeared to have the permanent blush of sunburn. When her male companion commented upon this he was assured that it was only the reflection of her red sunshade that created the unfortunate complexion.[60] Charles Blanc, author of *Art in Ornament and Dress* (1877), would have been disappointed that this young maid felt compelled to match her red dress to her parasol, suggesting that "a pretty woman will never sacrifice her beauty, even to the rules of optical harmony." Instead Blanc insists that a "light flounce" or a "small fringe" of the dress fabric should be used to attain the desired effect. While a "parasol lined with rose de chine, or carnation coloured silk, sheds a youthful and animated colour over the face," a parasol covered in purple, red, or brown would dull the face. "Let us here recall the laws of complementary colours," he instructs. "By throwing a violet shade over the face, the skin becomes colourless and dull, because the flesh tints, always more or less yellowish, destroyed by the violet, are reduced to a neutral tint of pale gray." In the play of colors, the author suggests "the sunshade . . . resembles a varnish."[61] It is this "varnish" that older women relied upon to look younger than they were. This is the situation described in the song *The Parasol Parade*:

Figure 3.10 A woman uses her white parasol to maintain a pale complexion. 1906. 10004567, Mary Evans Picture Library.

At the seaside there's the girl that's rather haughty
On the prom there she will roam,
Well, when I say a girl, she's nearly forty,
And she looks it when at home;
But see her strolling out beneath a sunshade,
She looks charming—simply grand—
Though really her complexion
Is the pink and white reflection
Of the sunshade that she carries in her hand:—

And on the Parasol Parade,
There you will see this charming maid,
She smiles so sweetly
Though most discreetly
On the Parasol Parade;
And underneath a smart sunshade—
And though over thirty
She's still young and flirty.[62]

Here the pinkish hue of a parasol turns a forty-year-old spinster into a young maid, giving her a second chance at love and romance.

Women on promenade were famous for deploying their parasols as flirtatious toys that helped to highlight their beauty. Parasols, like fans, had the potential to attracted visual interest. The bright colors of the accessory indicated that they were "designed more for show than for use."[63] "You believe that [the parasol] was invented to shield the complexion from the sun?" adds another. "No doubt this is true, but how many resources has this necessity of shading their faces furnished women with, and how little they would think of the sun if it did not give them this pretext of defending themselves from its rays?"[64] Women, skilled in the elegant use of the parasol, twirled, hid behind, and snapped shut their parasols to attract attention.[65] An action-song designed for school concerts indicates that girls learned early how to wield their parasols to attract interest:

> We only care to use them for ornament,
> And whether the day be dull or fair,
> With pretty ones we're content.
> We put them up we put them down,
> We swing them daintily to and fro,
> By them we give effect to a frown,
> We hold them steadily out in a row.[66]

Victorians like Octave Uzanne, who wrote *The Sunshade, the Glove, the Muff* (1883), believed that adult women knowingly used parasols to their advantage: "Surely the sunshade adds new graces to women! It is her outside weapon, which she bears boldly as a volunteer, either at her side, or inclined over her shoulder. It protects her head-dress, in supporting her carriage it surrounds as with a halo the charms of her face."[67] Charles Blanc puts it more bluntly, saying "The sunshade is another weapon of coquetry."[68]

If suitors were attracted to parasol-clad women, the sunshade could then be used to facilitate social interaction. M. Cazal, a French manufacturer of parasols and author of *Umbrellas, Parasols, and Walking Sticks* (1884), suggests that the accessory was a great "cover" for couples in love: "Under its rosy azure dome, sentiment buds, passion broods or blossoms. . . . How many sweet smiles have played under its corolla! How many charming signs of the head, how many intoxicating and magic looks, has the Sunshade protected from jealousy and indiscretion! How many emotions, how many dramas, has it hidden with its cloud of silk!"[69] As an accessory for courtship the parasol was also the subject of many songs of the early twentieth century that promised that love would blossom and perhaps come to fruition *Underneath a Parasol*:

You have seen a hundred lovers' billing
Cooing that their hearts are true,
Honey-woney does you love your Billie
Tootsey-wootsey course I do.
There's nothing like a little girlie-wirlie,
Not too short or not too tall,
And the place to hear her say
You may name the happy day,
Is underneath a parasol.[70]

The parasol had an advantage over the fan as a flirtation device: in both size and shape, it was inclusive. A couple felt "togetherness" when covered by a sunshade that had only a slim stick to divide lovers. In contrast, the folding fan was almost a barricade between would-be lovers with the man on one side and the woman on the other.

Instead of involving sunny days and parasols, a secondary type of courtship tale centered around men gallantly coming to the aid of women by offering

Figure 3.11 A gentleman gallantly offers a woman shelter from the rain. 1913. 10135461, Mary Evans Picture Library.

them shelter under umbrellas. Consider, for example, the story of a banker who "owed an excellent wife to the interposition of an umbrella. . . . On returning home one day in a heavy shower of rain," or so the story goes, "he found a young lady standing in his doorway. Politeness induced him to invite her to take shelter under his roof, and eventually to offer her the loan of an umbrella. Of course the gallant banker called for it the next day, and the acquaintance thus accidentally made, soon ripened into mutual affection."[71] In another tale written by J. S. Lloyd, a neighborhood picnic was interrupted by a sudden downpour. The one man who had brought an umbrella offered to share it with a young lady as they walked to safety. Underneath the protective silk the couple came to know each other and the tale ends with a marriage proposal: "My little queen," whispered the man, "how fortunate it was that I brought my umbrella! Otherwise I might never have gained you for my wife."[72] These stories of men rescuing women indicate how the umbrella became gendered as a male object (figure 3.11).

DEMOCRACY AND CHARACTER: THE UMBRELLA AS A MASCULINE ACCESSORY

Over the last four decades, historians have generally posited that by the eighteenth century, the connections between inner character and material objects were restricted to women. The general argument has been that prior to the Great Masculine Renunciation of 1688, when aristocratic men gave up their finery for more modest dress, men's characters like those of women could be read in their beautiful and varied choice of clothing.[73] The more modest and sober style of aristocratic clothing that emerged after the Glorious Revolution, however, separated men and women in terms of the equation of character and fashion. While men's characters were now understood to be interpreted through their actions, women were purported to display their inner selves through their garments. With the example of the umbrella, however, we can see that this gender distinction is not entirely accurate.

An alternative perspective is explored by sociologist Pierre Bourdieu who posits that, partly through clothing, men's class could be read by observers. Bourdieu's study of 1960s France shows that different classes make their position in life apparent by creating distinctions between themselves and other groups. Bourdieu shows that lifestyle, the cultivation of certain tastes, and the consumption of goods were means by which different social groups objectified their status.[74] The use of the umbrella is an excellent example of how elite nineteenth-century men sought to differentiate themselves from middle-class professionals and working-class poseurs through the consumption of a particular good.

Writings from the popular press in the late Victorian period often used humor to make clear that within the West the umbrella was an article that helped to reveal class differences. An anonymous author of an 1889 article entitled "Umbrellas" attests to this point: "In the days of its restricted employment the umbrella sufficiently indicated the status of its possessor. Has it, in its more widely extended use, lost its suggestion of character? I think not. . . . The subject is worth a moment's thought, for 'if the proper study of mankind is man,' and man is known by his umbrella, its investigation is an imperative duty."[75] Noting the absurdity of reading men's class through their umbrellas, turn-of-the-century author Herbert Howard writes a gossipy and intentionally comic article in *Harmsworth Magazine.* Howard jests that if you tell him what kind of umbrella a man possesses he can "tell you what manner of man he is!"[76] The authors of such articles suggested that observers could discern the character and class of those around them by focusing on characteristics of their umbrellas, including the material of the handle and covering, the general repair of the object, the precision with which its owner folded the umbrella, and how a man used his umbrella.

In his article "The Gossip about Umbrellas," A. B. Reach described the umbrellas of each class of society in ludicrously specific detail. According to the article the elite umbrella was subdivided into three classes. Each umbrella represented a different rank of the upper class, from a lord to a gentleman of limited means. The first class, "the perfectly aristocratic umbrella,"[77] had very thin steel ribs, an ivory or silver handle inscribed with the owner's initials or carved into an animal head, and was covered in silk from Lyon, France. The second class of aristocratic umbrellas "would be characterized as handsome, serviceable implements."[78] Their silk was not as soft and refined and their knobs not as beautifully ornamented as the first class of umbrella. The third class was possessed by gentlemen of limited means. The silk was either so worn and in need of repair that it was "as thin as a cobweb,"[79] or it was so inferior that one could see the sky through the protective cover. The ribs of this umbrella were made of whalebone, an older, heavier material typical of middle-class umbrellas; the shaft of stained wood; and the handle of horn.

Further specifying the "distinctions of taste" Reach explains that the ideal upper-class umbrella, at first glance, appeared to be a walking stick (figure 3.12).[80] The cane and the umbrella were both descendants of the sword, which eighteenth-century gentlemen carried with them as a sign of their position.[81] Howard went so far as to seek out umbrella-folding advice from Messrs. Sangster and Co. Ltd.—umbrella suppliers to the Queen.[82] The company explained in detail how to fold an umbrella so that a gentleman might appear to be part of the aristocratic set: "The left hand should grasp the silk firmly, but not very tightly, and the right hand by a series of half-turns—never releasing the tops of the ribs—should steadily work the umbrella through the other hand until it is entirely rolled up."[83] As if the phallic symbol of the sword-come-umbrella were not enough, these suggestive instructions include specifications for the correct hand and gesture to be exacted upon this most

Figure 3.12   The Earl of Hardwicke leans on his slim umbrella. Robarts Library, University of Toronto, "The Earl of Hardwicke," *The Illustrated London News* III, no. 64 (July 22, 1843): 57.

precious of men's objects. If an elite man could not properly control his accessory, suggested Howard, his upper-class masculine identity would be at stake. Those who did not attain the well-folded umbrella shape revealed a host of character flaws: "untidiness, lack of method, finnicking nicety, hurry, temper [and even] carelessness."[84] Another author goes so far as to twist William Shakespeare's famous line from *Much Ado about Nothing* to make the point that only a man of upstanding character could properly furl an umbrella: "to be a well favoured man is a gift of fortune; but to fold an umbrella in an artistic manner comes by nature"[85] (figure 3.13).

Other authors lightheartedly suggest that some umbrella users teetered on the edge of elite gentility and threatened class definitions. For example, an umbrella invented especially for gentlemen's clubs had as its distinguishing feature a handle that could be unscrewed. This innovation would ensure that when a gentleman left his umbrella in the hallstand at his club, he was

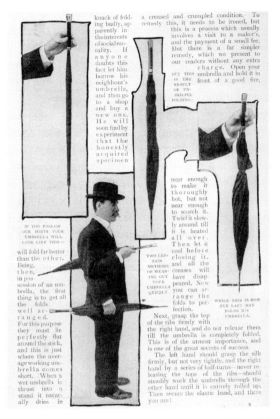

Figure 3.13 How to properly fold an umbrella. Robarts Library, University of Toronto, Herbert Howard, "Can You Fold Your Umbrella?: A Few Hints on a Practical Subject," *The Harmsworth Magazine* 3, no. 18 (January 1900): 608.

sure to find it untouched upon his return. The underlying assumption being that "no one would care to 'borrow' a handleless umbrella."[86] Despite the fact that clubmen were notorious for pinching one another's umbrellas, the invention failed "because it was felt to be an unclubable act for a man to enter his club with an umbrella that implied a distrust of the honesty of the members of his joint-stock home."[87] Of course the very invention of this object suggests that the "borrowing" of umbrellas was a major problem. With full knowledge of the possibility that his umbrella might be stolen, it was rumored that one man refused to ever part with or even use his perfectly folded silk: "he never takes it out but in sunny weather, when he displays it ostensibly for the sake of the shade, but really as a treat to mankind. . . . When he goes to a party with it, he has a little chain and padlock with which he makes it fast." He even goes so far as to "frequent the second boxes of the theater and amphitheater of the opera, that he may carry his dear umbrella with him."[88] Well aware that his upper-class masculinity would be defined through his umbrella, this man thwarted gentlemanly behavior for a symbol of this status. Victorians knew people who exhibited some of the characteristics of this anonymous gentleman, but the author was likely compounding the examples to make a joke of those who displayed these characteristics.

In other instances, men's personalities were examined using umbrellas as metaphors for their characters. In the story "A Study about the Umbrella-Mender," a gentleman craftsman had fallen on hard times because he and his fortune were abused by a wayward son. According to the tale the father was "not unlike a thin umbrella—a threadbare, shabbily-genteel umbrella, with an uncompromising handle, and a long drawn piece of elastic, and an ancient button, and a well-worn stick which wanted re-tipping (figure 3.14)."[89] Umbrella metaphors could just as easily reveal the rotten character of a "nouveaux riche." In another story, an umbrella seller found out that the postmistress's daughter has been seduced by the son of the wealthiest man in town. The

Figure 3.14   An umbrella-mender at work. Circa 1890. 10020852, Mary Evans Picture Library.

seller compared the character of the philandering son to a hackneyed umbrella: "Common gingham, that's what he's made of—nary silk about that umbrella, for all he speaks so genteel."[90] The son was identified as a "gingham" or an ordinary cotton fabric typical of middle-class umbrellas.

The above examples reflect that the move from the aristocratic to the middle-class umbrella was indicated by a change in fabric from silk to cotton. With this adjustment in material, we find a change in the rhetoric as well. One author notes: "there is always a sort of gentility about silk, but cotton descends into the region of respectability."[91] A. B. Reach indicates that there were two classes of umbrellas carried by middle-class men. The first class of cotton umbrella was said to be used by middle-class professionals. It was known by its good, strong cotton, and its ribs of whalebone. In terms of furling a cotton umbrella "may fold nearly, but not quite, as close as silk."[92] The second-class article was said to be used by merchants and was of coarser cotton and had a handle of horn.

When a middle-class man's umbrella was in disarray, the popular press applied a more sympathetic interpretation than was the case for aristocracy in parallel circumstances. That is, such disarray was thought to demonstrate certain details of his professional or personal life and did not necessarily carry with it the same loss of class status as a threadbare silk umbrella would in the aristocratic set. For example, the umbrellas of the middle classes were often seen as an extension of their professional identities. The headmaster's umbrella was characterized as "severe and somber," a symbol of the "pedantic authority" that he exerted in the school playground.[93] The umbrella of a politician tended to be unsewn in places and have a frayed cover, signs of an "absorbing preoccupation" with his employment.[94] The umbrella of a family man was a little worse for wear with "raspberry jam and treacle on the knob," suggesting that his fatherly responsibilities came above all else.[95] And finally, the inelegant, worn, and hastily furled umbrella was said to "betray a [doctor's or a parson's] devotion to duty." These two employments "leave little leisure for a consideration of appearances" and their umbrellas "indicate the haste with which a summons to the bed of a sick or dying person has been answered." The author goes on to argue that the middle-class umbrella served its purpose though it represented a respectable rather than a genteel type of manhood: "Should we be quite as satisfied with the fitness of things if the comforters of the afflicted in mind, body, or estate copied the airs of Bond Street and Pall Mall? I think not: there is a congruity in this negligence which satisfies our sense of right, and we would not have it otherwise."[96]

Working-class umbrellas took two forms: the abused, formerly middle-class umbrella and the distinctly working-class umbrella. Many working-class umbrellas were cotton accessories once owned by the middle class. When the ribs were bent, the cotton frayed, and the fastening gone, they were bought by umbrella hawkers who sold them to unsuspecting servant girls in need of protection from the rain.[97] One such umbrella was described as "particularly cumbersome about the handle, has clumsy whalebone ribs starting though its skin, no ferule, and a piece of rope dividing its ruins with a kind of waist in the middle."[98] This umbrella was furled in such a way that it mimicked the cinched waist of a woman rather than the strait, tight figure of a gentleman (figure 3.15). Though to the astute observer these umbrellas would not pass as respectable, they were often thought of by their owners as objects to be used for special occasions. The divide between an umbrella in fairly good repair and one in disrepair, however, was so marked that the working class tended not to "pass" as middle class through the display of this accessory.

There was also a distinctly working-class umbrella. The cover was made of alpaca wool. This superabsorbent fabric, which debuted at the Great Exhibition of 1851, became known as a working-class fabric once it was used by street sellers to keep themselves dry in the rainy British climate (figure 3.16).[99]

Umbrellas (like clothing) were often read by people to ascertain what class the umbrella carrier was from. Authors who wrote about umbrellas as

Figure 3.15 Music-hall entertainer George Robey poses as
a working-class upstart with
his misshapen umbrella. Circa
1905. 10088458, Mary Evans
Picture Library.

GEORGE ROBEY

representative of class used a mocking tone as they dissected the practice—
becoming the "reduction ad absurdum" of umbrella readers. The authors are
participating in a joke, and the joke lies in the fact that some Victorians actually looked at umbrellas and thought, "That man is dressed very well, but his
accessories do not match the rest of him. Perhaps he is not as wealthy as he
is presenting himself to be." The humor lies in the use of exaggeration by the
authors, who describe the umbrella and how to read it in obsessively minute
detail. Those reading the newspaper articles were in on a joke that was ultimately about themselves and a culture that prized hierarchy and rank.

The umbrella in the West remained a marker of wealth and power just as
it did in non-Western nations. Though in England men of all ranks were welcome to use umbrellas, not all umbrellas (or the men who owned them) were
created equal. The distinctions between classes were maintained by subtle
differences in material makeup, wear, and folding. Britons could read these
signs of class as readily as Indians understood the power associated with
their sultan's umbrella.

Figure 3.16 Knife grinder working at a street market under an
umbrella. 10107157, Mary Evans
Picture Library.

NOTES

1. Anon., "The Evolution of the Umbrella," *Chambers's Journal of Popular Literature, Science and Arts* 67 (1890): 394–96; Octave Uzanne, *The Sunshade, the Glove, the Muff* (London: J.C. Nimmo and Bain, 1883), 15; Walking Stick and Article tear-away from *The Woman's World*, 1888, John Johnson Collection, Box: Umbrellas and Trunks, Bodleian Library, 150.
2. Margaret R. Somers, "The Narrative Constitution of Identity: A Relational and Network Approach," *Theory and Society* 23, no. 5 (1994): 606.
3. James R. Barrett, "Whiteness Studies: Anything Here for Historians of the Working Class?," *International Labour and Working-Class History* 60 (Fall 2001): 33; Matthew Frye Jacobson, *Whiteness of a Different Color: European Immigrants and the Alchemy of Race* (Cambridge, MA: Harvard University Press, 1998), 2.
4. Somers, "The Narrative Constitution of Identity," 613–14.
5. John Stuart Mill, *Considerations on Representative Government* (London: Blackwell, 1946), 112.
6. Uzanne, *The Sunshade, the Glove, the Muff*, 11. See also: Anon., "The Story of the Umbrella," *Pearson's Magazine* 6 (July 1898): 39; Anon., "Umbrellas," *Household Words: A Weekly Journal* 6, no. 138 (1852): 202.
7. Anon., "Umbrella Evolution: The Umbrella and Parasol in History," *The Bag, Portmanteau and Umbrella Trader* 2, no. 35 (1909): 36.
8. Uzanne, *The Sunshade, the Glove, the Muff*, 12. See also: Walking Stick and Article tear-away from *The Woman's World*, 1888, John Johnson Collection, Box: Umbrellas and Trunks, Bodleian Library, 150.
9. Anon., "The Story of the Umbrella," 41; Uzanne, *The Sunshade, the Glove, the Muff*, 27. Sapna Reedy, "Be Sure to Get under Your *Ombra*: Ever Wonder about the Umbrella? A Glance at How People down the Ages Used It," *The Hindu*, August 26, 2005; Walking Stick and Article tear-away from *The Woman's World*, 1888, John Johnson Collection, Box: Umbrellas and Trunks, Bodleian Library, 151.
10. Anon., "Pagodas, Aurioles, and Umbrellas: Umbrellas, Ancient and Modern Part II," *The English Illustrated Magazine* 5 (July 1888): 656.
11. Anon., "The Umbrella," *The Perruquier* 2 (1879): 147.
12. Walking Stick and Article, John Johnson Collection of Printed Ephemera, Box: Umbrellas and Trunks, Bodleian Library, 150.
13. Uzanne, *The Sunshade, the Glove, the Muff*, 12.
14. Anon., "Umbrellas in the East," *The Penny Magazine of the Society for the Diffusion of Useful Knowledge* 4, no. 235 (1835): 480.
15. Anon., "Umbrellas in the East," 479.
16. Anon., "Umbrellas in the East," 479.
17. Anon., "Pagodas, Aurioles, and Umbrellas," 657; Anon., "The Religious Character of Umbrellas," *The Saturday Review* 55 (1883): 498; Anon.,

"The Story of the Umbrella," 39. Arthur Robinson Wright, "Umbrellas and Parasols," in *A Collection of Newspaper Cuttings on Walking Sticks, Umbrellas, Parasols, Fans and Gloves* (London: Author, 1932). This clipping was labeled "West. Gaz. Jan. 24, 1923" and was from an article entitled "Back to the Eleventh Century: Umbrellas that were State Symbols."

18. Anon., "The Story of the Umbrella," 38.
19. Anon., "Umbrellas," *Household Words*, 201. According to this article the funerals of mandarins were denoted by umbrellas of blue-and-white silk embroidered with yellow dragons. Minor government officials were allowed cloth umbrellas at these occasions, while the common people were distinguished by the use of stout paper parasols at their burial sites.
20. Anon., "Umbrellas in the East," 480.
21. Each location acquired its subservient position differently. Persia, formerly an imperial power in its own right, lost many of its colonies to Britain and had become economically dependent on Europe during the nineteenth century. India had been informally colonized by British investors since 1757 and became an official colony in 1857. Burma ceded some control of its coastal territories to the British in 1826 and 1851 and became a British colony in its entirety in 1885. China was forced to open fifteen ports to British traders after losing the Opium Wars of 1839–1842 and 1856–1860. And Turkey, which had been a strong imperial power in the sixteenth and seventeenth centuries, entered a decline just before the Victorian period. In order to maintain a balance of power in Europe, Britain protected a weak Ottoman Empire from Russian expansion, which led to Turkey's economic and diplomatic dependence on Britain.
22. Max von Boehn, *Modes and Manners: Ornaments; Lace, Fans, Gloves, Walking-Sticks, Parasols, Jewelry and Trinkets* (London: J.M. Dent & Sons, 1929), 147.
23. Anon., "Pagodas, Aurioles, and Umbrellas," 657.
24. Anon., "Pagodas, Aurioles, and Umbrellas," 657.
25. Anon., "Pagodas, Aurioles, and Umbrellas," 658.
26. Anon., "The Story of the Umbrella," 41.
27. Anon., "On Umbrellas," *The Michigan Freemason: A Monthly Magazine Devoted to Masonic and Home Literature* 6 (1875): 149.
28. For a similar example of stealing imperial spoils as a sign of British superiority see: Sarah Cheang, "Women, Pets and Imperialism: The British Pekingese Dog and Nostalgia for Old China," *Journal of British Studies* 45, no. 2 (2006): 359–87.
29. Anon., "Umbrellas," *The Gentleman's Magazine* 266 (1889): 537.
30. Anon., "The Religious Character of Umbrellas," 498. The use of umbrellas by all religious observers is an alternative narrative to the one where royalty has the exclusive right to use the sunshade.

31. Anon., "The Story of the Umbrella," 40.

32. Anon., "The Story of the Umbrella," 39.

33. Uzanne, *The Sunshade, the Glove, the Muff*, 9, 17. Anon., "Pagodas, Aurioles, and Umbrellas," 664; Anon., "The Umbrella," *Chambers's Journal of Popular Literature, Science and Arts* 49 (1896): 591–92. There is an alternative history of the umbrella that occasionally appears in the sources connecting umbrellas with Renaissance men. In Italy the umbrella was seen as an appendage of horsemen in 1611. Ten years later the umbrella had made its way to France where it was a large cumbersome object employed by hunting parties. Anon., "The Umbrella," 591; Anon., "Pagodas, Aurioles, and Umbrellas," 665; Uzanne, *The Sunshade, the Glove, the Muff*, 29.

34. Anon., "The Story of the Umbrella," 276.

35. Mashers are fashionable men who frequent theaters and think themselves irresistible to women. Anon., "Umbrellas," *The Gentleman's Magazine*, 538.

36. Uzanne, *The Sunshade, the Glove, the Muff*, 35.

37. Wright, "Umbrellas and Parasols." This clipping was labeled "West. Gaz. Jan. 24, 1923" and was from an article entitled "Back to the Eleventh Century: Umbrellas That Were State Symbols."

38. Anon., "Pagodas, Aurioles, and Umbrellas," 666. *Kersey's Dictionary* states "Umbrellas, or umbrella; a kind of broad fan or screen commonly used by women to shelter them from rain." *Baily's Dictionary* defines the word *umbrella* as "A little shadow, which women bear in their hands to shade them," and the *parasol* as "a sort of little canopy, or umbrella, which women carry to keep off the rain." It is interesting to note here that the differentiation of parasol and umbrella has not yet occurred in the early 1700s.

39. Anon., "Umbrellas," *Household Words*, 202. See also: Reedy, "Be Sure to Get under Your *Ombra*."

40. Anne Buck, *Victorian Costume and Costume Accessories*, 2nd ed. (Carlton: Ruth Bean, 1984), 180.

41. Anon., "The Story of the Umbrella," 42. See also: Reedy, "Be Sure to Get under Your *Ombra*."

42. Alexis Krausse, "Something about Umbrellas," *Cassell's Family Magazine* XXV (1879): 278–79.

43. Anon., "Umbrellas," *The Penny Magazine of the Society for the Diffusion of Useful Knowledge* 5 (1836): 7.

44. Anon., "Pagodas, Aurioles, and Umbrellas," 667. See also: Anon., "Umbrella Evolution," 38.

45. Fannie Roper Feudge, "Umbrellas," *St. Nicholas: Scriber's Illustrated Magazine for Girls and Boys* II (August 1875): 623.

46. Anon., "Umbrella Evolution," 38.

47. Peter N. Stearns, *Consumerism in World History: The Global Transformation of Desire* (London: Routledge, 2006), 22.

48. Uzanne, *The Sunshade, the Glove, the Muff*, 61.

49. Anon., "Umbrellas," *Household Words*, 203.

50. Anon., "The Evolution of the Umbrella," 396; Anon., "Umbrellas," *Household Words*, 203.

51. Anon., "Pagodas, Aurioles, and Umbrellas," 665.

52. Anon., "Umbrellas," *The Gentleman's Magazine*, 541.

53. Anon., "Umbrellas in the East," 479. See also: Anon., "Umbrellas," *Household Words*, 201.

54. Anon., *The Royal Umbrella: A Ballad of the Isle of Wight* (London: John Lee 1844), 3. In this publication it says that the original story was from the *Morning Post*, October 21, 1844. This story appears once more as a slightly different tale and poem in Orientalis, *The Umbrella; an o'er True and Regal Romaunt, or Legend of Osborne House* (Cowes: John R. Smith, Media Press, 1844).

55. Anon., *The Royal Umbrella: A Ballad of the Isle of Wight*, 16.

56. For a discussion of the lack of marriage-aged men in the Victorian period see: Lucy Bland, *Banishing the Beast: English Feminism and Sexual Morality, 1885–1914*, Penguin Women's Studies (London: Penguin, 1995), 162; Penny Kane, *Victorian Families in Fact and Fiction* (London: Macmillan, 1995), 93.

57. Mrs. Robert Noble, *Every Woman's Toilet Book* (London: George Newnes, 1908), 122. See also: Anon., *The Ladies' Hand-Book of the Toilet: A Manual of Elegance and Fashion* (London: H. Gt. Clarke and Co., 1843), 7.

58. Noble, *Every Woman's Toilet Book*, 122.

59. Noble, *Every Woman's Toilet Book*, 122.

60. Anon., "Editorial," *The Parasol* 1, no. 1 (1905): n.p.

61. Charles Blanc, *Art in Ornament and Dress*, trans. Alexandre Auguste (London: Chapman and Hall, 1877), 198–99.

62. David Worton, Charles Heslop, and K. L. Duffield, "The Parasol Parade" (London: Shapiro, von Tilzer Music Co., 1908), 4.

63. Anon., "Editorial," 1; Uzanne, *The Sunshade, the Glove, the Muff*, 40; Margaret Visser, *The Way We Are* (Toronto: HarperCollins, 1994).

64. Blanc, *Art in Ornament and Dress*, 197.

65. Uzanne, *The Sunshade, the Glove, the Muff*, 40; Visser, *The Way We Are*, 90; Anon., "For Every Woman," *Pall Mall Gazette* (1914): 8. For a sociological discussion of the way that flirtation functions see: Georg Simmel, *On Women, Sexuality and Love*, trans. Guy Oakes (New Haven, CT: Yale University Press, 1984). For a discussion of flirtation in Victorian novels see: Richard A. Kaye, *The Flirt's Tragedy: Desire without End in Victorian and Edwardian Fiction* (Charlottesville: University Press of Virginia, 2002). For information about the fan as a flirtatious object see chapter 2 in this

volume, " 'The Language of the Fan': Pushing the Boundaries of Middle-Class Womanhood."

66. "The Chinese Umbrella, An Action Song for School Concerts," words by A. J. Foxwell, music by C. Hutchins Lewis (London: J. Curwen and Sons, 1890).

67. Uzanne, *The Sunshade, the Glove, the Muff*, 61.

68. Blanc, *Art in Ornament and Dress*, 197.

69. As quoted in Blanc, *Art in Ornament and Dress*, 62.

70. Lester Keith and John Kemble, "Underneath a Parasol" (New York: Harry von Tilzer Music Pub. Co., 1906), 3–4. See also: Tom Mellor, Alf. J. Lawrance, and Harry Gifford, "A Parasol for Two" (London: Monte Carlo Publishing Co., 1907); Harold Orlob and Ned Rayburn, "Underneath a Parasol" (New York: Hitchy Koo, 1918).

71. Clyde and Black Co., *Umbrellas and Their History* (New York: Riverside Press, 1864), 70. Stories of love brought about by umbrellas seem to be a preoccupation for Victorian writers. In an etiquette manual by Mrs. Humphrey men are told: "A young man once asked me if it would be etiquette to offer an unknown lady an umbrella in the street, supposing she stood in need of one. I replied 'No *lady* would accept the offer from a stranger, and the other sort of person might never return the umbrella.' In large towns women of breeding soon learn to view casual attentions from well-dressed men with the deepest distrust. They would suffer any amount of inconvenience rather than accept a favour from a stranger, knowing that so many men make it their amusement to prowl about the streets, looking after pretty faces and graceful figures, and forcing their attentions on the owners. . . . It cannot be denied, however, that there is a corresponding class of women and girls who make promiscuous male acquaintances in the streets and the young men learn to distinguish these from respectable members of the community." Mrs. Humphrey, *Manners for Men* (London: James Bowden, 1897).

72. J. S. Lloyd, "Under an Umbrella," *Tinsley's Magazine* 32 (1883): 329. See also: Anon., "Mr. Thompson's Umbrella," *All the Year Round: A Weekly Journal* 15 (1866): 356–60.

73. The original idea of the Great Masculine Renunciation was published by J. C. Flugel, *The Psychology of Clothes* (New York: International University Press, 1969). The idea of the renunciation has been challenged by David Kuchta, "The Making of the Self-Made Man: Class Clothing and English Masculinity 1688–1832," in *The Sex of Things: Gender and Consumption in Historical Perspective*, ed. Victoria De Grazia and Ellen Furlough (Berkeley: University of California Press, 1996), 55–62, on the grounds that both the aristocracy and the middle class went through this trend of sober clothing, and by Brent Shannon, "Refashioning Men: Fashion, Masculinity, and the Cultivation of the Male Consumers in Britain,

1860–1914," *Victorian Studies* 46, no. 4 (2004): 598–99. Shannon argues that though men renounced flamboyant fashions they were still defined by their fashion; they were conspicuously inconspicuous consumers.

74. Pierre Bourdieu, *Distinction: A Social Critique of the Judgment of Taste*, trans. Richard Nice (Cambridge, MA: Harvard University Press, 1984).

75. Anon., "Umbrellas," *The Gentleman's Magazine*, 541.

76. Herbert Howard, "Can You Fold Your Umbrella?: A Few Hints on a Practical Subject," *The Harmsworth Magazine* 3, no. 18 (January 1900): 606–8.

77. A. B. Reach, "The Gossip about Umbrellas," *Sharpe's London Magazine of Entertainment and Instruction for General Reading* 3, no. 18 (1853): 373.

78. Reach, "The Gossip about Umbrellas," 373.

79. Reach, "The Gossip about Umbrellas," 373.

80. Reach, "The Gossip about Umbrellas," 373.

81. Reginald L. Hine, *The Cream of Curiosity—Being an Account of Certain Historical and Literary Manuscripts of the XVIIIth and XIXth Centuries* (London: George Routledge & Sons, 1920), 378; Daniel Pool, *What Jane Austen Ate and Charles Dickens Knew: From Fox Hunting to Whist—the Facts of Daily Life in 19th-Century England* (New York: Touchstone, 1994), 217–18.

82. Howard, "Can You Fold Your Umbrella?," 607.

83. Howard, "Can You Fold Your Umbrella?," 607. While folding one's own umbrella may have been a demonstration of upper-class precision, in reality few men of this class rolled their own umbrellas. This chore would have been the duty of a manservant who furled umbrellas as part of his duty to look after all details of his employer's dress. If a manservant was not skilled enough, high-end shops were known to iron and refold umbrellas for clients at a fee.

84. Howard, "Can You Fold Your Umbrella?," 606–7. For information on the ideal polite, honorable, sober, and serious aristocratic gentleman of the Victorian era see: Kuchta, "The Making of the Self-Made Man"; Alexander Saxton, *The Rise and Fall of the White Republic: Class Politics and Mass Culture in Nineteenth-Century America* (London: Verso, 1990); John Tosh, "Gentlemanly Politeness and Manly Simplicity in Victorian England," *Transactions of the Royal History Society* 12 (2002): 455–72; David Castronovo, *The English Gentleman: Images and Ideals in Literature and Society* (New York: Ungar, 1987). Castronovo's fourth and fifth models of gentlemanly behavior are especially relevant here. For a discussion of the permeable boundaries of the idea of the gentleman at the end of the nineteenth century see: Karen Volland Waters, *The Perfect Gentleman: Masculine Control in Victorian Men's Fiction, 1870–1901* (New York: P. Lang, 1997). For a discussion of the everyday practices of gentleman in the Victorian period see: Michael Brander, *The Victorian Gentleman* (London: Gordon Cremonesi, 1975).

85. Reach, "The Gossip about Umbrellas"; William Shakespeare, *Much Ado about Nothing*, ed. Claire McEachern (London: Arden Shakespeare, 2006). The original line is spoken by Dogberry at the beginning of the third act of *Much Ado about Nothing*. It reads: "God hath blessed you with a good name: to be a well-favored man is the gift of fortune; but to write and read comes by nature."

86. Anon., "The Umbrella," *The Perruquier* 2 (1879): 147.

87. Anon., "The Umbrella," *The Perruquier,* 147. Sporting an umbrella with an unscrewable handle in a club would be an indication of bad character that could have a very real impact on a man's class status, for men were sometimes blackballed from their clubs for "ungentlemanly behaviour." Amy Milne-Smith, "Clubland: Masculinity, Status, and Community in the Gentlemen's Clubs of London, c. 1880–1914" (PhD diss., University of Toronto, 2006). See chapter 2: "Exclusion and Inclusion I: Looking for the 'Right Sort' of Member."

88. Reach, "The Gossip about Umbrellas," 373.

89. B. Harraden, "A Study about the Umbrella-Mender," *Blackwood's Edinburgh Magazine* 146 (1889): 122.

90. C.C. Rothwell, "The Umbrella-Man," *Belgravia, A London Magazine* 69 (1889): 344.

91. Reach, "The Gossip about Umbrellas," 373.

92. Reach, "The Gossip about Umbrellas," 374.

93. Uzanne, *The Sunshade, the Glove, the Muff*, 58.

94. Anon., "Umbrellas," 543.

95. Anon., "Umbrellas," 542.

96. Anon., "Umbrellas," 543.

97. Anon., "Umbrellas," 543.

98. Anon., "The Umbrella," *The Perruquier*, 147.

99. Clyde and Black Co., *Umbrellas and Their History*, 53.

—4—

"The Real Thing": The Celluloid Vanity Set and the Search for Authenticity

In the nineteenth and early twentieth centuries, women's hairstyles had specific meanings, with certain styles marking the transition from girlhood to womanhood, from innocence to sexuality. The bound "updo" symbolized maturity, the mark of a woman who was grown-up, married, and sexually unavailable. This hairstyle coexisted with two other iconic feminine styles: the long, loose hair of the innocent young girl, and the unkempt tresses of the hypersexed prostitute, stage actress, or vaudeville singer.[1]

In Victorian culture, a well-kept appearance indicated respectability. The brush, mirror, and comb—the three basic items in the vanity set—were the essential tools for creating the upswept coiffure that signified middle-class dignity and taste. The Victorian vanity set, then, was a gendered artifact that helped women to maintain the appearance so famously tied up with the middle class.

In the Victorian period, brides received vanity sets from male and female relatives at their weddings.[2] The vanity set marked the bride's journey from girlhood to womanhood, symbolizing maturity, much like the updo. The gift vanity set was proudly displayed on the wife's dresser in the couple's bedroom, the only place where respectable women could "let their hair down," both literally and metaphorically. There it was a material representation of the woman's sexual and marital status. Hairbrushing, done in the bedroom, was associated with sensuality. Women used the vanity set as a beautification tool when they prepared themselves to be seen in public. As a cultural artifact, the vanity set had three functions: it was an object for giving, marking a transition in a woman's life, an erotic item associated with hairbrushing and flirtatious foreplay, and a tool that helped to create a respectable middle-class public image.

The vanity set also had other cultural work to perform. As well as helping to represent middle-class femininity, the vanity set could be a luxury item used to imitate the rich and well traveled. "Once upon a time only kings knew the luxury of ivory." But times were changing, this advertisement crowed, and E. I. du Pont de Nemours and Company was offering middle-class ladies a new product fit for royalty. They could have a brush, mirror, and comb set that looked like those at the dressing tables of aristocrats. In 1917 E.I. du Pont de Nemours & Co. issued an advertisement promoting its new product, "Ivory Pyralin." This was in fact a form of the earliest plastic celluloid, which was made by combining nitric and sulphuric acid with vegetable oils and camphor. The company claimed that Pyralin mimicked tusk ivory almost exactly, democratizing a substance that was once owned only by the wealthy. "Today the caste of ivory fashion still lives, greater than before. It is brought home to more of us, too, by the twentieth-century cousin of those gleaming tusks of old—Ivory Py-ra-lin. Exquisite graining and inexpressible mellowness like from some ancient elephant combine with the most charming present day style in Ivory Py-ra-lin. Milady who knows, indeed, will have naught else for her toilet requisites."[3] For middle-class housewives, these inexpensive objects symbolized upward mobility, and allowed them to imagine themselves as elegantly groomed aristocrats. Because celluloid was most often produced in imitation of ivory, it also gave women a tangible—if false—connection to empire. At the height of imperial aspirations on both sides of the Atlantic, vanity sets became imitative pieces of empire held in the palm of the hand.

This chapter is an examination of celluloid vanity sets that imitated the look of ivory. A type of personal grooming accessory kept on the bedroom dressing table, vanity sets typically consisted of a comb, brush, and handheld mirror, with dozens of add-ons such as cuticle pushers, glove stretchers, and perfume bottles. Much can be discovered by an analysis of this constellation of goods, used by millions of women in their daily beauty routines from its invention in 1862 through to the interwar period in England and America. Celluloid vanity sets had cultural resonance for diverse groups of people, including brushmakers, medical doctors, arts and crafts theorists, and female consumers. Drawing on company records, documents of government committees, trade publications, medical journals, advertisements, union records, and hunters' memoirs, this chapter traces the controversial history of celluloid—a story of a British invention that gets taken over by American might.

The chapter ends with the exploration of an American interwar advertising campaign focused on Pyralin vanity sets. Here we will make a leap from Britain into America and from the nineteenth century into the twentieth. This expanded view is appropriate because the Pyralin vanity-set campaign deals with transnational trends in middle-class identity and material culture. This campaign brought together concerns discussed throughout the chapter that are relevant in Britain and America: the meaning of ivory in a world that would soon favor decolonization, the place of celluloid that was made to look like ivory in an increasingly modernist world that preferred real to fake, and the position of middle-class women who had carefully constructed a class identity that was dependent on the mass production of luxury goods. Through this advertising campaign we follow celluloid into the "new world" where we can begin to see how the Victorian concept of leisured, white, middle-class womanhood was beginning to crack and a new ideal of womanhood based on consumerism was beginning to emerge.

This book has shown that the meaning of middle-class women's accessories was destabilized in the late Victorian and Edwardian periods. The widening frame of reference created by engagement with ideas of the "other" and of empire was largely responsible for this. After fans and parasols, ivory accessories were the most destabilized women's fashionable object of the period under study. Ivory was largely replaced by the chemical imitation—celluloid—that evoked the connotations of empire and luxury at a price more women could afford. Celluloid products were supposed to externalize women's identity as did gloves, fans, and parasols. But the use of a "fake" product could suggest, to the circle of intimate friends and relatives allowed to enter her bedroom, that the woman herself was less than genuine. DuPont's advertising campaign addressed this problem by fetishizing its celluloid products, suggesting identity resided in the vanity sets rather than in women. Representing its vanity sets as ladylike and cosmopolitan, DuPont hoped to convince women that purchasing these objects would buy them this identity. Hence at the opening of the twentieth century, Victorian traditions were unsupportable—the age of plastic had arrived.

IVORY AND COLONIALISM

By the end of the nineteenth century it was generally understood that the elephant population was in serious crisis because of the ivory trade.[4] Between 1800 and 1850 ivory imports into the United Kingdom increased from 119 tons to 458 tons.[5] For the following sixty years (1850–1910), Britain imported an average of 500 tons of ivory annually.[6] Between 1885 and 1919 ivory imports into the United States jumped from about 120 tons to 300 tons a year.[7] Worldwide consumption of ivory in the later nineteenth century had reached 1,000 tons a year. According to contemporary approximations this meant that 65,000 elephants were killed annually.[8] Around the end of the century the British and American press began to bring this serious matter to the public's attention.[9] Despite the subsequent uproar against the slaughter of elephants, wealthy Europeans and Americans continued to covet the material, consuming it as part of a great number of goods such as snuff boxes, umbrella handles, and vanity sets (figure 4.1).

Ivory had a reputation among producers and consumers as a beautiful and useful material. Ivory was attractive because of its exotic origins, its reputation as a romantic material (sensual and soft to the touch),[10] and its resemblance to Caucasian skin (which was important to Victorians who believed a woman's "ivory white" skin symbolized her class and status).[11]

The material was coveted by makers of fancy goods because it could be processed in so many ways: it could be sawed, cut, etched, carved, ground,

Figure 4.1 An advertisement for a range of hairbrushes in ivory and erinoid from Harrods's toilet-brush department. 1929. 10000797, Mary Evans Picture Library.

or worked on a lathe. Once finished it could be dyed or painted. Ivory could be either flexible or hard; it could be cut so thinly that it became malleable enough to create riding whips, or it could be left in a mass to be made into billiard balls.[12] A growing number of consumer items were made of ivory in the nineteenth and early twentieth centuries. Until the early nineteenth century most imported ivory was used as cutlery handles. However, between the 1820s and 1840s, the material became popular for piano keys, billiard balls, and combs.[13] During the second half of the nineteenth century, ivory craft in Europe and America flourished as factories in Aberdeen in Scotland, Sheffield in England, Deep River, Connecticut, in the United States, Erbach in Germany, and Dieppe in France became famous for carved articles as diverse as bracelets, beads, napkin rings, doorknobs, fans, and teapot handles.[14] As ivory was incorporated into greater and greater numbers of household objects, the increased visibility of the material gave concerned consumers the impression that this precious material would soon disappear.[15]

As each subcontinent found its elephant populations waning, either because of overhunting or because the elephants retreated from the coastal areas, independent (nongovernment-sponsored) hunters, primarily from Britain but also from Europe and America, sought new ground for the hunting and exporting of ivory. The peak of elephant killing in India occurred in the 1860s. Scarcity in India led hunters to move to Central Africa where elephant trackers were most prolific in the early 1870s. But it was East Africa that proved to be the greatest of all sources of ivory in the early 1880s (figure 4.2).[16]

Elephant hunting and colonialism were inextricably linked. Though independent gamesmen who killed large animals for profit preceded the European scramble for African colonies that took place after 1872, the work of independent hunters was understood as paving the way for colonialism. Through stories about big-game hunters, authored by the men themselves and disseminated throughout Britain, ordinary citizens got the impression that wild animals were obstacles to progress that had to be eliminated before India and Africa could begin the march toward civilization.[17] Who better to kill the

Figure 4.2 Three men stand in front of a store of ivory in Congo. Robarts Library, University of Toronto, "The Emin Pasha Relief Expedition. Tippoo Tib's Ivory," *The Illustrated London News* XCV, no. 2645 (December 28, 1889): 817.

beasts and usher in a new world than white Westerners? These sentiments were reinforced by tales of natives seeking out European hunters to help protect their crops and provide meat for their diet. To locals in this early period the white man's ability to shoot large game likened him to a powerful chief who could feed his people in abundance.

Many independent hunters were sought by the British government to become official imperial employees once territories became British colonies. Such was the case for Frederick Lugard who, after making his fortune in ivory, worked for the British East Africa Company; Sir Alfred Sharpe, a famed adventurer, author, and big-game hunter, who subsequently accepted a position as the governor of Nyasaland; and Robert Coryndon who, after shooting and trading ivory throughout Africa, became the governor of Uganda and Kenya.[18] The British government assumed that any man who had the physical rigor to subdue the great beasts of Africa could also control the natives and thereby establish proper colonial rule.

So strong were the connections between colonialism and hunting that the act of killing large beasts became a royal symbol of control not unlike the capture of umbrellas. During his visit to India in 1876, Edward Prince of Wales embodied the qualities of a true ruler through his success in the hunt: "The impression made on people at a distance—an impression of manly vigor and power of endurance which pleased everyone, Europeans and natives

Figure 4.3 Edward VII, when Prince of Wales, shooting a tiger from the safety of his howdah on the back of an elephant in India. Robarts Library, University of Toronto, "The Prince of Wales in India," *The Illustrated London News* LXVIII, no. 1913 (March 25, 1877): 308.

alike . . . proved he possessed royal qualities of courage, energy and physical power"[19] (figure 4.3). Significantly, only a year after this symbolic conquering of the Indian subcontinent by Prince Edward, Queen Victoria was crowned Empress of India.

In Britain and America board games, novels, and world exhibitions familiarized the general populace with the primary resources of Africa and India.[20] In the Great Exhibition of 1851, the India court featured a live display of Bengali men carving ivory tusks (figure 4.4).[21] The 1904 St. Louis World's Fair had a "Mysterious Asia" exhibit, which had a bazaar that sold crafts made of ivory.[22] Board and card games, made in Germany and exported worldwide, demonstrated a concerted effort to remind children of the colonial origins of everyday domestic items. These included cotton, indigo, coffee, cocoa, tea, rubber, and ivory.[23] And literate adults were offered a plethora of heroic novels and memoirs about ivory hunters who sought riches and adventure in the exotic regions of the world.[24]

Partly as a result of the associations of ivory with imperial power there was a growing demand in both America and Britain for domestic items made of ivory. Some desired objects were overtly masculine. Consider, for example, a page from *The Barret Book of Beautiful Presents* that featured a cigar lighter and corkscrew only slightly altered from their natural state as tusks (figure 4.5).[25] Consumer items featured on this page had an association with

Figure 4.4   A group of Bengalis carving ivory in a live exhibit at the Great Exhibition of 1851. Robarts Library, University of Toronto, "Indian Ivory Carvers for the Great Exhibition," *The Illustrated London News* XVIII, no. 480 (April 26, 1851): 335.

Natural
Elephant
Tusks
make
Unique
Gifts.

PRICES.

No. 1 Cigarette Box
£18:10:0
No. 2 Inkstand with
Clock £13:10:0
No. 3 Thermometers
from £2:10:0
No. 4 Match Stands
from 12/6 to
£5:5:0
No. 5 Corkscrew
£1:1:0
No. 6 Matchstand
10/6 to £5:5:0
No. 7 Cigar Lighter
£6:15:0 - £10:10:0
No. 8 Smokers Com-
panion £10:10:0
No. 9 Cigar Cutter
£3:15:0
No.10 Smokers Ash
Tray £1:15:0

Sporting Trophies
such as Ivory Tusks, Hoofs, Horns, Claws, Tails, Feet, Skins, etc.,
made up in interesting and unique designs. Sketches on request.

BARRETT'S—THE IVORY HOUSE

Figure 4.5 Male accessories made out of ivory. May 1937. Bodleian Library, University of Oxford: John Johnson Collection: Beauty Parlour 5 (27).

masculinity and Western superiority, combining the exotic material of ivory with such symbols of Western advances as clocks, inkstands, and thermometres.

Feminine domestic items made of ivory were highly processed so that they no longer looked like tusks, but the advertisements and trade catalogues that featured them reminded the consumer of their exotic origin. Another page of *The Barrett Book of Beautiful Presents* features a woman's vanity set with a bold reminder of the imperial origins of the toilet article: "Fine African Ivory Toilet Sets for Ladies" (figure 4.6).[26] The ad's image of an elephant head with a long trunk hanging vertically, ears extended as if ready to charge, valuable large tusks, and blank white eyes further reminds consumers of the great African beast from which their vanity set originated. The head of the elephant appears as if it is a trophy—stuffed and mounted. The rest of its body is absent. Though the elephant's extended ears show that it is a threat to humankind, the blank white eyes of the taxidermic specimen indicate the power that the hunter (and ultimately the consumer) holds over these great beasts. To solidify the colonial connection, a British royal crown appears above the images of the set.

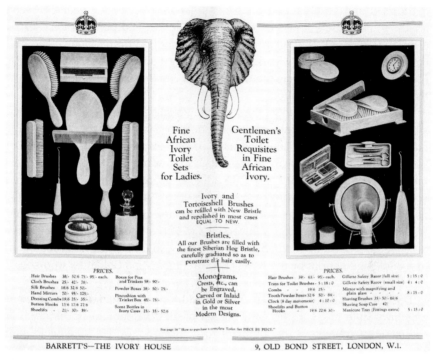

Fine
African
Ivory
Toilet
Sets
for Ladies.

Gentlemen's
Toilet
Requisites
in Fine
African
Ivory.

Ivory and
Tortoiseshell Brushes
can be refilled with New Bristle
and repolished in most cases
EQUAL TO NEW.

Bristles.
All our Brushes are filled with
the finest Siberian Hog Bristle,
carefully graduated so as to
penetrate the hair easily.

PRICES.

Hair Brushes   38/- 52/6 75/- 95/- each.
Cloth Brushes 25/- 42/- 70/-
Silk Brushes   18/6 32/6 50/-
Hand Mirrors   70/- 95/- 125/-
Dressing Combs 19/6 25/- 35/-
Button Hooks   13/6 17/6 27/6
Shoelifts   . 21/- 30/- 39/-

Boxes for Pins
and Trinkets 58/- 90/-
Powder Boxes 38/- 50/- 75/-
Pincushion with
Trinket Box 43/- 75/-
Scent Bottles in
Ivory Cases 25/- 35/- 52/6

Monograms.
Crests, &tc., can
be Engraved,
Carved or Inlaid
in Gold or Silver
in the most
Modern Designs.

PRICES.

Hair Brushes   38/- 63/- 95/- each.
Trays for Toilet Brushes - 5 : 18 : 0
Combs   -   19/6 25/-
Tooth Powder Boxes 32/6 52/- 84/-
Clock (8 day movement) 4 : 10 : 0
Shoelifts and Button
   Hooks   -   19/6 22/6 30/-

Gillette Safety Razor (full size) 5 : 15 : 0
Gillette Safety Razor (small size) 4 : 4 : 0
Mirror with magnifying and
   plain glass -   .   .   .   8 : 15 : 0
Shaving Brushes 35/- 50/- 60/6
Shaving Soap Case 42/-
Manicure Tray (Fittings extra)   5 : 15 : 0

See page 14 " How to purchase a complete Toilet Set PIECE BY PIECE."

BARRETT'S—THE IVORY HOUSE   9, OLD BOND STREET, LONDON, W.1.

Figure 4.6 Women's accessories made out of ivory. May 1937. Bodleian Library, University of Oxford: John Johnson Collection: Beauty Parlour 5 (27).

CELLULOID AND COLONIALISM

The early attempts to find an ivory substitute were due to the increasing expense of tusk ivory because of overhunting. In 1862, the year that celluloid made its first public appearance, 556 tons of ivory were imported into the United Kingdom at a cost of £455 per ton. Just over a decade later, in 1875, the amount of ivory imported into the country had increased to 813 tons, but the want of ivory was such that the price per ton had increased to £950. By the end of the nineteenth century leading trade journals and popular newspapers all over the Western world generated a virtual frenzy about the inevitable extinction of the elephant and disappearance of the material that "every civilized country needs."[27]

In order to reduce the overreliance on tusk ivory inventors in Britain and America almost simultaneously began experimentation to create a substitute ivory substance. They found that a mixture of cellulose nitrate (which had cotton as its base), camphor (a substance extracted from the bark of the camphor laurel tree), and ether alcohol combined with dye would create an ivory-like substance that was easily moldable into various shapes. There were two major problems with this recipe: (1) it shared the same basic components (nitric acid and cellulose) as smokeless gunpowder, making celluloid highly unstable, flammable under certain circumstances, and perhaps even explosive; and (2) camphor, the key solvent, was imported from China, Japan, and Formosa, and was at risk of deforestation. By 1900 it was available only in Formosa and was jealously protected by the Japanese government, which at that time controlled the area.[28]

At the time of its invention, however, the sourcing of material and the instability of the substance were not major concerns; inventors simply wanted to create a substance that could be used as an inexpensive form of ivory. Celluloid's connection with ivory dates back to its debut in London at the Great International Exhibition of 1862.[29] In a leaflet accompanying the substance's first appearance, the inventor, Alexander Parks of Birmingham, advertised that celluloid could be "hard as ivory."[30] One year later, in 1863, an American, John Wesley Hyatt, experimented with versions of Parks' formula.[31] Hyatt also saw a connection between his substance and ivory. In fact, Hyatt was responding to a challenge put out by the American firm Phelan and Collander who sought a substitute for ivory billiard balls.[32]

Despite early associations of celluloid with ivory, celluloid only appeared as a yellowy-white mass in the early stages of its development—a far cry from the intricate graining of the elephant tusk. However, by 1883 celluloid manufacturers developed a technique that imitated ivory's granulations.[33] They achieved this look by stacking sheets of celluloid tinted in varying colors on top of one another and compressing them with heat to create a solid block. This block was then cut across the grain producing an ivory-like effect. Because of the imprecision of this technique, the lines within the celluloid were imperfect, mimicking the irregular look of ivory. The substance even yellowed with age, just like real ivory. The only indications that celluloid was not real ivory were its expense, costing as little as one shilling per pound,[34] and its lack of density, which made celluloid weigh very little in comparison with ivory.

With ivory graining perfected, celluloid manufacturers in Britain and the United States began to develop ways to solidify the connections between celluloid and ivory. Such product names as "Ivorine," "Ivaleur," "French Ivory," "Parisian Ivory," "Grained Ivory," and "Ivory Pyralin" helped the consumers imagine that they were purchasing beautiful ivory tusks imported from Africa rather than a synthetic made in London, Toronto, or New Jersey. The British Xylonite Company used a trademark that featured an elephant and a tortoise walking upright arm in arm as if from some children's story (figure 4.7).

In America a similar process of equating ivory and celluloid was underway. In 1919 *DuPont Magazine* published an article that suggested that tusk ivory had been totally replaced by its chemical substitute: Ivory Pyralin. "Many a swain of bygone centuries has risked life and limb to secure an ivory tusk from which to fashion a comb for the lady of his heart." The ad copy exclaimed,

Figure 4.7 Trademark image of the British Xylonite Company. Science Museum and Library, British Xylonite Company, *Catalogue of Articles Manufactured from Xylonite and Other Plastics* (Hasell: Watson and Viney Ltd., 1936).

"the genuine ivory comb of centuries ago is no more, but in its place, today, upon the dressing table of the modern woman of refinement, rests its exact replica. . . . The resources of science and the skill of man have overcome nature's parsimony in the production of ivory by bringing into being an exquisite 'sister product'—Ivory Py-ra-lin."[35] Underlying this statement is the idea that the West had outdistanced foreign lands so thoroughly that it had found a way to reproduce imperial spoils without even leaving home soil.

Statistics from the United States in 1913 reveal that roughly 8.4 million pounds of celluloid were produced in the United States (not all would be made into imitation ivory).[36] Two years previously about 550,000 pounds of ivory were imported into America.[37] In other words, roughly sixteen times more celluloid was produced than tusk ivory imported into the United States by the 1910s. Furthermore, celluloid could be made for less than a third of the cost of hunting and shipping ivory, per pound.[38] In 1913 the standard price for celluloid ivory was 75 cents.[39] In contrast in 1912 ivory cost roughly $4.50 per pound on the New York market.[40] It stands to reason that more people were familiar with celluloid ivory than with tusk ivory.

PREJUDICES AGAINST CELLULOID

The fact that celluloid was a broadly used imitation of ivory generated concern at various levels of society. Though overall the nineteenth-century culture was delighted and fascinated by imitations, there were some segments of society that were nervous about inauthentic materials. This section explores the overall perception of celluloid in Britain and America. We will look at concerns expressed by the Arts and Crafts Movements about imitative objects, the British brushmakers' distress over losing their craft to factory-made celluloid, the British medical community's fear that celluloid was flammable and even explosive, and the British government's apprehensions about the dangers of celluloid, which resulted in investigations by a Select Committee.

American Studies scholar Miles Orvell shows that the nineteenth century was a "culture of imitation." Before the beginning of the twentieth century, Orvell suggests, the art of imitation and allusion was celebrated.[41] This was the case in Britain as well where cast iron was commonly used on building faces to create the texture and outline of stone and papier-mâché was placed upon chairs to mimic intricately carved wood. Reproductions were generally understood as democratizing agents that allowed the middle class to enjoy versions of rare and expensive luxuries that in previous centuries had been available only to the wealthy.[42] And middle-class men and women found it inspiring that machine-manufactured items could mimic natural materials. Jeffrey Meikle states that "far from indicating shoddiness or dishonesty, imitation in the nineteenth century expressed a brash exuberance and offered provocative evidence of the extension of human artifice through new technologies."[43]

Groups like the Arts and Crafts Movement reacted against the middle-class consumerist ethic that wanted objects at all cost whether they be "the real thing" or fake imitations. Members of the movement represented a small but influential element in the middle and upper classes that feared the overabundance of factory-made imitative goods. Beginning early in the Victorian period in Britain, the movement consisted of a number of privileged and educated male architects, theorists, designers, and craftsmen who sought to integrate art and life.[44] John Ruskin, William Morris, C.R. Ashbee, and Eric Gill valued an " 'organic' correspondence between design, materials, work process, and use."[45] For the craftsman/artist this meant the reintegration of the physical and mental labor that it took to create an object.[46] Theorists believed that this reintegration made the craftsmen's work pleasurable and this helped them to create beautiful, well-thought-out, and well-crafted pieces.[47] The joy of crafts-manship represented in the object would then be felt by the consumer. In contrast modern production practices, usually centered on the factory, separated the designer from the craftsman, creating a division of labor that alienated workers from the objects they made. Products that resulted from the factory system were thought by the movement to be cheap, fake, and shoddy because care of workmanship was not part of the process of creation.[48]

By 1875 America had begun to experience some of the social circumstances that British arts and crafts theorists were working to subdue, such as urbanization and an overreliance on the factory system.[49] As Americans established their Arts and Crafts Movement, there was a healthy exchange between the two countries. However, some of the British ideals were not transferred into the American context.[50] Though the American movement started out with a strong aversion to machines, some practitioners, like Ernest Batchelder, saw machines as a blessing, arguing that they represented a way to alleviate the drudgery of repetitive work and the social abomination of sweatshops.[51] This was a central point of divergence between the British and American movements; while the British were tied to the idea of reforming the social aspects of craftsmanship, the American movement believed more strongly in the democratization of luxury.[52] The reason why the movement took these particular forms and appealed to Americans so strongly was that the movement helped to define American national identity at a critical juncture in American history. After the Civil War Americans were desperate to redefine their place in the world and their understandings of themselves as a nation.

An important element of the arts and crafts theory that was prominent in both Britain and America was the idea that the craftsman should be true to whatever material was being used. Morris suggested that materials should be known and uses should be appropriate: "Not only should it be obvious what your material is, but something should be done with it which is specially natural to it, something that could not be done with any other. This is the very *raison d'être* of decorative art: to make stone look like ironwork, or wood like silk, or pottery like stone is the last resource of the decrepitude of art."[53]

The arts and crafts theorists believed that every substance had a history that could be used as an educational tool.[54] In opposition to natural materials, imitative substances broke down the learning process and "falsely claimed a natural or cultural richness they did not possess."[55] Just like those who owned them, imitative goods "assume a semblance of decoration far beyond either their means or their station."[56]

It was the difficulty in telling maid from mistress, prostitute from lady shopper, and well-dressed poseur from elite gentleman that inspired the fear of imitative items. Arts and crafts writers envisioned a topsy-turvy world where none were able to tell reality from fakery. Pushing their theories to the limit they suggested that even those who could afford and appreciate "the real thing" might ultimately give up in their battle against all things fake, finding themselves buried in objects that were "so common and so cheap that a refined taste, sick of the vulgarity of the imitation, cares little even for the reality."[57]

The Arts and Crafts Movement's concern about imitative products, like celluloid, offered a theoretical and often impractical solution to the repercussions of consumerism. Be that as it may, its ideals were shared by others in the society. Traditional brushmakers, for example, were concerned about the onslaught of factories that made inexpensive brushes in large quantities, which would eventually make their craft system obsolete. In many ways brushmakers were the epitome of what the Arts and Crafts Movement was attempting to preserve. Brushmakers were independent craftsmen, laboring with natural materials in small workshops, who understood and participated in all aspects of brush manufacture. This included the making of hairbrushes typically included in vanity sets. Furthermore, brushmakers were protected by an organization that provided for their social welfare.

Brushmaking was one of the few crafts that continued to thrive at the end of the nineteenth century. In 1895 the brushmaking trade of England and Wales included as many as 16,000 craftsmen. Of these about 2,500 worked with bone, horn, ivory, and tortoiseshell and were likely to produce hairbrushes and clothing brushes appropriate for vanity sets. The brushmaking craft had a strong society that originated in the 1700s. By 1810 the independent brushmaker societies that had been formed up to that point joined together to create the United Society of Brush Makers, which successfully regulated apprentices, journeymen, and master craftsmen throughout the nineteenth century.

The United Society of Brush Makers specified that a brushmaker's career would begin with a seven-year apprenticeship with a master brushmaker.[58] During this time the apprentice learned how to make every type of brush. This included items as simple as brooms and as complex as carved ivory hairbrushes. The typical brushmaker produced many different types of brushes in his workshop; in 1888, for instance, one brushmaker had nearly 5,000 kinds of brushes in his price list.[59] Before becoming a journeyman, apprentices learned how to work wood, separate and dress bristles, bore holes in the brush stock, and fasten bristles through various techniques such as wire drawing and pan searing (figure 4.8).[60] After their apprenticeship, brushmakers who proved to the society that they were well trained began paying society dues, and became journeymen. As a journeyman the brushmaker would seek work with masters who complied with society standards.[61] The system that the society set up was socialist, providing for the brushmakers when they found themselves in hard times. When employment was scarce journeymen might travel between twenty and thirty miles a day to find work. They tramped a route that incorporated towns in both England and Wales.[62] If the

Figure 4.8 Women threading bristles into ebony brushes. 1930s. 10145069, Mary Evans Picture Library.

journeyman brushmaker traveled the entire route without finding work he became known as a "receiver" and would be given 10 shillings a week from his home society. Brushmakers could also receive sick pay, pension benefits, and grants to help them emigrate.[63] Some journeymen eventually became master brushmakers. These men continued to pay a nominal fee to the society in case they returned to the bench as a journeyman.

Traditional brushmakers began to fuel the prejudice against celluloid when celluloid started to make inroads into the brushmaking business around 1877.[64] Brushmakers were resistant to new technology in general, but their aversion to innovation became very obvious when it came to celluloid brush manufacturing.[65] By the later 1880s *The Brush Journal*, whose audience was tradesmen and the general public, was engaged in an anticelluloid campaign. On the grounds that celluloid was dangerous brushmakers pleaded with the public not to use hair combs or toiletware made of the material: "We are strongly of the opinion that such inflammable substances as celluloid are utterly unsuitable either for ornamental or useful purposes on the person, since they expose the wearer to such serious risks."[66] Authors of the trade press urged consumers to save themselves by revisiting traditional materials: "a return to the employment of the good old-fashioned substances, like horn and other non-inflammable materials, in the manufacture of these articles intended for the toilette."[67]

The prejudice against celluloid in England was backed not only by the brushmaking trade, but also by the medical community. Celluloid was an unstable substance made partly from nitric acid and cellulose, the same basic components of smokeless gunpowder. It was especially dangerous when not mixed in the right proportions or created from ingredients that had impurities. As consumers reported that their celluloid products were defective, dangerous reports confirming these allegations appeared in such medical journals as the *Lancet* and the *British Medical Journal*.

As early as 1892, doctors writing for the *Lancet* experimented with celluloid to determine its rate of combustion when exposed to heat.[68] At this time an article was published that cautioned the public against buying this dangerous substance.[69] However, five years later the medical community found that these warnings had not been taken seriously. The *British Medical Journal* reported an incident where a hair comb that held the hair in place ignited as a young woman attempted to curl her hair, causing the girl to be badly burned, "the face, and eyes sharing in the injury."[70] This led to further research by the medical experts at both journals. In 1898 the *Lancet* writers ran experiments in which they exposed celluloid hair combs to hot curling tongs. They found that celluloid items were "highly inflammable" and pleaded with manufacturers to indicate this on their products, especially those that appeared to be natural substances.[71] The *British Medical Journal* went even further in its assessment of celluloid, claiming that it was not only inflammable but had the potential to explode spontaneously: "Very little is sufficient to cause them to burn with explosive violence; thus in the case of gun cotton, confinement with a canvas bag is sufficient for the purpose" of creating an explosion.[72] From this the author drew the conclusion that items made of the substance may "explode without any apparent cause."[73] These claims were conjecture and largely unfounded, but they helped to fuel the prejudice against celluloid.

By 1913 British concerns about celluloid proved to be so great that the House of Commons approved a Celluloid Committee. The committee found that there were special risks involved in using celluloid combs in hair; hair protects the head from feeling the true heat of gas stoves and fireplaces and such heat was known to cause celluloid hair combs to ignite without warning. The committee discussed the necessity of marking celluloid items so that the public would not mistake the substance for ivory or tortoiseshell. In the end, however, the committee was convinced that "the inflammable nature of celluloid is . . . generally understood by the purchasing public."[74] This allowed celluloid manufacture in Britain to continue unabated. It also allowed middle-class consumers to carry on purchasing products that resembled ivory at a moderate price, imitating the rich as they did so.

THE CULTURE OF AUTHENTICITY AND THE PROBLEM
OF ADVERTISING IVORY CELLULOID

Nineteenth-century advertising techniques for celluloid in both Britain and America consisted mainly of trade exhibitions and mail catalogues. Not until World War I did celluloid sales in Britain and America take off. In America this was particularly true for the E.I. du Pont de Nemours and Company, which supplied ammunition to the Allies. After the war, DuPont expanded its celluloid marketing by targeting the consumer directly, launching a campaign that lasted from 1920 to 1928 to sell Ivory-Pyralin vanity sets. This campaign contended with the issues of authenticity, middle-class buying patterns, and the desires and expectations of consumers. Marketers attempted to answer questions like: What meaning do women derive from their vanity sets? Can celluloid ivory be thought of as genuine? How can the hopes and dreams of consumers be used to sell celluloid toiletware? Can understandings of the true Victorian lady be harnessed to sell brushes and combs? When DuPont found that its first campaign was not working it introduced new advertisements targeting the modern woman, appealing to her wider worldview and heightened interest in fashion. DuPont also changed the look of its Pyralin line, introducing modern styling, brighter colors, and themes that tied in with interior-decorating trends, rather than women's inner beauty. Despite these efforts, sales of DuPont vanity sets slumped, forcing the firm to seek other markets for plastics during the 1930s. In many ways this is a story of a British invention stolen by the newly emerging American superpower. However, the interwar period saw such cultural change that the ideals established in the Victorian period did not transfer well to non-Victorian postwar America.[75]

During the nineteenth century advertising for celluloid vanity sets was limited. The only public advertising done by what would become the British Xylonite Company was at international exhibitions and smaller trade shows. While scholars often see these public gatherings as spectacles of luxury that helped to form certain conceptions of nation, race, and modernity, expositions were also an important aspect of Victorian and early twentieth-century commercial culture.[76] Fairs were marketplaces in which new products competed for prizes, found financial backing, and sought out wholesalers. Celluloid made its debut, as mentioned, in London at the Great International Exhibition of 1862. There it received a bronze medal in recognition of its quality.[77] The new invention caught the eye of a vendor named Daniel Spill who worked for a company that manufactured rubberized cloth.[78] Together Spill and Alexander Parkes, the inventor, began Parkesine Company Limited in 1866.[79] This company went through two bankruptcies within its first ten years before finally the Xylonite Company (later the British Xylonite Company Ltd.) was established in 1877.[80] After 1877, the Xylonite Company entered the brushmaking trade in force when it established a Comb Department that produced vanity sets *en masse*.[81] Stands were rented at trade exhibitions to display celluloid vanity sets; catalogues with images, descriptions, prices, and ordering information were also produced for retailers.[82] The general public knew about celluloid vanity sets from mail-order catalogues sent out by larger retailers such as department stores.

In America, vanity set marketing started out in much the same way; trade catalogues were used to sell toiletware to retailers leaving advertising to the larger firms. Then in 1920 E. I. du Pont de Nemours & Co. began a national advertising campaign that appeared in women's magazines such as *Vogue*, *Harper's Bazaar*, and *Vanity Fair*, reaching a total readership of eight million.[83] What was so new about DuPont's campaign was that it addressed the consumer directly, rather than relying on intermediaries such as mail-order catalogues or chance introductions at international exhibits.

The different financial circumstances of the British Xylonite and the American DuPont companies helps to explain why DuPont could afford to engage in an expensive advertising campaign where Xylonite could not. Both companies profited from the war; however, while Xylonite had a boost in its sales because the British government commissioned celluloid items such as combs and shaving equipment, DuPont made a fortune because of its sale of explosives to the Allies.[84] After the war, Xylonite was finally in the clear financially, no longer fearing bankruptcy, but DuPont had made a substantial profit from the war that could be put toward perfecting and marketing consumer items, like vanity sets. The American federal government's new "excess profits tax" also had an impact on DuPont's marketing strategy.[85] In effect, from 1917 to 1921 this federal policy enabled American businesses to lower their taxable income by deducting advertising expenses—making advertising essentially free. This tax policy may have motivated DuPont managers to launch the first national advertising campaign for Pyralin in 1920.[86]

The 1920s represents a distinctive phase in the history of American manufacturing, marketing, and advertising. Business historians have shown that this decade was a transitional period between the decline of the independent craftsman and self-promoter, and the rise of the professional industrial design and marketing consultant.[87] During this time of flux, national advertising grew by leaps and bounds, as American manufacturers sought to stimulate demand for new consumer products. In this golden age of national advertising, manufacturers and advertising agencies embraced dramatic new tactics for creating desire. Rejecting Victorian advertising methods that emphasized the product's inherent qualities, advertisers in the 1920s began to sell feelings, benefits, and experiences. They replaced "reason-why" copy with "atmospheric" themes that suggested how products might transform a consumer's life.[88] In other words, 1920s advertisers attributed new meanings to their goods, using psychological ploys to engage the attention of consumers.

While the British Xylonite Company did not engage in a national advertising campaign in the interwar period, the American campaign contended with issues that were also relevant to the British context. They both grappled with the problems of imitation and the issues of selling to a lower-income market. Furthermore, as we will see, both cultures subscribed to a similar concept of beauty and self-presentation. DuPont advertising managers tried to harness the Victorian ideals of womanly charm and beauty to sell vanity sets, but in doing so they altered these principles as they were set out in Britain. When this did not work the DuPont Company made yet another attempt at marketing celluloid by changing its name, look, and moving away from Victorian ideals of womanhood. But this too failed. In order to understand these claims we must examine the marketing campaign run by DuPont.[89]

The Sears, Roebuck & Co. catalogue advertised combs and hairbrushes in many different materials and prices. Between 1884 and 1918, celluloid appeared next to silver, ivory, ebony, and a few inferior woods.[90] Imitation ivory was among the lower-priced items on the list, giving the impression that celluloid was inferior to most other materials.[91] Such advertising eroded DuPont's hope to position Pyralin Toilet Ware as a quality product competitive with ivory and other precious materials. DuPont's Advertising Department challenged this bias by attempting to build a highbrow image for the celluloid vanity set. Borrowing the famous General Motors description of its ladder of automobiles, DuPont's national campaign for Pyralin offered vanity sets for "every taste and pocket book."[92] These claims about imitation ivory encouraged consumers of modest means to imagine themselves owning an article once enjoyed only by the wealthy.

Despite the references to elite consumers, promotional literature suggests that the principal audience for celluloid ivory in both Britain and America consisted of "men and women of limited means."[93] In 1924 DuPont's Advertising Department may have taken advantage of the Revenue Act of 1918, which stipulated that names and addresses of U.S. residents who filed tax returns be made public record.[94] This federal mandate enabled advertising agencies, which were pioneering the new field of market research, to gather information on consumers. The Sales Department made good use of statistics about possible Pyralin consumers in every American city by 1924.[95] In a trade catalogue, *Selling Pyralin to Your Toilet Ware Market*, retailers were encouraged to "look in the following table and see the actual figures in *your own* city, and in the surrounding towns as well."[96] The family income bracket at which Pyralin vanity sets were aimed was the lowest taxable income bracket of $2,000 per year. This was a lower-middle-class level. Men and women of this class considered themselves to be upwardly mobile, and consumer economists of the time believed that the class as a whole sought to emulate their social betters, leaving them susceptible to the advertising of goods that remained just beyond their reach.[97]

Further evidence that the Advertising Department imagined its consumers to be from households of modest lower-middle-class incomes is found in advertising pamphlets encouraging women to see vanity sets as affordable fancy goods. A 1923 leaflet, *Directing the Demand to You*, assured consumers that "exquisite" Shell Pyralin was "quite within your means." The brochure encouraged women to "build up a complete set of perfectly matched articles by starting with just a few pieces."[98] Similarly a Xylonite trade catalogue suggests: "The first cost of a full range of first quality articles, such as will last the owner a lifetime, is sometimes sufficiently heavy to make some members of the public hesitate; then is the opportunity to suggest the gradual building up of a collection."[99] Pyralin and Xylonite retailers thus capitalized on the 1920s craze for installment buying, but with a twist.[100] While there were some installment buying plans for Pyralin vanity sets, a more popular tactic was to suggest that women could buy their sets piece by piece as household money became available. Vanity sets were different from most consumer durables because they had many components, while a car or watch was purchased in its entirety. A vanity set could be purchased on an "installment plan" of the consumer's own making.

The second strand of Pyralin advertising (not used by the Xylonite Company) promoted celluloid as a desirable replacement for other household materials. One such advertisement claimed that "Ivory Pyralin does not tarnish like metal, . . . shrink and swell like wood, nor chip and break like fragile compositions."[101] These types of arguments could be interpreted as indirect answers to concerns about the explosive potential of celluloid—by stating that the substance is better than natural materials, celluloid's less desirable qualities are deemphasized.

Occasionally these appeals stressed celluloid's superiority to real ivory, claiming "the man-made product proved definitely superior to ivory—it did not crack or discolor with age."[102] Celluloid was described as an improvement because it retained its original color and was not likely to crack along the grain. This appeal strategy was directed toward practical consumers who wanted durable, long-lasting products rather than fragile fancy goods.

The third series of advertisements claimed that Pyralin was "the real thing," an authentic form of ivory from elephant tusks. Advice to sales clerks clouded the distinction between tusk ivory and Ivory Pyralin.[103] Once a customer entered the store, the sales clerk might suggest that Pyralin was in fact genuine. In a 1917 pamphlet clerks were given a dubious definition of ivory: " 'ivory' in the toilet goods trade means manufactured or artificial ivory."[104] This was an attempt to resignify the meaning of the word *ivory* from a natural substance to a chemical invention. If this strategy proved successful the customer might believe that Pyralin was real ivory—the same material wealthy women proudly displayed on their vanity tables.

Along the same lines, the 1920 booklet *Autobiography of an Ivory Pyralin Brush* pits "authentic" Pyralin against other brands of celluloid toiletware. The hairbrush speaks for itself in the booklet and proclaims that only Ivory Pyralin is genuine, while all other celluloid products are false. "I was mighty pleased to discover that I was solid Ivory Pyralin through and through," the hairbrush declared. "They might have used a wooden core for me and, after building it up with wax, have wrapped around it a thin veneer of Ivory Pyralin. I mention no names, but I know some toilet brushes which put on great airs which are made in this fashion. But there is no sham about me, and although I say nothing, I know that these impostors will soon disappear from the face of the earth, while I am handed down from generation to generation."[105] The Pyralin brush accuses its counterfeit rival of "putting on airs," much like consumers who dressed above their station. The *Autobiography* implied that vanity sets, like people, came from different classes. In a world that could not distinguish tusk ivory from celluloid, Pyralin was upheld as genuine. Here we see the arts and crafts realization that the difference between real and imitation would become indistinguishable.

The original trick—making plastic appear to be ivory—was common in both Britain and America. The middle classes used objects to demonstrate their status in an increasingly impersonal urban world.[106] In both Britain and America, consumers were told how to represent themselves: look as if you are the ideal. Pretending that inauthentic objects were authentic was an essential part of this process.

As we have seen in the case of the glove and the fan Victorians believed that the moral character of a woman became evident on her body and therefore could be read by those around her. To change their appearances for the better, according to this model, a moral re-education was required. Guides began with pious references to the simplicity of olden days. Mrs. Noble reassured women that they could improve their external beauty by simply cultivating a good character: "Where do you see the most beautiful women as a rule . . . ?" she asks, her answer as quick as her question, "In a Quaker meeting-house, in a Sisters of Charity convent, in a home where the spiritual life and the domestic duties are the two important factors; not among the gay society butterflies, [who] let every art of coiffeur and complexion, artist and dressmaker be cultivated to its most exotic perfection. No. If we want to keep back plainness, keep attractive, we must give our soul leisure to expand and feed our minds."[107] A similar statement can be found in an American etiquette manual: "you cannot wear lies on your outside and not feel it in your soul."[108] The concept that the innermost character of a woman could be read in her external appearance was a throwback from conduct manuals of the eighteenth century, which relied on the concept of inner character rather than external appearance as the marker of a person's social class. However, once one gets beyond these remarks, etiquette manuals contain extensive practical advice on how to alter a woman's appearance.

The practical advice one finds within the manuals is epitomized by Florence Jack and Rita Strauss's manual *The Woman's Book* (1911), which explains that a woman must maintain her hair in order to be seen as a proper lady: "No woman who values her appearance can afford to neglect her hair, for a fine, well-kept head of hair forms indeed a 'woman's crowning glory,' whereas dull-looking, ill-kept tresses tend to show . . . that she lacks that dainty and scrupulous care of her person which should prove one of the chief character-istics of her sex."[109] Here the tables have been turned. The inner goodness of a woman did not miraculously generate a great head of hair, rather the hairdo had to be created and maintained for her inner beauty to shine through. In-stead of revealing a lady's inner qualities, it was a woman's class and gender aspirations that were made evident as she sought to attain physical beauty by coiffing and purchasing the correct accessories.

Along the same lines, etiquette manuals suggested that the objects that a woman purchased, particularly those things worn on her person, like clothes and makeup, were indicative of her inner character. A recurring example of this can be seen in the figure of the maid-of-all-work who puts on airs (fig-ure 4.9).[110] In a *Punch* cartoon the maid's adornment impedes her work; her crinoline hits a dainty table, breaking its contents while she dusts. The mes-sage is that if a woman purchased clothing that reflected her proper station, it would fit correctly and could be referred to as an indication of her upstanding character.[111] Of course, this sort of argument is upheld by the middle class who benefited from its circular logic. Women who had the time and money to create an appropriate physical impression were thought to be good domestic women. Those who did not, or could not, rise to the proper standard of loveli-ness were thought to have intentions of social climbing or a blemished soul. Because time and money were important factors in determining a woman's physical appearance, the lower classes were generally unable to rise to the middle-class ideal. If working-class women made attempts in this direction, advice literature reassured their middle-class readership that malintentions would appear physically. Using this logic the middle class secured its position in an unstable social structure.

In 1896 Maud Cooke wrote *Social Etiquette; or, Manners and Customs of Polite Society*, which became influential in both America and England and un-derwent numerous editions. The book is important because it extended the consumable items associated with the inner character beyond clothing and makeup to include objects that were not worn on the body—like accessories. For example, in order to avoid misrepresenting themselves in public, Cooke suggested women should "suit all accessories to her own personality."[112] Fol-lowing this logic, any object that was closely associated with women had the

Figure 4.9 This cartoon entitled "Cause and Effect" shows that a maid's crinoline is too large and misshapen to wear while she works. Robarts Library, University of Toronto, Anon., *Punch; or, The London Charivari* XLVI (March 26, 1864): 123.

potential of revealing their inner ambitions and social class. Here we come back to the vanity set and its implications.

In a national advertising campaign for Ivory Pyralin Toilet Ware DuPont attempted to harness the cultural assumption that a woman's inner beauty could be reflected in the objects she consumed. In this campaign the woman and her toiletware were both considered a beautiful ornament: "Its grace and dignity makes Pyralin a fitting complement for a beautiful woman. With daily intimate use, it seems to become a part of herself. It has the simple beauty which never grows irksome and a mellow luster which richens as the years pass by"[113] (figure 4.10). This advertising campaign took the Victorian notion that the woman's inner self becomes reflected in her personal items and skews the logic by imbuing the vanity set with the qualities most sought after by middle-class women. The vanity set's "simple beauty" could now

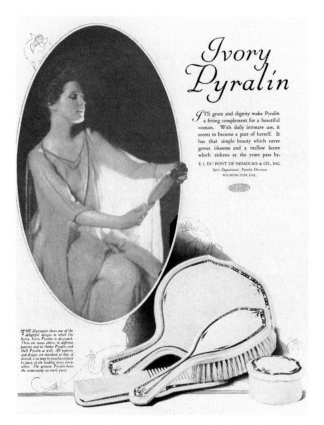

Figure 4.10 Advertisement for Ivory Pyralin. Anon., *Twenty Million* (Wilmington, DE: E.I. du Pont de Nemours & Co., Pyralin Division, 1920). Trade Catalogue Collection, Hagley Museum and Library.

be purchased by women desiring this reputation. In attributing meanings to goods, DuPont took meaning away from the woman herself.

This seems like it would be a good place to tie up the story until we realize that ivory vanity sets sold by DuPont were not flying off the shelves as expected. DuPont company records show that the Sales Department lost money on its vanity sets during the early 1920s. In part, the deficit stemmed from the costs associated with Pyralin as a start-up business. DuPont poured money into retail trade literature, national advertising, and implementing new production strategies such as standardization. Until 1924, the department kept prices artificially low, based on consumer expectations rather than actual costs.[114] Also, the postwar recession of 1920–1921 stunted sales of Pyralin and other luxury goods.[115] To put the Pyralin Department on a profitable basis, Pyralin executives recognized they must make changes. In 1924, the Pyralin Division was split into separate units for toilet articles and plastic sheeting.[116] In early 1925, new products such as fountain pens and radio dials were introduced. Later that year DuPont executives merged the Pyralin Department with the newly purchased Viscoloid Company into a single subsidiary called the DuPont Viscoloid Company.[117]

The economic boom of the mid-1920s may have provided F. B. Davis Jr., general manager of the Pyralin Department and later president of the Viscoloid Company, with the impetus to introduce new vanity-set colors and styles. In a memo dated January 1925, Davis noted "the recent trend has been away from the conservative heavy ivory articles and toward the lighter vari-colored and more flashy lines." In another letter Davis encouraged Fin Sparre, general manager of the Development Department, to seek an expert in the "psychology of colors" to advise DuPont on style matters. Like other big-business managers of the 1920s, Davis had begun to acknowledge "fickle female tastes." The toiletware market, he wrote, was "dominated by the whims and fancies of the buyers, principally women. . . . If we had a tint which would produce subconsciously a favorable attitude of mind, the problem of making sales and popularizing the articles would be very much simplified."[118]

Davis implemented his plan for enticing female consumers with new styles and colors between 1925 and 1927. The Viscoloid Company began to experiment with exceptionally bright, unnatural colors, such as pink, green, and yellow pearl, as it designed a new product for a new consumer. The throwback Victorian ideals used in earlier advertisements were outdated. National advertising now had to target women who wore their hair bobbed and wanted personal-care tools in modern shapes and colors.

Back in 1911, managers had realized that the new bobbed hairstyle popularized by dancer Irene Castle starting in 1909 affected Pyralin sales.[119] After World War I the bob grew in popularity, affecting DuPont's Pyralin toiletware business. In 1925 Davis expressed concern, noting that "the recent fad of bobbed hair" had "entirely upset" the hair ornament and accessories trade, reducing DuPont's sales of Pyralin vanity sets (along with Pyralin sheeting, bought by other toiletware manufacturers).[120] By the late 1920s, DuPont managers realized that they had to take action to secure the interests of bob-haired women.

To reach this new market, the Viscoloid Company and the Development Department took stock of the ivory appearance of the vanity set and saw that it was outdated. The Consumer Durables Revolution, with its emphasis on products such as radios and automobiles, promised radical changes in the everyday lives of Britons and Americans. Historian Lois W. Banner argues that a new type of woman—the flapper—represented the hope and vitality of these new developments.[121] As the dominant physical ideal of the 1920s, the flapper, with her bobbed hair, heavy makeup, and slim, androgynous, flat-chested shape, represented a new model of femininity. Advertisements and movies depicted flappers as free-spirited women functioning as secretaries, saleswomen, or college students, who danced the night away doing the Charleston. These young flappers did not have time to make themselves up in the privacy of their boudoirs, so they adopted the portable compact as a fashion accessory. Unlike Victorian women who hid their beauty rituals, the modern flapper coiffed herself in public—in the workplace, at restaurants, in dance halls—bringing attention to herself and the performance of her womanhood.[122] Vanity sets, with their Victorian associations, did not have much appeal to these women. The Advertising Department had to change its sales pitch, marketing strategies, and advertising iconography to fit this new model of womanhood.

In 1928, the newly formed Viscoloid Company announced the invention of a "new material" called Lucite.[123] Advertised as an entirely new substance, Lucite in fact was a celluloid product, just like Pyralin. Vanity sets made from Lucite, however, came in translucent bright colors and modern designs.[124] DuPont explained the rationale for Lucite toilet sets to retailers. "A new vogue in toiletware was needed—expressly keyed to the modern mode, purposely designed to harmonize with the present-day trends in interior decoration—something so radically different, so smart, so modern—that people who owned toilet sets of the old conventional type would recognize that they were out of date, and buy these new up-to-date creations."[125] The Viscoloid Company launched Lucite with a brand-new ad campaign.

This time, DuPont looked to fashion intermediaries "to find out what the public wanted and needed" from their toiletware.[126] By the mid-1920s fashion experts, such as DuPont's premier colorist, H. Ledyard Towle, had successfully interpreted color fads, making Duco paints the trend setter in automobile finishes.[127] Seeking to repeat this success, DuPont hired six consultants with a mandate to create "a new vogue in toiletware."[128] These specialists included color experts, architects, and market researchers. The two women in the group contributed design expertise and knowledge of the "woman's viewpoint," while the men were managers and engineers who supervised the overall project.[129] The inclusion of women was due to the general recognition that women were the primary consumers, and that as market researchers, they were admitted more readily into homes, where they could solicit frank discussions about products.[130] Once the designers had proposed new styles, Rose Estelle Brown, one of the six consultants hired for her expertise as a stylist and field researcher, led a team of investigators to test the potential success of the product. During the research Brown and her team showed Lucite to women of different incomes and social classes, from students at Columbia College to YMCA members. They discovered that seven out of ten women preferred the new Lucite sets over older designs.[131] With the help of fashion intermediaries, who had their fingers on the pulse of consumer wants, DuPont tracked public demand and made plans to adjust its toiletware line. With Lucite, DuPont created "a new vogue in toiletware," marketed toward the modern woman.

Based on this market research, DuPont Viscoloid introduced five new vanity-set designs: Ming, Watteau, Empire, Orchis, and Wedgwood. Advertisements for Lucite Toilet Ware featured a woman's slim white hand holding a mirror, so that the viewer could see the pattern on the back of the mirror but not the woman's face (figure 4.11). The images on the backs of the mirrors varied, but all the patterns emphasized the exoticism of far-off places and times. This advertising imagery represented a break from the Victorian idea that a woman's possessions reflected her inner character and beauty. The Lucite campaign turned the mirror around, shifting emphasis from the woman to the wider world.

Lucite marketers also capitalized on what historian Roland Marchand has called "the mystique of the ensemble," a 1920s design strategy that emphasized coordinated colors and styles in interior design.[132] Advertisements for Lucite vanity sets emphasized how the new hues and designs would "harmonize with the present-day trends in interior decoration," especially with the "colorful *ensemble* of the modern boudoir."[133] In this formula, women's responsibilities,

Figure 4.11 Advertisement for Ming pattern vanity set showing a white woman's hand and a reflection of imagined China. Late 1920s. *Beauty from China, France, and the Tropics* (Wilmington, DE: E.I. du Pont de Nemours & Co., Pyralin Division). Trade Catalogue Collection, Hagley Museum and Library.

which had long revolved around interior decoration and self-beautification, were updated for the Jazz Age. The modern, cultured woman had to understand the vocabulary of modernism, as expressed in the new Lucite designs.

Lucite colors marked a complete departure from the Ivory Pyralin tradition. DuPont invented new hues for the Lucite color palette and gave them exotic names: Napoleonic blue, imperial green, colonial buff, and mandarin red.[134] Should these exotic references be lost on consumers, the Lucite hand mirrors were decorated with foreign motifs. The Ming design featured a Chinese woman surrounded by calligraphy and miniature manicured trees (figure 4.11). The female consumer, who had loomed large in earlier iconography, rarely appeared in the new advertisements. The Lucite campaign focused on the broader world, rather than inner-looking feminine vanity, appealing to women who saw themselves as worldly and modern. Unfortunately, DuPont soon found the vanity-set market in permanent decline.

THE DEMISE OF THE VANITY SET

The romantic ideal of womanhood was partially embodied and maintained through the vanity set. At the moment when plastic vanity sets became accessible to middle-class consumers, the values embodied in them were being replaced by a modern viewpoint. With bobbed hairstyles, women stopped using vanity sets, needing only a single comb to style their hair. As it happened, Lucite vanity sets were introduced on the eve of the 1929 stock-market crash. By 1930, DuPont managers reported an overall reduction of vanity-set consumption in the United States.[135] By 1931, many American department stores no longer stocked vanity sets, so few consumers were buying them. Sales slumped even in December, traditionally the month with the highest turnover due to the gift-giving holiday season.[136] Though DuPont continued to advertise vanity sets until 1940, by the late 1920s the firm extended its plastics portfolio beyond women's boudoir accessories to include a wide variety of items, from toilet seats to airplane windshields. By 1937, the vanity set was no longer a profit-making consumer line. That year DuPont managers noted that more than 40 percent of the products it made in 1937 had not been on the market ten years earlier.[137] The vanity-set market had vanished. In 1936 a new Plastics Department took charge of Pyralin and Lucite, gradually phasing out vanity sets and focusing on other products.[138]

During the 1920s DuPont tried to establish a market for Pyralin plastics by attributing new meanings to the vanity set. In the national ad campaign of 1920–1927 ad copy reinforced Victorian ideology suggesting that a woman's character was reflected in her appearance and the objects that she used. DuPont abandoned this approach in 1928, as advertising managers acknowledged shifting cultural ideals, changing tastes, and women's expanded worldview. In the Lucite advertising campaign, DuPont encouraged women to see their toilet accessories as extensions of themselves as cultured individuals. However, DuPont found it could not entice women to buy the new product. The downfall of the vanity set was due to a number of factors: new trends in modern life, an unstable world market prone to booms and busts, and new chemical innovations that took precedence over celluloid toilet sets at DuPont. By the late 1920s, the heyday of the vanity set had passed.

NOTES

Excerpted by permission of the Publishers from "Coiffing Vanity: A Study of the Manufacture, Design, and Meaning of the Celluloid Hairbrush in America, 1900–1930," in *Producing Fashion: Commerce, Culture, and Consumers*, ed. Reggie Balszczyk (Philadelphia: University of Pennsylvania Press, 2007), 229–54. Copyright © 2007.

1. On the sexual symbolism of hair, see: Elisabeth G. Gitter, "The Power of Women's Hair in the Victorian Imagination," *Publications of the Modern Language Association* 99 (October 1984): 936–54; Wendy Cooper, *Hair: Sex, Society, Symbolism* (New York: Stein and Day, 1971); Raymond Firth, *Symbols: Public and Private* (London: Allen and Unwin, 1973); and Heidi Humphrey, *Hair* (Baskerville: Eastern Press, 1980).
2. See, for example: "Phillips's Minton China: Wedding Presents," *The Illustrated London News* 98 (May 1891): 583.
3. Ivory Py-Ra-Lin, August 1917, DuPont Archive, Folder 7, Box 6, Accession 1803, Hagley Museum and Library.
4. R. F. du Toit, S. N. Stuart, and D.H.M. Cumming, *African Elephants and Rhinos: Sattus Survey and Conservation Action Plan* (Gland, Switzerland: Nature Conservation Bureau, 1990), 3.
5. Abdul Sheriff, *Slaves, Spices and Ivory in Zanzibar: Integration of an East African Commercial Empire into the World Economy, 1770–1873* (London: James Currey, 1987), 257–58. See Sheriff also for a table that indicates the amount of tons of ivory imported into the United Kingdom from 1792 to 1875.
6. Martin Meredith, *Africa's Elephant: A Biography* (London: Hodder and Stoughton, 2001), 111.
7. Robert Friedel, *Pioneer Plastic: The Making and Selling of Celluloid* (Madison: University of Wisconsin Press, 1983), 33.
8. Meredith, *Africa's Elephant*, 112.
9. See, for example: Anon., "The Dying Fauna of an Empire," *The Saturday Review. Politics, Literature, Science and Art* (November 24, 1906): 635–36; Anon., "The Supply of Ivory," *The New York Times*, July 7, 1867, 3. For other sources citing the inevitable extinction of elephants see: Anon., "Elephants

and the Ivory Trade," *The Brush Journal* 11, no. 8 (1896): 115–16; Anon., "The Ivory Trade," *Journal of the Society of the Arts* 12 (1864): 190. "The Wonderful World of Chemistry" pamphlet, 1936, DuPont Archive, Folder: Viscoloid Company 49, Box 37, Accession 228, Advertising Department, Hagley Museum and Library.

10. Ramesh Bedi, *Elephant: Lord of the Jungle*, trans. J.P. Uniyal (New Delhi: National Book Trust, India, 1969), 91. For information on ivory as a romantic material see: Meredith, *Africa's Elephant*, 111.

11. Meredith, *Africa's Elephant*, 108.

12. Meredith, *Africa's Elephant*, 107.

13. John M. MacKenzie, *The Empire of Nature: Hunting, Conservation and British Imperialism* (Manchester: Manchester University Press, 1988), 148; Sheriff, *Slaves, Spices and Ivory in Zanzibar*, 87.

14. Meredith, *Africa's Elephant*, 108–10. There was a constant increase in the price of ivory throughout the nineteenth century because of demand. Fortunately for the consumer, the price of manufactured items remained steady, and sometimes even decreased, as a result of the capitalist competitions and innovations in the industrial process. Sheriff, *Slaves, Spices and Ivory in Zanzibar*, 2, 77.

15. Friedel, *Pioneer Plastic*, 31–32; Jeffrey L. Meikle, *American Plastic: A Cultural History* (New Brunswick, NJ: Rutgers University Press, 1995), 17.

16. MacKenzie, *The Empire of Nature*, 124, 148, 183.

17. For examples of such hunting narratives see: Roualeyn Gordon-Cumming, *Five Years of a Hunter's Life in the Far Interior of South Africa: With Notices of the Native Tribes, and Anecdotes of the Chase of the Lion, Elephant, Hippopotamus, Giraffe, Rhinoceros, &c.* (New York: Harper, 1850); Frederick Courteney Selous, *A Hunter's Wanderings in Africa: Being a Narrative of Nine Years Spent amongst the Game of the Far Interior of Africa, Containing Accounts of Explorations beyond the Zambesi, on the River Chobe, and in the Matabele and Mashuna Countries, with Full Notes upon the Natural History and Present Distribution of All the Large Mammalia*, 4th ed. (London: R. Bentley and Sons, 1895); Robert Briggs Struthers, *Hunting Journal: 1852–1856, in the Zulu Kingdom and the Tsonga Regions*, ed. Patricia L. Merrett and Ronald But (Pietermaritzburg, South Africa: University of Natal Press, 1991).

18. MacKenzie, *The Empire of Nature*, 127.

19. Quoted in Philip Magnus, *King Edward the Seventh* (London: William Clowes & Sons, 1964), 141.

20. For further sources on imperialism and popular culture see: Annie E. Coombes, *Reinventing Africa: Museums, Material Culture and Popular Imagination in Late Victorian and Edwardian England* (New Haven, CT: Yale University Press, 1994); John M. MacKenzie, ed., *Imperialism and Popular Culture* (Manchester: Manchester University Press, 1986); Ruth

B. Phillips and Christopher B. Steiner, eds., *Unpacking Culture: Art and Commodity in Colonial and Postcolonial Worlds* (Berkeley: University of California Press, 1999).

21. Jeffrey Auerbach, *The Great Exhibition of 1851: A Nation on Display* (New Haven, CT: Yale University Press, 1999), 102.

22. 1904 World's Fair Society, "1904 St Louis World's Fair, The Pike: Foreign Cultures," http://ftp.apci.net/~truax/1904wf/Pike%20Foreign%20Cultures.htm (accessed October 8, 2008).

23. Jeff Bowersox, *Raising Germans in the Age of Empire: Youth and Colonial Culture, 1871–1914* (Oxford: Oxford University Press, 2012).

24. MacKenzie, *The Empire of Nature*, 168, 136, 126.

25. *The Barrett Book of Beautiful Presents Catalogue*, May 1937, John Johnson Collection, Box: Beauty Parlour 5, Bodleian Library, 11.

26. *The Barrett Book of Beautiful Presents Catalogue*.

27. Anon., "The Supply of Ivory," 3. Sheriff, *Slaves, Spices and Ivory in Zanzibar*, 257–58.

28. Camphor sold for 22 cents a pound in 1891, between 27 and 67 cents a pound in 1895, and between 55 and 60 cents a pound in 1903. Keith Lauer and Julie Robinson, *Celluloid: Collector's Reference and Value Guide* (Paducah, KY: Collector Books, 1999), 266; Meikle, *American Plastic*, 20–21; Walter A. Durham Jr., "The Japanese Camphor Monopoly: Its History and Relation to the Future of Japan," *Pacific Affairs* 5, no. 9 (September 1932): 799.

29. Sylvia Katz, *Early Plastics* (Buckingham: Shire Publications, 1986), 19.

30. Exhibit, "London Exhibition 1862," in Spill v. Celluloid Mfg. Co.; this is reprinted in Friedel, *Pioneer Plastic*, 44.

31. At the world exhibition of 1862 celluloid received a bronze medal in recognition of quality. Katz, *Early Plastics*, 19.

32. Anon., "The Supply of Ivory," 3. Sheriff, *Slaves, Spices and Ivory in Zanzibar*, 257–58.

33. Lauer and Robinson, *Celluloid*, 265.

34. Friedel, *Pioneer Plastic*, 10.

35. Anon., "The Career of the Comb," *DuPont Magazine* (August 1919): 10–11.

36. Meikle, *American Plastic*, 17.

37. Friedel, *Pioneer Plastic*, 33.

38. Meikle, *American Plastic*, 17.

39. Meikle, *American Plastic*, 17.

40. Friedel, *Pioneer Plastic*, 32.

41. Miles Orvell, *The Real Thing: Imitation and Authenticity in American Culture, 1880–1940* (Chapel Hill: University of North Carolina Press, 1989), xv.

42. Meikle, *American Plastic*, 14.

43. Meikle, *American Plastic*, 12.

44. Elizabeth Cummin and Wendy Kaplan, *The Arts and Crafts Movement* (London: Thames and Hudson, 1991), 9.

45. Eileen Boris, *Art and Labor: Ruskin, Morris and the Craftsman Ideal in America* (Philadelphia: Temple University Press, 1986), 14.

46. Wendy Kaplan, *"The Art That Is Life": The Arts and Crafts Movement in America, 1875–1920* (Boston: Museum of Fine Arts, 1987), viii.

47. Boris, *Art and Labor*, 29.

48. Boris, *Art and Labor*, 29. The British movement had a socialist agenda. English arts and craft founders believed that in supporting the work of designer/craftsmen they could challenge the existing factory system. To this end architects, designers, and craftsmen including C.R. Ashbee and Eric Gill went to the country to establish small working communities that integrated work, home, and schooling. Along the same lines John Ruskin founded the Guild of St. George, which was based on his idea of the Middle Ages in which work and life were fully integrated. And William Morris established the business Morris, Marshall, Faulkner & Co., which incorporated the work of painters, carvers, furniture makers, and metal workers into a single firm. It was perhaps due to the company's overwhelming success that Morris realized it was impossible to reach his ideal of hand-crafted art for the masses. Morris later lamented that his products were too expensive to be bought by anyone but the very rich, leading him to ask "What business have we with art at all, unless all can share it?" Kaplan, *The Arts and Crafts Movement*, 13–18; quoted by Kaplan, *"The Art That Is Life,"* 55.

49. Kaplan, *"The Art That Is Life,"* viii.

50. Kaplan, *"The Art That Is Life,"* 55–57. Arts and crafts books written by English authors were widely read in America (John Ruskin and William Morris being among the most popular). There was also a fair amount of exchange of goods and advice between the two countries. Though Morris never made the voyage to America, he fabricated wall coverings for American clientele; his daughter, May, went on a lecture tour in America disseminating some of her father's ideas; and Morris's work was given much attention in American periodicals. Another important point of exchange was established by Ashbee who stirred American arts and crafts societies with frequent lecture tours between 1895 and 1915, and whose ideas about rural workshops inspired the establishment of the Handicraft Shop of the Boston Society of Arts and Crafts. Ruskin was also indirectly involved in the American movement through his forty-five year friendship with Charles Eliot Norton, Harvard's first professor of the fine arts.

51. Kaplan, *"The Art That Is Life,"* 29.

52. Cummin and Kaplan, *The Arts and Crafts Movement*, 150–54.

53. William Morris, "Art and the Beauty of the Earth," in *The Collected Works of William Morris* (London: Longmans Green, 1914), 169.

54. John Ruskin, *The Stones of Venice*, 3 vols., vol. 3 (New York: John Wiley and Sons, 1880), 28–29.

55. Meikle, *American Plastic*, 13.

56. A.W.N. Pugin, *The True Principles of Pointed or Christian Architecture: Set Forth in Two Lectures Delivered at St. Marie's, Oscott* (London: W. Hughes, 1841), 67.

57. Mary E. Turner, "Of Modern Embroidery," in *Arts and Crafts Essays by Members of the Arts and Crafts Exhibition Society* (London: Longmans Green and Co., 1903), 362.

58. John K. Boyd, Thomas Elliott, Joseph Willis, and A.J. Cockburn, "United Society of Brush Makers, 43 Stanhope Street, Newcastle-on-Tyne" (Newcastle-on-Tyne: United Society of Brush Makers, 1894), Collection of Leaflets etc., British Library, 4; United Society of Brush Makers, *General Trade Rules of the United Society of Brush Makers* (London: Printed by F.W. Worthy, Trade Union Printer, 1894), Collection of Leaflets etc., British Library, 4.

59. M.G. Jones, *The Story of Brushmaking: A Norfolk Craft* (Norwich: Briton Chadwick, 1974), 4.

60. Jones, *The Story of Brushmaking*, 10–12; Michael R. Snow, *Brushmaking: Craft and Industry* (Oxford: Oxford Polytechnic Press, 1984), 67.

61. United Society of Brush Makers, *List of Fair Employers* (London: Issued by the Society, 1892, 1893); William Kiddier, *The Brushmaker and the Secrets of His Craft: His Romance* (London: Sir Isaac Pitman & Sons, 1928), 66–67; United Society of Brush Makers, *General Trade Rules of the United Society of Brush Makers*, 4. According to the rules of the United Society of Brush Makers, master brushmakers would be allowed only one apprentice. A second apprentice could be taken on if the brushmaker had employed three journeymen for at least a year. Master brushmakers could not employ their wives or other female family members to draw the bristles through the brush. Master brushmakers would be removed from the tramping list if they did not follow union rules.

62. Snow, *Brushmaking*, 19.

63. Kiddier, *The Brushmaker and the Secrets of His Craft*, 115–17; Snow, *Brushmaking*, 19.

64. Exhibit, "London Exhibition 1862," in Spill v. Celluloid Mfg. Co.; this is reprinted in Friedel, *Pioneer Plastic*, 44; Peter C. Ashlee, "Tusks and Tortoiseshell: The Early Development of the British Plastics Industry with Special Reference to the British Xylonite Company 1877–1920" (BA degree, University of Nottingham, 1982), 63.

65. By the 1860s the brush trade was beginning to become mechanized. Between 1869 and 1871 two young Americans, J. Sheldon and E.F. Bradley, designed and patented a revolutionary machine for making solid-back brushes that included a boring and filling function. They found it difficult to sell their machine in Britain, perhaps because the brushmaking craft at

this time was made up of small workshops that could not accommodate larger machinery or perhaps the brushmakers themselves were resistant because such machines would reduce the amount of jobs in the craft or both. The anonymous author of the article "Brush Making by Machinery" claimed that in the 1890s the British brushmaking trade was being over-shadowed by its foreign competitors that had converted to machinery. The author calls on brushmakers to invent new ways of pursuing their craft: "It is high time that those who are chiefly interested in maintaining our manufacturing supremacy should turn their attention to devising the means by which it may be most efficiently maintained." An aversion to machinery may have further prejudiced traditional brushmakers against celluloid. Anon., "Brush-Making by Machinery," *The Brush Journal* I, no. 11 (1896): 163.

66. Anon., "Celluloid Combs and Their Dangers," *The Brush Journal* IV, no. 1 (1898): 1–2.

67. Anon., "Celluloid Combs and Their Dangers," 2.

68. Anon., "Experiments with Celluloid," *Lancet* 1 (1892): 708–9.

69. Anon., "Inflammable Hair Combs: A Grave Danger," *Lancet* 1 (1898): 661.

70. Anon., "Explosive Combs," *British Medical Journal* (1897): 1741.

71. Anon., "Inflammable Hair Combs," 661.

72. Anon., "Explosive Combs," 1741.

73. My own experience with celluloid is that it is not explosive. When left in the sun, or in confined spaces celluloid sometimes sweats and melts taking on the form of objects that are laid upon it. Celluloid also acquires sun spots of a darker color than the original light-colored ivory. It is eas-ily melted with a hot pin, but does not ignite when in contact with heat. Hagley Museum and the Museum of London (Ontario), which have exten-sive celluloid collections, store pieces in confined spaces, but this has not led to explosions.

74. Celluloid Committee, *Report of the Departmental Committee on Celluloid Presented to Both Houses of Parliament by Command of His Majesty* (Lon-don: His Majesty's Stationary Office by Eyre and Spottiswoode, 1913), 6.

75. This argument was first published in Ariel Beaujot, "Coiffing Vanity: A Study of the Manufacture, Design, and Meaning of the Celluloid Hair-brush in America, 1900–1930," in *Producing Fashion*, ed. Reggie Blaszc-zyk (Philadelphia: University of Pennsylvania Press, 2007), 229–54.

76. Auerbach, *The Great Exhibition of 1851*, 1, 4–5, 159–92.

77. Katz, *Early Plastics*, 19.

78. Celluloid's apparent flexibility and ability to withstand water caught the attention of Daniel Spill who was looking for a new substance for rain-proofing the company's fabric. Spill was intrigued by Parkesine, believing that it would make an excellent substitute for rubber, which gave off a noxious smell.

79. S.T.I. Mossman, "Parkesine and Celluloid," in *The Development of Plastics*, ed. S.T.I. Mossman and P.J.T. Morris (Cambridge: The Royal Society of Chemistry, 1994), 12.
80. Lauer and Robinson, *Celluloid*, 16.
81. Exhibit, "London Exhibition 1862," in Spill v. Celluloid Mfg. Co.; this is reprinted in Friedel, *Pioneer Plastic*, 44. Ashlee, "Tusks and Tortoiseshell," 63.
82. Ashlee, "Tusks and Tortoiseshell," 65.
83. *Catalogue of Dealer Advertisements and Electrotypes* (Wilmington, DE: E.I. du Pont de Nemours & Co., Pyralin Division, 1921), Trade Catalog Collection, Hagley Museum and Library, Wilmington, DE (hereafter cited as TC-HML).
84. Ashlee, "Tusks and Tortoiseshell," 67–68, 102. *Catalogue of Articles Manufactured from Xylonite and Other Plastics by the British Xylonite Company Limited* (Hasell: Watson and Viney, 1936), Science Museum and Library, Bakelite Xylonite Ltd. Collection, 1.
85. Beaujot, "Coiffing Vanity," 233.
86. Roland Marchand, *Advertising the American Dream: Making Way for Modernity, 1920–1940* (Berkeley: University of California Press, 1985), 6.
87. Regina Lee Blaszczyk, *Imagining Consumers: Design and Innovation from Wedgwood to Corning* (Baltimore: Johns Hopkins University Press, 2000), 12.
88. Marchand, *Advertising the American Dream*, 9–16.
89. The same analysis can be found in: Beaujot, "Coiffing Vanity."
90. As of 1918, pyralin was separated from other materials within the mail-order catalogues. By 1910, catalogues changed from using the generic name *celluloid* and began to use brand names such as "Parisian Ivory," the name later replaced by "Pyralin Ivory."
91. "Celluloid Combs," *Sears, Roebuck & Co.* 106 (1897): 641; "Combs," 113 (1904): 961; "Combs, Curling Irons and Hair Brushes," 121 (1910/11): 914; "Combs, Pocket Cases and Infant Hair Brushes of Quality," 125 (1912/13): 614; "Combs and Pocket Necessities," 137 (1918): 773. For a similar analysis of mail-order catalogues, see: Orvell, *The Real Thing*, 43–45.
92. *Pyralin Toilet Ware: The Leader in Popular Demand, Now Complete and Standardized in Every Price Class* (Wilmington, DE: E.I. du Pont de Nemours & Co., Pyralin Division, 1925), TC-HML.
93. *Pyralin Toilet Ware.*
94. Gerald Carson, *The Golden Egg: The Personal Income Tax—Where It Came From, How It Grew* (Boston: Houghton Mifflin, 1977), 104–5.
95. Although the advertising agency for DuPont in the late 1920s was Frank Seaman, it is unclear which agency the company was using for the 1924 pyralin campaign.

96. *Selling Pyralin to Your Toilet Ware Market* (Wilmington, DE: E. I. du Pont de Nemours & Co., Pyralin Division, 1924), 16, TC-HML.

97. Daniel Horowitz, *The Morality of Spending: Attitudes toward the Consumer Society in America, 1875–1940* (Baltimore: Johns Hopkins University Press, 1992), 138–39; Robert A. Wilson and David E. Jordan, *Personal Exemptions and Individual Income Tax Rates, 1913–2002*, bulletin prepared for the Internal Revenue Service, Publication 1136 (Washington, DC: Government Printing Office, 2002), 219.

98. *Directing the Demand to You* (Wilmington, DE: E. I. du Pont de Nemours & Co., Pyralin Division, 1923), TC-HML.

99. *Catalogue of Articles Manufactured from Xylonite and Other Plastics by the British Xylonite Company Limited*, 6.

100. The 1920s experienced what the economic historian Martha Olney called a "Consumer Durables Revolution," evidenced by increased purchasing of major durable goods (cars, appliances, radios) and steady purchasing of minor durable goods (china and tableware, jewelry and watches). This revolution coincided with a burgeoning credit economy and a fundamental change in middle-class attitudes toward acquiring credit and accumulating debt.

101. *Ivory Pyralin*, 1922, Folder: Trade Catalogues, Pamphlets, 1917–1921, Box 34, Advertising Department, E. I. du Pont de Nemours & Co., Hagley Museum and Library, Wilmington, DE.

102. "The Wonderful World of Chemistry," 1936.

103. Anon., *Points on Ivory Py-Ra-Lin for the Retail Clerk* (Wilmington, DE: E. I. du Pont de Nemours & Co., Arlington Division, 1917), 3, TC-HML.

104. Anon., *Points on Ivory Py-Ra-Lin for the Retail Clerk*.

105. *Autobiography of an Ivory Pyralin Brush* (Wilmington, DE: E. I. du Pont de Nemours & Co., Pyralin Division, 1920), 10–12, TC-HML.

106. An increase in migration to great cities, such as London, Manchester, Birmingham, and Liverpool, left city dwellers feeling alienated and uneasy about the strangers they encountered on a day-to-day basis. These anxieties were new to Britons. Though industrialism and urbanization began to pick up in the mid-1700s these trends skyrocketed in the nineteenth century. In 1801 only London had a population of more than 100,000. By 1841 there were six British cities of more than 100,000, by 1871 there were sixteen, and by 1901 there were thirty cities of this size. It was challenging for Britons to become accustomed to the new urban living. In small-scale cities and rural communities, people were intimately acquainted with one another. Even if small-town folk encountered strangers, whose family and class background were not known to them, they would have been able to garner such information through close observation of their dialect, manners, and dress. A combination of tradition, sumptuary laws, small disposable incomes, and a lack of

privacy confined smaller-town dwellers to the social class to which they belonged. This situation was a stark contrast to the city where most day-to-day interactions were between strangers who had little hope of getting to know each other's backgrounds. The anonymity of the city brought with it a fear that people could disguise their social and economic statuses with impunity. In the urban environment there was widespread fear that strangers were not always what they appeared to be. For an excellent analysis of the anxieties generated by city dwelling see: James E. Côté, "Sociological Perspectives on Identity Formation: The Culture-Identity Link and Identity Capital," *Journal of Adolescence* 19 (1996): 417–28; Marjorie Morgan, *Manners, Morals and Class in England, 1774–1858* (Houndmills: Macmillan, 1994), 42–51. Statistics on city dwelling were taken from: Walter L. Arnstein, *Britain Yesterday and Today: 1830 to the Present*, 8th ed., *A History of England* (Boston: Houghton Mifflin, 2001), 82.

107. Mrs. Robert Noble, *Every Woman's Toilet Book* (London: George Newnes, 1908), 11.
108. Charlotte Perkins Gilman, "The Shape of Her Dress," *Woman's Journal* (1904): 226.
109. Florence B. Jack and Rita Strauss, *The Woman's Book: Contains Everything a Woman Ought to Know* (London: T.C. & E.C. Jack, 1911), 456.
110. Anon., "Cause and Effect," *Punch; or, The London Charivari* XLVI (March 26, 1864): 123.
111. MacKenzie, *The Empire of Nature*, 68–69; Rob Schorman, *Selling Style: Clothing and Social Change at the Turn of the Century* (Philadelphia: University of Pennsylvania Press, 2003), 68–69; Mariana Valverde, "The Love of Finery: Fashion and the Fallen Woman in Nineteenth Century Social Discourse," *Victorian Studies* 32, no. 2 (1989): 169–88.
112. Maud C. Cooke, *Social Etiquette; or, Manners and Customs of Polite Society: Containing Rules of Etiquette for All Occasions* (London: McDermid & Logan, 1896), 389. This book was republished in 1899 in the United States: Maud Cooke, *Twentieth Century Hand-Book of Etiquette* (Philadelphia: Co-Operative Publishing, 1899).
113. Anon., *Twenty Million* (Wilmington, DE: E.I. du Pont de Nemours & Co., Pyralin Division, 1920), unpaginated.
114. Irénée du Pont to F.B. Davis Jr., January 2, 1924, Folder: Plastics Department, October 1921–August 1927, Box 62, Papers of the President's Office, E.I. du Pont de Nemours & Co., Hagley Museum and Library, Wilmington, DE (hereafter cited as PP-HML).
115. Graham D. Taylor and Patricia E. Sudnik, *DuPont and the International Chemical Industry* (Boston: Twayne, 1984), 79.
116. F.B. Davis Jr., General Notice, September 20, 1924, Folder: Plastics Department, October 1921–August 1927, Box 62, PP-HML.

117. Irénée du Pont to department heads, April 28, 1925, Folder: Plastics Department, October 1921–August 1927, Box 62, PP-HML.

118. F.B. Davis Jr. to Fin Sparre, January 8, 1925, Folder: Plastics Department, October 1921–August 1927, Box 62, PP-HML; Regina Lee Blaszczyk, "The Importance of Being True Blue: The Du Pont Company and the Color Revolution," in *Cultures of Commerce: Representation and American Business Culture, 1877–1960*, ed. Elspeth H. Brown, Catherine Gudis, and Marina Moskowitz (New York: Palgrave Macmillan, 2006), 34.

119. In 1911 the Arlington Company, not DuPont, owned and marketed Pyralin. As it diversified into plastics, DuPont bought the Arlington Company, one of the nation's largest celluloid manufacturers, for $8 million in 1915. Originally known for its high-quality celluloid collars and cuffs, this New Jersey firm had expanded into the vanity-set business when the market for these detachable fashions began to decline. In 1910, Arlington had introduced a line of vanity sets sold under the brand name "Pyralin." At the time of the merger, DuPont managers knew that Pyralin toilet accessories had been profitable for Arlington; they hoped to use the line to move into consumer markets. "History of DuPont's Plastics Department," November 28, 1965, Folder: Plastics Department History, Box 42, Accession 1410: Public Affairs Department Records, E. I. du Pont de Nemours & Co., Hagley Museum and Library, Wilmington, DE; David A. Hounshell and John Kenly Smith Jr., *Science and Corporate Strategy: DuPont R&D, 1902–1980* (New York: Cambridge University Press, 1988), 73; Taylor and Sudnik, *DuPont and the International Chemical Industry*, 61.

120. Davis to Sparre, January 8, 1925, 2.

121. Lois W. Banner, *American Beauty* (New York: Knopf, 1983), 279.

122. Kathy Peiss, *Hope in a Jar: The Making of American's Beauty Culture* (New York: Metropolitan Books, 1998), 186.

123. *Behind the Scenes: How a New Vogue Has Been Created* (Wilmington, DE: E. I. du Pont de Nemours & Co., Viscoloid Company, 1928), 14, TC-HML.

124. *DuPont Boudoir Accessories: Lucite-Pyralin 1929: Dealers' Price List for 1929* (Wilmington, DE: E. I. du Pont de Nemours & Co., Viscoloid Company, 1929), 2, TC-HML.

125. *DuPont Boudoir Accessories*.

126. *Behind the Scenes*, 10.

127. Blaszczyk, "The Importance of Being True Blue," 29.

128. *Behind the Scenes*, 12.

129. *Behind the Scenes*, 10.

130. Marchand, *Advertising the American Dream*, 34–35.

131. *Behind the Scenes*, 12.

132. Marchand, *Advertising the American Dream*, 132.

133. *Behind the Scenes*, 14.

134. *DuPont Toilet Ware: Lucite & Pyralin* (Wilmington, DE: E.I. du Pont de Nemours & Co., Viscoloid Company, 1928), n.p., TC-HML.

135. Sales Report to Willis F. Harrington, September 1930, Folder 6: 1930 DuPont Viscoloid Company, Box 3, Accession 1813: Willis F. Harrington Papers, Vice President, Hagley Museum and Library, Wilmington, Delaware (hereafter cited as WFH-HML).

136. Sales Report to Willis F. Harrington, WFH-HML.

137. Taylor and Sudnik, *DuPont and the International Chemical Industry*, 145.

138. "History of DuPont's Plastics Department," 4.

Conclusion

While my objects appear to be unique they often shared space on the same dresser. The glove, fan, parasol, and vanity set were all part of a certain definition of female beauty and femininity. Those that used these accessories wanted to be white and leisured; they could afford to consume and proudly displayed status on their person by showing off the things they bought. The book tells a micro story about women—their struggle to fit in, their strategies to find a husband—but it also tells a macro history. No item, despite its size or apparent frivolous use, was innocent of far-reaching political implications. Each accessory speaks of an empire that inscribes itself on the culture's smallest artifacts, forcibly defining not only gender and beauty, but also race and class, empire and colony. Women brushing their hair in the morning had occasion to imagine the great elephants hunted in Africa sacrificed to create their combs; others putting up their umbrellas on a rainy day might remember an article they read about colonial nations and their strange use of the object to protect them from the hot rays of the sun. But with World War I, the Victorian consciousness and mores that kept these accessories in constant use began to change.

This book began with a chapter about the glove and its place in the creation and maintenance of the middle class. I argued that the "look" of middle-class women helped to consolidate their class and was dependent on visible signs of domesticity and leisure such as the white color of a woman's skin, signifying her lack of exposure to the elements, and supple, small hands, which demonstrated that a woman did not engage in manual labor. It was partly by means of their tiny, soft white hands that middle-class women defined themselves and became differentiated from other classes. Using etiquette manuals, fashion plates, printed ephemera, women's magazines, and dance hall songs, this chapter showed how class became physically manifested on women's bodies not only in their fashion, but also in the shape, size, and state of their hands.

The second chapter, about the fan, used sources such as the woman's press, fashion plates, professional periodicals, department store catalogues, novels, plays, select committees, and government petitions. This chapter argued that the fan helped extend the traditional category of leisured domestic womanhood identified in the chapter about gloves. The chapter dealt with the imagined problem of female redundancy due to what Victorians thought was a marriage market overpopulated by women. Though the problem was largely a figment of the Victorian imagination, the fan offered two real solutions to "the surplus women question": the design and manufacture of fans created paid employment for women, and fans became props that could be used to flirt with potential husbands. In these ways middle-class women challenged their domestic boundaries and participated in the public sphere by taking up paid employment and actively seeking a husband. The chapter ends with a reaction to women's encroachment into the public sphere as Victorians began to view the Japanese belle, who hid behind her fan, as a representative of the vanishing ideal domestic British wife.

Building upon this understanding of the role of the fan in gender and racial formation, the third chapter, about parasols and umbrellas, began with a discussion of the place of these artifacts in non-Western countries. Through a study of the popular press, popular history books, and advertising ephemera, we came to see that Victorians believed there was a divergent use of the umbrella in the East and the West. This difference became a way for Britons to define the political positions in these two areas of the world. The East, explained British authors in the popular press, had sumptuary laws that restricted umbrella use to royalty, while the West made umbrellas available to every class and gender. Through this narrative, umbrella usage in the East became symbolic of despotic, tyrannical rule, and their use in the West was representative of the democracy that European citizens generally enjoyed. From here, drawing on sources such as etiquette manuals, dance hall songs, and short stories, the chapter explored the meaning of the umbrella within Victorian culture by investigating two of the themes of the previous two chapters: the performance of white middle-class womanhood and the use of an accessory as a flirtatious toy to attract a husband. Finally there is a discussion of masculine character as represented through umbrellas, a topic that I will be taking up further in my forthcoming book about masculinity and Victorian male fashion.

The book is concluded with a chapter about faux ivory vanity sets, which could be seen as the last hurrah of the Victorian concept of womanhood explored throughout the book. This chapter uses sources as diverse as company records, government reports, medical journals, mail order catalogues, union records, and hunting journals. Returning to the question of colonialism and the empire, the chapter began with an exploration of the meaning assigned to goods made of ivory during the nineteenth century. Throughout the period, objects made of ivory were important reminders of colonial rule for rich citizens who never left the metropole. By 1883 the look of ivory was mimicked by celluloid, the first plastic, allowing middle-class as well as aristocratic women to hold small pieces of empire in the palm of their hands. However, the imitative qualities of celluloid ivory sparked concerns within some

Victorian circles about the cultural currency of inauthentic objects, and the intentions of the women who owned them. The chapter ended with the exploration of an American interwar advertising campaign that attempted to bring all of these issues together: the meaning of ivory in a world that would soon favor decolonization, the place of celluloid ivory in an increasingly modernist world that preferred real to fake, and the position of middle-class women who had carefully constructed a class identity that was dependent on the mass production of luxury goods. Through this advertising campaign, that ultimately failed, we began to see how the Victorian concept of leisured, white, middle-class womanhood was beginning to crack.

In 1929 Max von Boehn lamented the disappearance of women's fashionable accessories of the 1800s and by extension the particularities of Victorian femininity. He mourned the departure of the delicate complexion of Victorian women's hands, saying "a sunburned tint, formerly considered unbecoming, is thought beautiful to-day—or at least a guarantee of health. Since white hands are no longer fashionable, what is the use of gloves?"[1] He went on to observe that modern women had no use for fans, "What does she want with a plaything?" he bemoans, when "she prefers a cigarette."[2] The parasol was also missed by von Boehn who observed that "by 1900 sunshades began to be rarer." He surmised that "a complexion of lilies and roses [became] less highly prized," instead "to be burnt coffee-brown had suddenly become cool."[3] By the postwar period the ideal of the domestic, dainty white woman of the Victorian period was being replaced by the independent, sporty woman of the Jazz Age—a woman who thought nothing of pulling out a compact and applying her brazen red lipstick.

It is no coincidence that von Boehn wrote in 1929; profound changes in women's behavior and fashion had been brought on by World War I. The war occasioned a shortage of various materials due to restrictions in trade. For example, camphor, a key ingredient of celluloid, could no longer be imported from Japan.[4] Germany, the premier manufacturer of fabric gloves and Britain's major continental enemy, refused to trade with the United Kingdom, and the manufacture of folding fans in France was temporarily put on hold in preparation for the war effort.[5] Not only did these accessories suffer owing to the war economy, they also waned in the postwar period because modern women broke from the ideologies of their Victorian mothers. The war created a break in the aesthetics of beauty, encouraging a shift toward robust and active women who saw beyond their individual homes and looked for ways to help their nation. New trends in skin coloration created a drop in the consumption of such protective coverings as gloves and parasols. The fan, which fluttered to cool overheated and overdressed Victorian women, was not necessary to refresh interwar women because their clothing was cooler, shorter, and less layered. Furthermore, women marching for the vote sought to represent themselves as respectable citizens rather than flirtatious coquettes, and this meant women had to do away with frivolous accessories such as fans. Finally, the vanity set, once used to perfect long Victorian tresses, was replaced by a single comb for the new bob-haired woman on the go.[6] As these new cultural and social phenomena increased, Victorian accessories were no longer necessary; in fact, their very existence came to represent times past.

NOTES

1. Max von Boehn, *Modes and Manners: Ornaments; Lace, Fans, Gloves, Walking-Sticks, Parasols, Jewelry and Trinkets* (London: J.M. Dent & Sons, 1929), 93.
2. von Boehn, *Modes and Manners*, 67.
3. von Boehn, *Modes and Manners,* 149.
4. Keith Lauer and Julie Robinson, *Celluloid: Collector's Reference and Value Guide* (Paducah, KY: Collector Books, 1999), 266; Jeffrey L. Meikle, *American Plastic: A Cultural History* (New Brunswick, NJ: Rutgers University Press, 1995), 20–21; Walter A. Durham Jr., "The Japanese Camphor Monopoly: Its History and Relation to the Future of Japan," *Pacific Affairs* 5, no. 9 (September 1932): 799.
5. Arthur Robinson Wright, "Gloves," in *A Collection of Newspaper Cuttings on Walking Sticks, Umbrellas, Parasols, Fans and Gloves* (London: Author, 1932).
6. Ariel Beaujot, "Coiffing Vanity: A Study of the Manufacture, Design, and Meaning of the Celluloid Hairbrush in America, 1900–1930," in *Producing Fashion*, ed. Reggie Balszczyk (Philadelphia: University of Pennsylvania Press, 2007), 229–54.

Bibliography

NEWSPAPERS AND PERIODICALS

All the Year Round: A Weekly Journal
The Art-Journal
The Athenaeum Journal of Literature, Science and the Fine Arts
The Bag Portmanteau and Umbrella Trader
Beauty and Fashion: A Weekly Illustrated Journal for Women
Belgravia: A London Magazine
Blackwood's Edinburgh Magazine
The British Essayists; with Prefaces Biographical, Historical and Critical
British Medical Journal
The Brush Journal
Cassell's Family Magazine
Chamber's Journal of Popular Literature, Science and Art
The Connoisseur
Cosmopolitan
The English Illustrated Magazine
The Gentleman's Magazine
The Harmsworth Magazine
Household Words: A Weekly Journal
The Illustrated London News
Le Journal des Demoiselles
Journal of the Society of the Arts
Ladies' Cabinet
Ladies' Magazine
The Ladies' Monthly Museum
The Lancet
The London Times
The Michigan Freemason: A Monthly Magazine Devoted to Masonic and Home
    Literature
Myra's Journal of Dress and Fashion
The New York Times
The Nineteenth Century
Pearson's Magazine
The Penny Magazine of the Society for the Diffusion of Useful Knowledge
The Perruquier: A Monthly Trade Journal for Hairdressers, Perfumers, Brush and
    Comb Manufacturers
Punch; or, The London Charivari

The Queen: The Lady's Newspaper
The Quiver: An Illustrated London Magazine for General Reading
St. Nicholas: Scribner's Illustrated Magazine for Girls and Boys
Sartain's Union Magazine of Literature and Art
The Saturday Review
Sharpe's London Magazine
The Tailor and Cutter
Tinsley's Magazine
Townsden's Monthly Selection of Paris Fashions
Westminster Review
Woman's Journal

ARCHIVAL SOURCES

Bakelite Xylonite Ltd. Collection, Science Museum and Library
A Collection of Newspaper Cuttings on Walking Sticks, Umbrellas, Parasols, Fans and Gloves, British Library
Celluloid Corporate Archives, Smithsonian Institution
DuPont Archive, Hagley Museum and Library
John Johnson Collection of Printed Ephemera
United Society of Brush Makers, Collection of Leaflets etc., British Library
Worshipful Company of Fan Makers, Guildhall Library

MUSEUMS

Museum of Costume at Bath
Axminster Museum
The Museum of London
The Fan Museum
Victoria and Albert Museum
Hagley Museum
Museum of London (Ontario)

PARLIAMENTARY PAPERS

Celluloid Committee, *Report of the Departmental Committee on Celluloid Presented to Both Houses of Parliament by Command of His Majesty.* London: His Majesty's Stationary Office by Eyre and Spottiswoode, 1913.
Select Committee on the School of Design, "Report from the Select Committee on the School of Design: Together with Proceedings of the Committee, Minutes of Evidence, Appendix and Index." London: House of Commons, 1849.

PRIMARY SOURCES

Addison, Joseph. "I Do Not Know Whether to Call the Following a Letter." *The Spectator* 2 (1897): 76–79.

Addison, Joseph. "Mr Spectator." *The Spectator* 1 (1826): 134–35.

Allen, G. "Are We Englishmen?" *Fortnightly Review* XXVIII (1880): 472–87. Reprinted in *Images of Race*, edited by M. Biddiss, 238–56. Leicester: Leicester University Press, 1979.

Anon. "Brush-Making by Machinery." *The Brush Journal* I, no. 11 (1896): 162–63.

Anon. "The Career of the Comb." *DuPont Magazine* (August 1919): 10–11.

Anon. "Cause and Effect." *Punch; or, The London Charivari* XLVI (March 26, 1864): 123.

Anon. "Celluloid Combs and Their Dangers." *The Brush Journal* IV, no. 1 (1898): 1–2.

Anon. *Complete Etiquette for Ladies and Gentlemen: A Guide to the Rules and Observances of Good Society.* London: Ward, Lock and Co., 1900.

Anon. "Delamira Resigns Her Fan." *The Tatler* 3, no. 52 (1814): 311–14.

Anon. "Description of Illustrations." *The Queen* 69 (1881): 100.

Anon. "Design for Fan Painted on Silk." *Myra's Journal of Dress and Fashion*, no. 300 (1881): 582.

Anon. "The Dying Fauna of an Empire." *The Saturday Review. Politics, Literature, Science and Art* (November 24, 1906): 635–36.

Anon. "Editorial." *The Parasol* 1, no. 1 (1905): n.p.

Anon. "Elephants and the Ivory Trade." *The Brush Journal* 11, no. 8 (1896): 115–16.

Anon. *Etiquette for All; or, Rules of Conduct for Every Circumstance in Life: With the Laws, Rules, Precepts, and Practices of Good Society.* Glasgow: George Watson, 1861.

Anon. *Etiquette for Ladies: A Guide to the Observances of Good Society.* London: Ward, Lock and Co., n.d.

Anon. *Etiquette for Ladies; with Hints on the Preservation, Improvement, and Display of Female Beauty.* Philadelphia: Lea & Blanchard, 1840.

Anon. *Etiquette for Ladies and Gentlemen.* London: Frederick, Warne and Co., 1876.

Anon. *Etiquette for the Ladies: Eighty Maxims on Dress, Manners and Accomplishments.* London: Charles Tilt, 1837.

Anon. *The Etiquette of Love, Courtship and Marriage.* London: Simpkia, Marshal & Co., 1847.

Anon. *The Etiquette of Modern Society: A Guide to Good Manners in Every Possible Situation.* London: Ward, Lock and Co., n.d.

Anon. "The Evolution of the Umbrella." *Chambers's Journal of Popular Literature, Science and Arts* 67 (1890): 394–96.

Anon. "Excess of Widows over Widowers." *Westminster Review* 131 (1889): 501–5.

Anon. "The Exhibition of Fans." *Illustrated London News* LVII, no. 1602 (1870): 42.

Anon. "Experiments with Celluloid." *Lancet* 1 (1892): 708–9.

Anon. *Explanatory Report of the Working Ladies' Guild*. London: Hatchards Publishers, 1877.

Anon. "Explosive Combs." *British Medical Journal* (1897): 1740–41.

Anon. "Fan." *Library of Universal Knowledge*. New York: American Book Exchange 5 (1880).

Anon. "Fan Making: An Employment for Women." *The Queen, The Lady's Newspaper* 48 (1870): 64.

Anon. "Fancies in Fans." *Beauty and Fashion: A Weekly Illustrated Journal for Women* 1, no. 9 (1891): 176.

Anon. "The Fanmakers' Company." *The Perruquier* II (1879): 93.

Anon. "Fans." *The Perruquier* 1, no. 3 (1878): 44.

Anon. "Fans in Past and Present Times." *The Queen* 72 (1882): 41.

Anon. "The Female School of Design." *The Art-Journal* XII (1850): 130.

Anon. "Flirts and Flirting." *Beauty and Fashion: A Weekly Illustrated Journal for Women* 1, no. 22 (1891): 430.

Anon. "For Every Woman." *Pall Mall Gazette* (1914): 8.

Anon. "Inflammable Hair Combs: A Grave Danger." *Lancet* 1 (1898): 661.

Anon. "The Ivory Trade." *Journal of the Society of the Arts* 12 (1864): 190.

Anon. *The Ladies' Hand-Book of the Toilet: A Manual of Elegance and Fashion*. London: H. Gt. Clarke and Co., 1843.

Anon. *The Lady's Pocket Companion and Indispensable Friend Comprising the Whole Art of True Politeness, Dressing, the Toilette, Evening Amusements, Games, the Ball Room, Needle Work, Crochet and Netting, Knitting etc. Also Hints on Courtship and Marriage*. New York: Leaville and Allen, c. 1850.

Anon. "M. Duvelleroy's Fan Manufactory." *The Art-Journal* XIII (1851): 99.

Anon. "A Master of the Fan: The Art of Charles Conder." *Illustrated London News—Supplement to the* CXLII, no. 3847 (1913): ii.

Anon. "Mr. Thompson's Umbrella." *All the Year Round: A Weekly Journal* 15 (1866): 356–60.

Anon. "On Umbrellas." *The Michigan Freemason: A Monthly Magazine Devoted to Masonic and Home Literature* 6 (1875): 149.

Anon. "Ornamentation of China, Glass and Fans." *The Queen* (April 9, 1881): 351.

Anon. "Pagodas, Aurioles, and Umbrellas: Umbrellas, Ancient and Modern Part II." *The English Illustrated Magazine* 5 (July 1888): 654–67.

Anon. *Points on Ivory Py-Ra-Lin for the Retail Clerk*. Wilmington, DE: E. I. du Pont de Nemours & Co., Arlington Division, 1917.

Anon. "The Queen Fan in Brussels Point Lace." *The Queen* 48 (1870): 390–91.

Anon. "The Religious Character of Umbrellas." *The Saturday Review* 55 (1883): 497–98.

Anon. *The Royal Umbrella: A Ballad of the Isle of Wight*. London: John Lee, 1844.

Anon. *The Science of Dress for Ladies and Gentlemen*. London: Groombridge and Sons, 1857.

Anon. "The Season's Prettiest Fans." *The Ladies' Home Journal* (1893): 15.

Anon. "Sic Itur Ad Astra; or, How Pelham Jones Gets into 'Society.' " *Punch; or, The London Charivari* (1880): 203.

Anon. "The Story of the Umbrella." *Pearson's Magazine* 6 (July 1898): 37–42.

Anon. "Suggestions for Fan Painting, Art Needlework &c." *The Queen* 69 (1881): 617.

Anon. "The Supply of Ivory." *The New York Times*, July 7, 1867, 3.

Anon. *Thackerayana: Notes and Anecdotes Illustrated by Hundreds of Sketches*. New York: Hansell House, 1901.

Anon. "The Toilet." *The Perruquier: A Monthly Trade Journal for Hairdressers, Perfumers, Brush and Comb Manufacturers* 2, no. 2 (1879): 38.

Anon. *Twenty Million*. Wilmington, DE: E. I. du Pont de Nemours & Co., Pyralin Division, 1920.

Anon. "The Umbrella." *Chambers's Journal of Popular Literature, Science and Arts* 49 (1896): 591–92.

Anon. "The Umbrella." *The Perruquier* 2 (1879): 147.

Anon. "Umbrella Evolution: The Umbrella and Parasol in History." *The Bag, Portmanteau and Umbrella Trader* 2, no. 35 (1909): 36–38.

Anon. "Umbrellas." *The Gentleman's Magazine* 266 (1889): 536–44.

Anon. "Umbrellas." *Household Words: A Weekly Journal* 6, no. 138 (1852): 201–4.

Anon. "Umbrellas." *The Penny Magazine of the Society for the Diffusion of Useful Knowledge* 5 (1836): 5–7.

Anon. "Umbrellas in the East." *The Penny Magazine of the Society for the Diffusion of Useful Knowledge* 4, no. 235 (1835): 479–80.

Anon. *The Woman of the Future*. London: J. G. Berger, 1869.

Anon. "Women and Work." *Westminster Review* 131 (1889): 270–79.

Anon. *Women Workers' Directory*. London: John Bale, Sons and Danielsson, 1909.

Arnold, Edwin. "A Japanese Belle." *Punch; or, The London Charivari* 98 (1890): 180.

Ballin, Ada S. *The Science of Dress in Theory and Practice*. London: Sampson Low, Marston, Searle & Rivington, 1885.

Barlow, George, and Henry Pontet. "The Ivory Fan Humourous Song." London: Marshalls, 1889.

Beale, Anne. "Finding Employment for Women." *The Quiver: An Illustrated London Magazine for General Reading* (1889): 113–16.

Beamish, Richard. *The Psychonomy of the Hand; or, The Hand: An Index of Mental Development*. London: Frederick Pitman, 1865.

Beard, Linda. "How to Make a Fan." In *How to Amuse Yourself and Others*. New York: American Girls Handbook, 1887.

Beck, William. "The Romance of Gloves." *Cosmopolitan* XIII (1892): 450–57.

Beeton, Mrs. *Manners of Polite Society: Complete Etiquette for Ladies, Gentlemen and Families*. London: Ward, Lock and Tyler, 1875.

Berguer, Reverend Lionel Thomas. "Delamira Resigns Her Fan." *The British Essayists; with Prefaces Biographical, Historical and Critical* 1 (1823): 97–100.

Bisbee Duffery, Elisa. *The Ladies' and Gentlemen's Etiquette: A Complete Manual of the Manners and Dress of American Society*. Philadelphia: Porter and Coats, 1877.

Blanc, Charles. *Art in Ornament and Dress*. Translated by Alexandre Auguste. New York: Scribner Welford, and Armstrong, 1877.

Boyd, John K., Thomas Elliott, Joseph Willis, and A. J. Cockburn. "United Society of Brush Makers, 43 Stanhope Street, Newcastle-on-Tyne." Newcastle-on-Tyne: United Society of Brush Makers, 1894.

British Xylonite Company. *Catalogue of Articles Manufactured from Xylonite and Other Plastics by the British Xylonite Company Limited*. Hasell: Watson and Viney, 1936.

British Xylonite Company. *Catalogue of Xylonite Articles*. London: Gale and Polden, 1931.

British Xylonite Company. *Halex: Export Price List*. London: Haleford Press, 1949.

British Xylonite Company. *Halex Catalogue*. London: The British Xylonite Company, 1950.

British Xylonite Company. *Halex Catalogue*. London: The British Xylonite Company, 1954.

British Xylonite Company. *Halex 1950*. London: The British Xylonite Company, 1950.

Brown, Lew, B. G. DeSylva, Ray Henderson, and George White. "Beware of a Girl with a Fan." New York: Harms, 1925.

Campbell, Lady Colin. *Etiquette of Good Society*. London: Cassell and Company, 1893.

Campbell, Lady Colin. *The Lady's Dressing Room*. London: Cassell and Company, 1893.

Carlton, Harry, and Horatio Nicholls. "Lady of the Fan." London: Lawrence Wright Music Co., c. 1938.

Catalog of Dealer Advertisements and Electrotypes (Wilmington, DE: E. I. du Pont de Nemours & Co., Pyralin Division, 1921), Trade Catalog Collection, Hagley Museum and Library, Wilmington, DE.

"Celluloid Combs." *Sears, Roebuck & Co.* 106 (1897): 641.

"Combs." *Sears, Roebuck & Co.* 113 (1904): 961.

"Combs, Curling Irons and Hair Brushes." *Sears, Roebuck & Co.* 121 (1910/11): 914.

"Combs, Pocket Cases and Infant Hair Brushes of Quality." *Sears, Roebuck & Co.* 125 (1912/13): 614.

"Combs and Pocket Necessities." *Sears, Roebuck & Co.* 137 (1918): 773.

Chambers, Epharaim. "Fan." In *Chambers's Encyclopaedia: A Dictionary of Universal Knowledge for the People* 4 (1862): 140–41.

Clayton, Ellen C. *English Female Artists*. London: Tinsley Brothers, 1876.

Clyde and Black Co. *Umbrellas and Their History*. New York: Riverside Press, 1864.

Collet, Clara. "Prospects of Marriage for Women." *The Nineteenth Century* 31 (1892): 537–52.

Cooke, Maud. *Twentieth Century Hand-Book of Etiquette*. Philadelphia: Co-Operative Publishing, 1899.

Cooke, Maud C. *Social Etiquette; or, Manners and Customs of Polite Society: Containing Rules of Etiquette for All Occasions*. London: McDermid & Logan, 1896.

Crampton, Earnest. "An Old Fan Song." London: Cary & Co., 1900.

Davin, Nicholas Flood. *Mr. Davin on "Fanning in Church," and Addison and Steele on the Use of the Fan*. Toronto: Globe, 1874.

De Bourrienne, M. *Memoirs of Napoleon Bonaparte*. London: Crosby Lockwood and Son, 1888.

De Lange, Louise, and Billee Taylor. "The Legend of the Fan." New York: M. Witmark & Sons, 1902.

Dent, Allcroft & Co. *A Brief Description of the Manufacture, History and Associations of Gloves: With Illustrations from Dent, Allcroft & Co.'s Manufactory, Worcester*. Worcester: Baylis, Lewis & Co., 189?

Dickens, Charles. *David Copperfield*. New York: Sheldon and Co., 1863.

Dickens, Charles. "The Female School of Design in the Capital of the World." *Household Words. A Weekly Journal. Conducted by Charles Dickens* 2, no. 51 (1851): 577–81.

Dickens, Charles. *Hard Times*. New York: Pearson Longman, 2004 [1854].

Diderot, Denis. "Evantailliste." *Encyclopedie; ou, Dictionnaire raisone des sciences, des arts et des métiers/mis en ordre & publie par M. Diderot; & quant a la Partie Mathematique, par M. D'Alembert*. Vol. 4. New York: Pergamon, 1969 [1751–1780], 306–7.

Disraeli, Benjamin. *Contarini Fleming: A Psychological Romance*. New York: Elbron Classic Series, 2005 [1904].

Duvelleroy, M. "Fabrication des Evantails." *Exposition Universelles. Paris 1867, Rapports du Jury International*. Vol. V.

Ellis, B. Eldred. *Gloves and the Glove Trade*. London: Sir Isaac Pitman & Sons, 1921.

Fann-makers. "The Case of the Fann-Makers Who Have Petitioned the Honorable House of Commons, against the Importation of Fanns from the East-Indies." In *Early English Books, 1641–1700; 1664: 5*, 1695.

Flory, M. A. *A Book about Fans: The History of Fans and Fan-Painting*. New York: Macmillan and Co., 1895.

Foxwell, A. J., and C. Hutchins Lewis. "*The Chinese Umbrella: An Action Song for School Concerts*." London: J. Curwen and Sons, 1890.

Gaskell, G. A. *Gaskell's Compendium of Forms, Educational, Social, Legal and Commercial*. Chicago: Fairbanks, Palmer & Co., 1881.

Gifford, Harry, Fred E. Cliffe, and George Arthurs. "Rotten Cotton Gloves." London: Montgomery & Co., 1928.

Gilbert, W. S. *The Mikado; or, The Town of Titipu*. Studio City, CA: Players Press, 1997.

Gilman, Charlotte Perkins. "The Shape of Her Dress." *Woman's Journal* (1904): 226.

Godey, Louis Antoine, and Sarah Josepha Buell Hale. *Godey's Magazine* 44–45 (1852): 13.

Gordon-Cumming, Roualeyn. *Five Years of a Hunter's Life in the Far Interior of South Africa: With Notices of the Native Tribes, and Anecdotes of the Chase of the Lion, Elephant, Hippopotamus, Giraffe, Rhinoceros, &c*. New York: Harper, 1850.

Greenwood, James, Hohn Birchall, Walter Marshaman, Eli Norton, Thomas Stonehouse, George Stonehouse, Henry Earnshaw, and George Hulme. "A Collection of Leaflets etc., Issued by the Society." Manchester: United Society of Brush Makers, 1894.

Greg, W. R. *Why Are Women Redundant?* London: N. Trubner & Co., 1869.

Halex Limited. *Catalogue of Articles Manufactured from Plastics and Other Materials by Halex Limited*. London: Halex Limited, 1939.

Harraden, B. "A Study about the Umbrella-Mender." *Blackwood's Edinburgh Magazine* 146 (1889): 122–31.

Hart, Ernest. *Fan Exhibition, 1894*. London: Liberty & Co., 1894.

Hart, Ernest. "The Fans of the Far East." *The Queen* (1893).

Hartley, Cecil B. *The Gentlemen's Book of Etiquette and Manual of Politeness*. Boston: DeWolfe, Fiske & Co., 1875.

Haweis, Mrs. H. R. *The Art of Dress*. London: Chatto and Windus, 1879.

Heard, Adrian. *The Ivory Fan*. London: T. Fisher Unwin, 1920.

Heather-Bigg, Ada. "Women and the Glove Trade." *Nineteenth Century* XXX, no. 178 (1891): 939–51.

Hichens, Robert. *The Woman with the Fan*. London: Methuen & Co., 1904.

Hine, Reginald L. *The Cream of Curiosity—Being an Account of Certain Historical and Literary Manuscripts of the XVIIIth and XIXth Centuries*. London: George Routledge & Sons, 1920.

Hoskin, Mary. "The Little Green Glove." In *The Little Green Glove and Other Stories*, edited by Mary Hoskin, 1–90. Toronto: Extension Print, 1920.

Howard, Herbert. "Can You Fold Your Umbrella?: A Few Hints on a Practical Subject." *The Harmsworth Magazine* 3, no. 18 (1900): 606–8.

Humphrey, Mrs. *Manners for Men*. London: James Bowden, 1897.

Jack, Florence B., and Rita Strauss. *The Woman's Book: Contains Everything a Woman Ought to Know*. London: T.C. & E.C. Jack, 1911.

Jameson, Mrs. *Sisters of Charity: Abroad and at Home*. London: Longman, Grown, Green & Longmans, 1855.

Jeaune, Lady. *Ladies at Work: Papers on Paid Employment for Ladies by Experts in the Several Branches*. London: A.D. Innes & Co., 1893.

Keene, H.G. *History of India—From the Earliest Times to the End of the Nineteenth Century*. Vol. II. Edinburgh: Grant, 1915.

Keim, DeB. Randolph. *Hand Book of Official and Social Etiquette and Public Ceremonials at Washington*. Washington, DC: DeB. Randolph Keim, 1886.

Keith, Lester, and John Kemble. "Underneath a Parasol." New York: Harry von Tilzer Music Publishing Co., 1906.

Kiddier, William. *The Brushmaker and the Secrets of His Craft: His Romance*. London: Sir Isaac Pitman & Sons, 1928.

Kirkland, Caroline Matilda, and John Sartain. "Academy for Instruction in the Use of the Fan." *Sartain's Union Magazine of Literature and Art* 7: (July–December 1850), 103.

Krausse, Alexis. "Something about Umbrellas." *Cassell's Family Magazine* XXV (1879): 276–79.

Lange, O. "Japanese Fans." London: W. Paxton & Co., 1934.

Lavater, John Casper. *Essays on Physiognomy: Designed to Promote the Knowledge and the Love of Mankind*. Translated by Thomas Holcroft. 12th ed. London: William Tegg, 1862.

Leigh-Smith, Barbara. "Women and Work (1857)." In *What Is a Woman to Do? A Reader on Women, Work and Art, c. 1830–1890*, edited by Kyriaki Hadjiafxendi and Patricia Zakreski, 39–46. Bern: Peter Lang, 2011.

Liberty & Company. *Fans: A Brief Sketch of Their Origin and Use*. London: Liberty & Company, 1896.

Linton, Eliza Lynn. *The Girl of the Period and Other Social Essays*. 2 vols. Vol. 1. London: Richard Bentley & Son, 1883.

Lloyd, J.S. "Under an Umbrella." *Tinsley's Magazine* 32 (1883): 321–30.

London, Jack. *The People of the Abyss*. London: Pluto Press, 1998 [1903].

Loudon, Jane. *Gardening for Ladies*. London: John Murray, 1840.

Lover, Samuel. "The Hand and the Glove Song." London: Duff & Hodgson, 1843.

Macaulay, Thomas Babington. *The History of England from the Accession of James II*. New York: Harper and Brothers, 1855.

Mantegazza, Paolo. *Physiognomy and Expression*. London: Walter Scott, 1890.

Mayhew, Henry. *London Labour and the London Poor*. New York: Dover Publications, 1968 [1851].

Mclan, Fanny. "On Porcelain Painting." *The Athenaeum Journal of Literature, Science and the Fine Arts*, no. 906 (1845): 249–50.

Mearns, Andrew. *The Bitter Cry of Outcast London*. New York: Humanities Press, 1970 [1883].

Mellor, Tom, Alf. J. Lawrance, and Harry Gifford. "A Parasol for Two." London: Monte Carlo Publishing Co., 1907.

Mew, J. "The Fan." *Pall Mall Magazine* IX, no. 40 (1896): 481–88.

Mill, John Stuart. *Considerations on Representative Government*. London: Blackwell, 1946.

Mill, John Stuart. "On Liberty." In *On Liberty; Considerations on Representative Government*, edited by C. H. Wilson and R. B. McCallum, 1–104. London: Blackwell, 1946.

Morris, William. "Art and the Beauty of the Earth." In *The Collected Works of William Morris*, 155–74. London: Longmans Green, 1914.

Mossoba, Marie. "Old Romance of the Glove: The Gay Hues of Today Recall the Bright Hand-Coverings Worn in a Glamorous Past." *The New York Times*, May 10, 1936, SM15.

Munby, Arthur. "Munby Diary." In *Munby, Man of Two Worlds: The Life and Diaries of Arthur J. Munby, 1812–1910*, edited by Derek Hudson, 17–415. London: J. Murray, 1972.

Nevin, Gordon Balch. "Painted on a Fan Song." Philadelphia: T. Presser Co., 1915.

Noble, Mrs. Robert. *Every Woman's Toilet Book*. London: George Newnes, 1908.

Norman, Henry. *The Real Japan: Studies of Contemporary Japanese Manners, Morals, Administrations, and Politics*. 5th ed. London: T. Fisher Unwin, 1908.

Norton-Kyshe, James William. *The Law and Customs Relating to Gloves, Being an Exposition Historically Viewed of Ancient Laws, Customs, and Uses in Respect of Gloves, and of the Symbolism of the Hand and Glove in Judicial Proceedings*. London: Stevens and Haynes, 1901.

Opie, Amelia Alderson. *Dangers of Coquetry*. Peterborough: Broadview Press, 2003 [1790].

Orientalis. *The Umbrella; an o'er True and Regal Romaunt, or Legend of Osborne House*. Cowes: John R. Smith, Media Press, 1844.

Orlob, Harold, and Ned Rayburn. "Underneath a Parasol." New York: Hitchy Koo, 1918.

Ostolle, Henri. *La Fleur Peinte Sur L'eventail*. Paris, 1892.

Pugin, A.W.N. *The True Principles of Pointed or Christian Architecture: Set Forth in Two Lectures Delivered at St. Marie's, Oscott*. London: W. Hughes, 1841.

Purnell, Thomas. "Women, and Art: The Female School of Design." *The Art-Journal* 23 (1861): 107–8.

Reach, A. B. "The Gossip about Umbrellas." *Sharpe's London Magazine of Entertainment and Instruction for General Reading* 3, no. 18 (1853): 372–76.

Redgrave, Sam. *Fans of All Countries: A Series of Twenty Photographs of Spanish, French, German, Italian and English Fans under the Sanction of the Science and Art Department, for the Use of Schools of Art and Amateurs*. London: Arundel Society for Promoting the Knowledge of Art, 1871.

Reports by the Juries of the Great Exhibition 1851. London: William Clowes & Sons, 1852.

Roper Feudge, Fannie. "Umbrellas." *St. Nicholas: Scribner's Illustrated Magazine for Girls and Boys* II (August 1875): 623–25.

Rothwell, C. C. "The Umbrella-Man." *Belgravia: A London Magazine* 69 (1889): 344.

Ruskin, John. *The Stones of Venice.* 3 vols. Vol. 3. New York: John Wiley and Sons, 1880.

Saunders, Captain L. H. "The Outer Man." *The Modern Man*, June 11, 1910, 24.

Selous, Frederick Courteney. *A Hunter's Wanderings in Africa: Being a Narrative of Nine Years Spent amongst the Game of the Far Interior of Africa, Containing Accounts of Explorations beyond the Zambesi, on the River Chobe, and in the Matabele and Mashuna Countries, with Full Notes upon the Natural History and Present Distribution of All the Large Mammalia.* 4th ed. London: R. Bentley and Sons, 1895.

Slade, Adlolphus Esq., Lieut. RN. *Records of Travels in Turkey, Greece, &c. and of a Cruise in the Black Sea, with the Captain Pasha, in the Years 1829, 1830 and 1831.* Vol. II. 2nd ed. London: Saunders and Otley, 1833.

Sladen, Douglas. *Queer Things about Japan.* London: Anthony Treherne & Co., 1904.

Smiles, Samuel. *Self-Help; with Illustrations of Character, Conduct, and Perseverance.* New York: Allison, 1859.

Smith, Adam. *An Inquiry into the Nature and Causes of the Wealth of Nations,* edited by A. S. Skinner, W. B. Todd, and R. H. Campbell, 99–520. Oxford: Claredon Press, 1967 [1776].

Smith, Walter. *Art Education, Scholastic and Industrial.* Boston: James R. Osgood and Co., 1872.

Smith, Willard M. *Gloves Past and Present.* New York: Sherwood Press, 1917.

Struthers, Robert Briggs. *Hunting Journal: 1852–1856, in the Zulu Kingdom and the Tsonga Regions.* Edited by Patricia L. Merrett and Ronald Butcher. Pietermaritzburg, South Africa: University of Natal Press, 1991 [1852–1856].

Sylvia. *How to Dress Well on a Shilling a Day: Ladies' Guide to Home Dressmaking and Millinery.* London: Ward, Lock & Tyler, 1876.

Talbot, Howard. "A Paper Fan." London: Hopwood & Crew, 1901.

Tallis, John, and Jacob George Strutt. *Tallis' History and Description of the Crystal Palace: And the Exhibition of the World's Industry in 1851.* Vol. 1, part 2. London: London Printing & Publishing Co., 1852.

Turner, Mary E. "Of Modern Embroidery." In *Arts and Crafts Essays by Members of the Arts and Crafts Exhibition Society,* 355–65. London: Longmans Green and Co., 1903.

United Society of Brush Makers. *Balance Sheets and Report with Names and Amounts Paid to Receivers to End of March 1894.* London: F. W. Worthy, Trade Union Printer, 1894.

United Society of Brush Makers. *General Trade Rules of the United Society of Brush Makers.* London: Printed by F. W. Worthy, Trade Union Printer, 1894.

United Society of Brush Makers. *List of Fair Employers*. London: Issued by the Society, 1892, 1893.

Uzanne, Octave. *The Sunshade, the Glove, the Muff*. London: J. C. Nimmo and Bain, 1883.

Veblen, Thorstein. *The Theory of the Leisure Class: An Economic Study of Institutions*. New York: New American Library, 1953 [1899].

Von Boehn, Max. *Modes and Manners: Ornaments; Lace, Fans, Gloves, Walking-Sticks, Parasols, Jewelry and Trinkets*. London: J. M. Dent & Sons, 1929.

Von Siebold, P. F. *Manners and Customs of the Japanese in the Nineteenth Century*. Rutland, VT: Charles E. Tuttle, 1973 [1841].

Weatherly, F. E., and Charlotte Helen Weatherly. "The Glove." London: Enoch and Sons, 1873.

Webb, Beatrice. "The Diary of Beatrice Webb: 1873–1892." Edited by Norman MacKenzie and Jeanne MacKenzie. Cambridge, MA: Belknap Press, 1982 [1873–1892].

Wedmore, Frederick. "The Art of Conder." *The Connoisseur* VIII (1904): 219–24.

Worton, David, Charles Heslop, and K. L. Duffield. "The Parasol Parade." London: Shapiro, von Tilzer Music Co., 1908.

Wright, Arthur Robinson. "Fans." In *A Collection of Newspaper Cuttings on Walking Sticks, Umbrellas, Parasols, Fans and Gloves*. London: Author, 1932.

Wright, Arthur Robinson. "Gloves." In *A Collection of Newspaper Cuttings on Walking Sticks, Umbrellas, Parasols, Fans and Gloves*. London: Author, 1932.

Wright, Arthur Robinson. "Umbrellas and Parasols." In *A Collection of Newspaper Cuttings on Walking Sticks, Umbrellas, Parasols, Fans and Gloves*. London: Author, 1932.

Young, John H. *Our Deportment; or, The Manners, Conduct and Dress of the Most Refined Society*. Harrisburg, PA: F. B. Dickenson and Co., 1882.

SECONDARY SOURCES

Agnew, Jean-Christophe. "Coming up for Air: Consumer Culture in Historical Perspective." In *Consumption and the World of Goods*, edited by John Brewer and Roy Porter, 19–39. London: Routledge, 1993.

Alexander, Hélène. *Duvelleroy King of Fans: Fan Maker to Kings*. London: Fan Museum, 1995.

Alexander, Hélène. *Fans*. Cromwell House: Shire Publications, 2002.

Allen, Theodore. *The Invention of the White Race*. Vol. 1, *Racial Oppression and Social Control*. London: Verso, 1994.

Ames, Kenneth L. "Meaning in Artifacts: Hall Furnishings in Victorian America." *Journal of Interdisciplinary History* 9, no. 1 (1978): 19–46.

Anderson, Gregory. *Victorian Clerks*. Manchester: Manchester University Press, 1976.

Appadurai, Arjun, ed. *The Social Life of Things: Commodities in Cultural Perspective*. Cambridge: Cambridge University Press, 1986.

Armitage, David. *The Ideological Origins of the British Empire*. Cambridge: Cambridge University Press, 2000.

Armstrong, Nancy. *A Collector's History of Fans*. London: Cassell & Collier, 1974.

Arnstein, Walter L. *Britain Yesterday and Today: 1830 to the Present*. 8th ed. *A History of England*. Boston: Houghton Mifflin, 2001.

Ashlee, Peter C. "Tusks and Tortoiseshell: The Early Development of the British Plastics Industry with Special Reference to the British Xylonite Company 1877–1920." BA degree, University of Nottingham, 1982.

Atkinson, Diane. *Love and Dirt: The Marriage of Arthur Munby and Hannah Cullwick*. London: Macmillan, 2003.

Auerbach, Jeffrey. *The Great Exhibition of 1851: A Nation on Display*. New Haven, CT: Yale University Press, 1999.

Auslander, Leora. *Taste and Power: Furnishing Modern France*. Berkeley: University of California Press, 1996.

Bailey, Peter. "Parasexuality and Glamour: The Victorian Barmaid as Cultural Prototype." *Gender & History* 2, no. 2 (Summer 1990): 148–72.

Bailey, Peter. *Popular Culture and Performance in the Victorian City*. Cambridge: Cambridge University Press, 1998.

Banks, Joseph Ambrose. *Prosperity and Parenthood: A Study of Family Planning among the Victorian Middle Classes*, International Library of Sociology and Social Reconstruction. London: Routledge & Kegan Paul, 1954.

Banner, Lois W. *American Beauty*. New York: Knopf, 1983.

Barrett, James R. "Whiteness Studies: Anything here for Historians of the Working Class?" *International Labour and Working-Class History* 60 (Fall 2001): 33–42.

Baudrillard, Jean. *For a Critique of the Political Economy of the Sign*. St Louis: Telos, 1981.

Baudrillard, Jean. *Simulacra and Simulation*. Translated by Sheila Faria. Ann Arbor: University of Michigan Press, 1994.

Beaujot, Ariel. "Coiffing Vanity: A Study of the Manufacture, Design, and Meaning of the Celluloid Hairbrush in America, 1900–1930." In *Producing Fashion*, edited by Reggie Balszczyk, 229–54. Philadelphia: University of Pennsylvania Press, 2007.

Beckow, Steven M. "Culture, History and Artifact." In *Material Culture Studies in America*, edited by T. J. Schlereth, 114–23. Nashville: American Association for State and Local History, 1982.

Bedi, Ramesh. *Elephant: Lord of the Jungle*. Translated by J. P. Uniyal. New Delhi: National Book Trust, India, 1969.

Beetham, Margaret. *A Magazine of Her Own? Domesticity and Desire in the Women's Magazine, 1800–1914*. London: Routledge, 1996.

Bell, Quentin. *On Human Finery*. London: Hogarth Press, 1976.

Berg, Maxine. *Luxury and Pleasure in Eighteenth-Century Britain*. Oxford: Oxford University Press, 2005.

Berg, Maxine, and Elizabeth Eger, eds. *Luxury in the Eighteenth Century: Debate, Desires and Delectable Goods*. New York: Palgrave Macmillan, 2003.

Berg, Maxine, and Helen Clifford, eds. *Consumers and Luxury: Consumer Culture in Europe 1650–1850*. Manchester: Manchester University Press, 1999.

Bernstein, Susan David, and Else B. Michie, eds. *Victorian Vulgarity: Taste in Verbal and Visual Culture*. Aldershot: Ashgate, 2009.

Berry, Christopher J. *The Idea of Luxury: A Conceptual and Historical Investigation*. Cambridge: Cambridge University Press, 1994.

Berry, Helen, and Jeremy Gregory, eds. *Creating and Consuming Culture in North-East England, 1660–1830*. Aldershot: Ashgate, 2004.

Bigelow, Marybelle S. *Fashion in History: Apparel in the Western World*. Minneapolis: Burgess, 1970.

Bland, Lucy. *Banishing the Beast: English Feminism and Sexual Morality, 1885–1914*. London: Penguin, 1995.

Blaszczyk, Regina Lee. *Imagining Consumers: Design and Innovation from Wedgwood to Corning*. Baltimore: Johns Hopkins University Press, 2002.

Blaszczyk, Regina Lee. "The Importance of Being True Blue: The Du Pont Company and the Color Revolution." In *Cultures of Commerce: Representation and American Business Culture, 1877–1960*, edited by Elspeth H. Brown, Catherine Gudis, and Marina Moskowitz, 27–50. New York: Palgrave Macmillan, 2006.

Bonnett, Alastair. "How the British Working Class Became White: The Symbolic (Re)Formation of Racialized Capitalism." *Journal of Historical Sociology* 11, no. 3 (1998): 316–40.

Bordo, Susan. *Unbearable Weight: Feminism, Western Culture, and the Body*. Berkeley: University of California Press, 2003.

Boris, Eileen. *Art and Labor: Ruskin, Morris and the Craftsman Ideal in America*. Philadelphia: Temple University Press, 1986.

Bourdieu, Pierre. *Distinction: A Social Critique of the Judgment of Taste*. Translated by Richard Nice. Cambridge, MA: Harvard University Press, 1984.

Bovey, Patricia E. *Bustles and Rosepetals Fashion Is Art: 1882–1910*. Winnipeg: Winnipeg Art Gallery, 1980.

Bowersox, Jeff. *Raising Germans in the Age of Empire: Youth and Colonial Culture, 1871–1914*. Oxford: Oxford University Press, 2012.

Bradfield, Nancy. *Costume in Detail: Women's Dress 1730–1930*. London: George G. Harrap and Co., 1986.

Bradley, Carolyn G. *Western World Costume: An Outline History*. New York: Appleton-Century Crofts, 1954.

Branca, Patricia. "Image and Reality: The Myth of the Ideal Victorian Woman." In *Clio's Consciousness Raised: New Perspectives on the History of Women*, edited by Mary S. Hartman, 179–90. New York: Octagon Books, 1976.

Branca, Patricia. *Silent Sisterhood: Middle-Class Women in the Victorian Home*. London: Croom Helm, 1975.

Brander, Michael. *The Victorian Gentleman*. London: Gordon Cremonesi, 1975.

Breward, Christopher. *The Culture of Fashion: A New History of Fashionable Dress*. New York: St. Martin's Press, 1995.

Breward, Christopher. *Fashioning London: Clothing and the Modern Metropolis*. Oxford: Berg, 2004.

Breward, Christopher. *The Hidden Consumer: Masculinities, Fashion and City Life 1860–1914*. Manchester: Manchester University Press, 1999.

Breward, Christopher, and Caroline Evans, eds. *Fashion and Modernity*. Oxford: Berg, 2005.

Breward, Christopher, Becky Conekin, and Caroline Cox, eds. *The Englishness of English Dress*. Oxford: Berg, 1995.

Briggs, Asa. *The Making of Modern England: The Age of Improvement*. New York: Harper and Row, 1965.

Briggs, Asa. *Victorian Things*. Chicago: University of Chicago Press, 1989.

Brodkin, Karen. *How Jews Became White Folks and What that Says about Race in America*. New Brunswick, NJ: Rutgers University Press, 1998.

Brucken, Carolyn. "In the Public Eye: Women and the American Luxury Hotel." *Winterthur Portfolio* 31, no. 4 (1996): 199–203.

Buck, Anne. *Victorian Costume and Costume Accessories*. 2nd ed. Carlton: Ruth Bean, 1984.

Budd, Louis J., ed. *Mark Twain: Collected Tales, Sketches, Speeches and Essays, 1891–1910*. New York: Literary Classics of the United States, 1992.

Buettner, Elizabeth. *Empire Families: Britons and Late Imperial India*. Oxford: Oxford University Press, 2004.

Bulpin, T. V. *The Hunter Is Death*. Cape Town, South Africa: Cape and Transvaal Printers, 1962.

Burke, Timothy. *Lifebuoy Men, Lux Women: Commodification, Consumption and Cleanliness in Modern Zimbabwe*. Durham, NC: Duke University Press, 1996.

Burton, Antoinette. *At the Heart of the Empire: Indians and the Colonial Encounter in Late-Victorian Britain*. Berkeley: University of California Press, 1998.

Burton, Antoinette. *Burdens of History: British Feminists, Indian Women, and Imperial Culture, 1865–1915*. Chapel Hill: University of North Carolina Press, 1994.

Bushman, Richard L. *The Refinement of America: Persons, Houses, Cities*. New York: Random House, 1993.

Butler, Judith. *Bodies That Matter: On the Discursive Limits of Sex*. New York: Routledge, 1993.

Butler, Judith. *Gender Trouble: Feminism and the Subversion of Identity*. New York: Routledge, 1990.

Butler, Judith. "Performative Acts and Gender Constitution: An Essay in Phenomenology and Feminist Theory." In *Performing Feminisms: Feminist Critical Theory and Theatre*, edited by Sue Ellen Case, 270–82. Baltimore: John Hopkins University Press, 1990.

Butterfield, H. *The Whig Interpretation of History*. New York: W. W. Norton, 1965.

Cadden, Joan. *Meanings of Sex Difference in the Middle Ages: Medicine, Science and Culture*. Cambridge: Cambridge University Press, 1993.

Caine, Barbara. *Victorian Feminists*. Oxford: Oxford University Press, 1992.

Campbell, Colin. "The Meaning of Objects and the Meaning of Actions: A Critical Note on the Sociology of Consumption and Theories of Clothing." *Journal of Material Culture* 1, no. 1 (1996): 93–105.

Carby, Hazel. "White Women Listen! Black Feminism and the Boundaries of Sisterhood." In *The Empire Strikes Back*, edited by The Centre for Contemporary Cultural Studies, 212–23. London: Hutchinson, 1982.

Carlson, Hannah. "Vulgar Things: James Fenimore Cooper's 'Clairvoyant' Pocket Handkerchief." *Common-Place* 7, no. 2 (2007). www.common-place. org. Accessed September 6, 2011.

Carson, Gerald. *The Golden Egg: The Personal Income Tax—Where It Came From, How It Grew*. Boston: Houghton Mifflin, 1977.

Castronovo, David. *The English Gentleman: Images and Ideals in Literature and Society*. New York: Ungar, 1987.

Centre for Contemporary Cultural Studies. *The Empire Strikes Back*. London: Hutchinson, 1982.

Chakrabarty, Dipesh. *Provincializing Europe: Postcolonial Thought and Historical Difference*. Princeton, NJ: Princeton University Press, 2000.

Chalmers, F. Graeme. "Fanny Mclan and London's Female School of Design, 1842–57: 'My Lords and Gentlemen, Your Obedient and Humble Servant'?" *Woman's Art Journal* 16, no. 2 (1996): 3–9.

Chalmers, F. Graeme. *Women in the Nineteenth-Century Art World: Schools of Art and Design for Women in London and Philadelphia*. Westport, CT: Greenwood Press, 1998.

Cheang, Sarah. "Women, Pets and Imperialism: The British Pekingese Dog and Nostalgia for Old China." *Journal of British Studies* 45, no. 2 (2006): 359–87.

Checkland, Olive. *Britain's Encounter with Meiji Japan, 1868–1912*. Houndmills: Macmillan, 1989.

Checkland, Olive. *Japan and Britain after 1859: Creating Cultural Bridges*. New York: Routledge, 2003.

Clancy-Smith, Julia, and Frances Gouda, eds. *Domesticating the Empire: Race, Gender, and Family Life in French and Dutch Colonialism*. Charlottesville: University Press of Virginia, 1998.

Cohen, Deborah. *Household Gods: The British and Their Possessions*. New Haven, CT: Yale University Press, 2006.

Colley, Linda. *Britons: Forging the Nation, 1707–1837*. New Haven, CT: Yale University Press, 1992.

Colley, Linda. *Captives: Britain, Empire and the World, 1600–1850*. London: Jonathan Cape, 2002.

Collins, Bernard Ross. *A Short Account of the Worshipful Company of Fan Makers*. London: Favil Press, 1950.

Conner, Patrick. *Oriental Architecture in the West*. London: Thames and Hudson, 1979.

Coombes, Annie E. *Reinventing Africa: Museums, Material Culture and Popular Imagination in Late Victorian and Edwardian England*. New Haven, CT: Yale University Press, 1994.

Cooper, Wendy. *Hair: Sex Society Symbolism*. New York: Stein and Day, 1971.

Cooter, Roger. *The Cultural Meaning of Popular Science: Phrenology and the Organization of Consent in Nineteenth-Century Britain*. Cambridge: Cambridge University Press, 1984.

Côté, James E. "Sociological Perspectives on Identity Formation: The Culture-Identity Link and Identity Capital." *Journal of Adolescence* 19 (1996): 417–28.

Cranfield, Geoffrey Alan. *The Press and Society: From Caxton to Northcliff*. London: Longman, 1978.

Crook, J. Mordaunt. *The Rise of the Nouveaux Riches: Style and Status in Victorian and Edwardian Architecture*. London: John Murray, 1999.

Crowley, John. *The Invention of Comfort: Sensibilities and Design in Early Modern Britain and Early America*. Baltimore: Johns Hopkins University Press, 2001.

Cullan-Swan, Betsy, and Peter K. Manning. "What Is a T-Shirt? Codes, Chorontypes, and Everyday Objects." In *The Socialness of Things: Essays on the Social-Semiotics of Objects*, edited by Stephen Harold Riggins, 415–33. New York: Nouton de Gruyer, 1994.

Cummin, Elizabeth, and Wendy Kaplan. *The Arts and Crafts Movement*. London: Thames and Hudson, 1991.

Cumming, Valerie. *Gloves*. Edited by Aileen Ribeiro, The Costume Accessories Series. London: B. T. Batsford, 1982.

Cunnington, C. Willett. *English Women's Clothing in the Nineteenth Century*. 2nd ed. New York: Dover Publications, 1990.

Cunnington, C. Willett, and Phillis Cunnington. *Handbook of English Costume in the Nineteenth Century*. 3rd ed. London: Faber and Faber, 1970.

Curtin, Michael. *Propriety and Position: A Study of Victorian Manners*. New York: Garland, 1987.

Davidoff, Leonore. "Class and Gender in Victorian England: The Diaries of Arthur J. Munby and Hannah Cullwick." *Feminist Studies* 5, no. 1 (1979): 87–141.

Davidoff, Leonore, and Catherine Hall. *Family Fortunes: Men and Women of the English Middle Class, 1780–1850*. Chicago: University of Chicago Press, 1987.

De Courtais, Georgine. *Women's Headdress and Hairstyles: In England from A.D. 600 to Present Day*. London: B.T. Batsford, 1973.

De Grazia, Victoria. *Irresistible Empire: America's Advance through Twentieth-Century Europe*. Cambridge, MA: Harvard University Press, 2005.

De Vere Green, Bertha. *A Collector's Guide to Fans over the Ages*. London: Frederick Muller, 1975.

De Vere Green, Bertha. *Fans over the Ages: A Collector's Guide*. Cranbury: A.S. Barnes and Co., 1975.

De Vries, Jan. *The Industrious Revolution: Consumer Behavior and the Household Economy, 1650 to the Present*. Cambridge: Cambridge University Press, 2008.

Dictionary of Proverbs. Ware: Wordsworth Editions, 1993.

Douglas, Mary. *The World of Goods*. New York: Basic Books, 1979.

Driver, Felix, and David Gilbert, eds. *Imperial Cities: Landscape, Display and Identity*. Manchester: Manchester University Press, 1999.

Dupont, Jean Claude. "The Meaning of Objects: The Poker." In *Living in a Material World: Canadian and American Approaches to Material Culture*, edited by Gerald L. Pocius, 1–18. St. John's, Newfoundland: Institute of Social and Economic Research, Memorial University of Newfoundland, 1991.

Durham, Walter A. Jr. "The Japanese Camphor Monopoly: Its History and Relation to the Future of Japan." *Pacific Affairs* 5, no. 9 (September 1932): 797–801.

Du Toit, R.F., S.N. Stuart, and D.H.M. Cumming. *African Elephants and Rhinos: Status Survey and Conservation Action Plan*. Gland, Switzerland: The Nature Conservation Bureau, 1990.

Dyer, Richard. "White." *Screen* 29, no. 4 (1988): 44–65.

Ellenberger, Nancy W. "The Transformation of London 'Society' at the End of Victoria's Reign: Evidence from the Court Presentation Records." *Albion* 22, no. 4 (1990): 633–53.

Fausto-Sterling, Anne. "Gender, Race, and Nation: The Comparative Anatomy of 'Hottentot' Women in Europe, 1815–1817." In *Deviant Bodies: Critical Perspectives on Difference in Science and Popular Culture*, edited by Jennifer Terry and Jacqueline Urla, 19–43. Bloomington: Indiana University Press, 1995.

Fendel, Cynthia. *Celluloid Hand Fans*. Dallas: Hand Fan Productions, 2001.

Fields, Jill. " 'Fighting the Corsetless Evil': Shaping Corsets and Culture, 1900–1930." In *Beauty and Business: Commerce, Gender and Culture in Modern America*, edited by Philip Scranton, 109–41. New York: Routledge, 2001.

Fields, Jill. *An Intimate Affair: Women, Lingerie, and Sexuality*. Berkeley: University of California Press, 2007.

Finkelstein, Joanne. *The Fashioned Self*. Cambridge: Polity Press, 1991.

Finley, Gregg. "The Gothic Revival and the Victorian Church in New Brunswick: Toward a Strategy of Material Culture Research." *Material Culture Bulletin* 32 (1990): 1–16.

Firth, Raymond. *Symbols: Public and Private*. London: Allen and Unwin, 1973.

Fleming, E. McClung. "Artifact Study: A Proposed Model." *Winterthur Portfolio* 9 (1974): 153–73.

Flugel, J.C. *The Psychology of Clothes*. New York: International University Press, 1969.

Foster, Vanda. *Bags and Purses*. Edited by Aileen Ribeiro, Costume Accessories Series. London: B.T. Batsford, 1982.

Foster, Vanda. *A Visual History of Costume in the Nineteenth Century*. London: B.T. Batsford, 1984.

Foucault, Michel. *The History of Sexuality: An Introduction*. New York: Pantheon Books, 1978.

Freedgood, Elaine. *The Ideas in Things: Fugitive Meaning in the Victorian Novel*. Chicago: University of Chicago Press, 2006.

Friedel, Robert. *Pioneer Plastic: The Making and Selling of Celluloid*. Madison: University of Wisconsin Press, 1983.

Frye, Marilyn. "On Being White: Thinking toward a Feminist Understanding of Race and Race Supremacy." In *The Politics of Reality: Essays in Feminist Theory*, edited by Marilyn Frye, 110–27. Trumansburg, NY: Crossing Press, 1983.

Furlough, Ellen, and Victoria de Grazia, eds. *The Sex of Things: Gender and Consumption in Historical Perspective*. Berkeley: University of California Press, 1996.

Gilbon, Craig. "Pop Pedagogy: Looking at the Coke Bottle." In *Material Culture Studies in America*, edited by Thomas J. Schlereth, 183–91. Nashville: American Association for State and Local History, 1982.

Gillett, Paula. *The Victorian Painter's World*. Gloucester: Alan Sutton, 1990.

Gilmore, Michael T., and Wai Chee Dimock. *Rethinking Class: Literary Studies and Social Formations*. New York: Columbia University Press, 1994.

Gilroy, Paul. *There Ain't No Black in the Union Jack*. London: Hutchinson, 1987.

Ginsburg, Madeleine. *Victorian Dress in Photographs*. New York: Holmes and Meier, 1983.

Gitter, Elisabeth G. "The Power of Women's Hair in the Victorian Imagination." *Publications of the Modern Language Association* 99 (October 1984): 936–54.

Glassie, Henry. "Folk Art." In *Folklore and Folklife: An Introduction*, edited by Richard Dorson, 253–80. Chicago: University of Chicago Press, 1972.

Goffman, Erving. *Gender Advertisements*. New York: Harper and Row, 1979.

Gowing, Margaret. "Science, Technology and Education: England in 1870." *Oxford Review of Education* 4, no. 1 (1978): 3–17.

Graham, Clare. "'A Noble Kind of Practice': The Society of Arts Art-Workmanship Competitions, 1863–71." *The Burlington Magazine* 135, no. 1083 (1993): 411–15.

Greenblatt, Stephen. *Renaissance Self-Fashioning: From More to Shakespeare*. Chicago: University of Chicago Press, 2005.

Grier, Katherine C. *Culture and Comfort: People, Parlors, and Upholstery 1850–1930*. Rochester: University of Massachusetts Press, 1988.

Gunn, Simon, and Rachel Bell. *Middle Classes: Their Rise and Sprawl*. London: Cassell, 2002.

Hale, Grace Elizabeth. *Making Whiteness: The Culture of Segregation in the South, 1890–1940*. New York: Pantheon Books, 1998.

Hall, Catherine. "William Knibb and the Constitution of the New Black Subject." In *Empire and Others: British Encounters with Indigenous Peoples, 1600–1850*, edited by Martin Daunton and Rick Halpern, 31–55. Philadelphia: University of Pennsylvania Press, 2000.

Hall, Catherine, and Sonya O. Rose, eds. *At Home with the Empire: Metropolitan Culture and the Imperial World*. Cambridge: Cambridge University Press, 2006.

Hamilton Hill, Margot, and Peter A. Bucknell. *The Evolution of Fashion: Pattern and Cut from 1066–1930*. London: B. T. Batsford, 1967.

"hand, n.1." *OED Online*. Oxford University Press. June 2011. http://oed.com/view/Entry/83801?rskey=A7O8QM&result=1&isAdvanced=false, 8a. Accessed September 7, 2011.

Hansen, Adam. "Exhibiting Vagrancy, 1851: Victorian London and the 'Vagabond Savage.'" In *A Mighty Mass of Brick and Smoke: Victorian and Edwardian Representations of London*, edited by Laurence Phillips. New York: Rodopi, 2007.

Harrison, John Fletcher Clews. *Early Victorians 1832–1851*. London: Weidenfeld and Nicolson, 1971.

Head, Raymond. *The Indian Style*. London: George Allen & Unwin, 1986.

Hebdige, Dick. *Subculture: The Meaning of Style*. London: Routledge, 1979.

Henderson, W. O. "The Anglo-French Commercial Treaty of 1786." *Economic History Review*, n.s. 10, no. 1 (1957): 104–12.

Hergenhahn, B. R. *An Introduction to the History of Psychology*. Belmont: Wadsworth Cengage Learning, 2009.

Hesseltine, William B. "The Challenge of the Artifact." In *Material Culture Studies in America*, edited by T. J. Schlereth, 93–100. Nashville: American Association for State and Local History, 1982.

Hobsbawm, Eric. *Industry and Empire: From 1750 to the Present Day*. New York: Penguin Books, 1999.

Hoganson, Kristin. "The Fashionable World: Imagined Communities of Dress." In *After the Imperial Turn: Thinking with and through the Nation*, edited by Antoinette Burton, 260–78. Durham, NC: Duke University Press, 2003.

Holland, Vivian. "On Collecting Fashion Plates." *The Book-Collector's Quarterly* 2 (1951): 10–28.

Hollander, Anne. *Seeing through Clothes*. New York: Penguin Books, 1988.

hooks, bell. "Travelling Theories: Traveling Theorists." *Inscriptions* 5 (1989): 177–88.

Horn, Pamela. *The Rise and Fall of the Victorian Servant*. Dublin: Gill and Macmillan, 1975.

Horowitz, Daniel. *The Morality of Spending: Attitudes toward the Consumer Society in America, 1875–1940*. Baltimore: Johns Hopkins University Press, 1992.

Hounshell, David A., and John Kenly Smith Jr. *Science and Corporate Strategy: DuPont R&D, 1902–1980*. Cambridge: Cambridge University Press, 1988.

Howe, Bea. *Lady with Green Fingers: The Life of Jane Loudon*. London: Country Life, 1960.

Hudson, Derek, ed. *Munby, Man of Two Worlds: The Life and Diaries of Arthur J. Munby, 1828–1910*. London: William Clowes & Sons, 1972.

Humphrey, Heidi. *Hair*. Baskerville: Eastern Press, 1980.

Hunt, John Dixon. "The Sign of the Object." In *History from Things: Essays on Material Culture*, edited by Steven Lubar and Kingery W. David, 293–98. Washington, DC: Smithsonian Institution Press, 1993.

Ignatiev, N. *How the Irish Became White*. New York: Routledge, 1995.

Jackson, Anna. "Imagining Japan: The Victorian Perception and Acquisition of Japanese Culture." *Journal of Design History* 5, no. 4 (1992): 245–56.

Jacobson, Dawn. *Chinoiserie*. London: Phaidon Press, 1993.

Jacobson, Matthew Frye. *Whiteness of a Different Color: European Immigrants and the Alchemy of Race*. Cambridge, MA: Harvard University Press, 1998.

Jarvis, Anthea. *Liverpool Fashion: Its Makers and Wearers: The Dressmaking Trade in Liverpool 1830–1940*. Liverpool: Saints and Co., 1981.

Johnson, Eleanor. *Ladies' Dress Accessories*. Cromwell House: Shire Publications, 2004.

Johnson, Sheila K. *The Japanese through American Eyes*. Stanford, CA: Stanford University Press, 1988.

Jones, Gareth Stedman. *Outcast London: A Study in the Relationship between Classes in Victorian Society*. London: Penguin Books, 1992.

Jones, M. G. *The Story of Brushmaking: A Norfolk Craft*. Norwich: Briton Chadwick, 1974.

Joyce, Patrick. *Democratic Subjects: The Self and the Social in Nineteenth-Century England*. Cambridge: Cambridge University Press, 1994.

Joyce, Patrick. *Visions of the People: Industrial England and the Question of Class, 1848–1914*. Cambridge: Cambridge University Press, 1991.

Kane, Penny. *Victorian Families in Fact and Fiction*. London: Macmillan, 1995.

Kaplan, Wendy. *"The Art That Is Life": The Arts and Crafts Movement in America, 1875–1920*. Boston: Museum of Fine Arts, 1987.

Katz, Sylvia. *Early Plastics*. Buckingham: Shire Publications, 1986.

Kaye, Richard A. *The Flirt's Tragedy: Desire without End in Victorian and Edwardian Fiction*. Charlottesville: University Press of Virginia, 2002.

Kidd, Alan, and David Nicholls, eds. *Gender, Civic Culture and Consumerism: Middle-Class Identity in Britain 1800–1940*. Manchester: Manchester University Press, 1999.

King, Shell, and Yaël Schlick. *Refiguring the Coquette: Essays on Culture and Coquettery*. Cranbury: Rosemount Publishing and Printing Corp., 2008.

Kouwenhoven, D. Reidel. "American Studies: Words or Things?" In *American Studies in Transition*, edited by William Marshall Finshwick, 15–35. Boston: Houghton Mifflin, 1964.

Kowaleski-Wallace, Elizabeth. *Consuming Subjects: Women, Shopping, and Business in the Eighteenth Century*. New York: Columbia University Press, 1997.

Kriegel, Lara. *Grand Designs: Labor, Empire, and the Museum in Victorian Culture*. Durham, NC: Duke University Press, 2007.

Kuchta, David. "The Making of the Self-Made Man: Class Clothing and English Masculinity 1688–1832." In *The Sex of Things: Gender and Consumption in Historical Perspective*, edited by Victoria de Grazia and Ellen Furlough, 55–62. Berkeley: University of California Press, 1996.

Kuchta, David. *The Three-Piece Suit and Modern Masculinity: England, 1550–1850*. Berkeley: University of California Press, 2002.

Kwint, Marius, Christopher Breward, and Jeremy Aynsley. *Material Memories*. Oxford: Berg, 1999.

Kybalova, Ludmila, Olga Herbenova, and Milena Lamarova. *The Pictorial Encyclopedia of Fashion*. Translated by Claudia Rosoux. London: Paul Hamlyn, 1970.

Lampela, Laurel. "Women's Art Education Institutions in Nineteenth Century England." *Art Education* 46, no. 1 (1993): 64–67.

Lancaster, William. *The Department Store: A Social History*. London: Leicester University Press, 1995.

Lansdell, Avril. *Fashion a La Carte 1860–1900: A Study of Fashion through Cartes-de-Visite*. Aylesbury: Shire Publications, 1985.

Lauer, Keith, and Julie Robinson. *Celluloid: Collector's Reference and Value Guide*. Paducah, KY: Collector Books, 1999.

Lee, Martyn J. "Introduction." In *The Consumer Society Reader*, edited by Martyn J. Lee, ix–xxvi. Malden, MA: Blackwell, 2000.

Leites, Edmund. "The Duty to Desire: Love, Friendship and Sexuality in Some Puritan Theories of Marriage." *Journal of Social History* 15 (1982): 383–408.

Lemire, Beverly. *Dress, Culture and Commerce: The English Clothing Trade before the Factory, 1660–1800*. London: Macmillan, 1997.

Lemire, Beverly. *Fashion's Favourite: The Cotton Treade and the Consumer in Britian, 1660–1800*. Oxford: Oxford University Press, 1991.

Lemire, Beverly. "Second-Hand Beaux and 'Red-Armed Belles': Conflict and the Creation of Fashions in England, c. 1660–1800." *Continuity and Change* 15, no. 3 (2000): 391–417.

Levell, Nicky. "Reproducing India: International Exhibitions and Victorian Tourism." In *Souvenirs: The Material Culture of Tourism*, edited by Michael Hitchcock and Ken Teague, 36–51. Aldershot: Ashgate, 2000.

Levi Peck, Linda. *Consuming Splendor*. Cambridge: Cambridge University Press, 2005.

Levitt, Sarah. *Victorians Unbuttoned: Registered Designs for Clothing, Their Makers and Wearers, 1839–1900*. London: Allen and Unwin, 1986.

Lewis, Perce F. "Axioms of Reading the Landscape: Some Guides to the American Scene." In *Material Culture Studies in America*, edited by Thomas J. Schlereth, 174–82. Nashville: American Association for State and Local History, 1982.

Lewis, Roy, and Angus Maude. *The English Middle Classes*. London: Phoenix House, 1949.

Lister, Margot. *Costume: An Illustrated Survey from Ancient Times to the Twentieth Century*. London: Herbert Jenkins, 1968.

Loeb, Lori Anne. *Consuming Angels: Advertising and Victorian Women*. Oxford: Oxford University Press, 1994.

Lowe, L. *Critical Terrains: French and British Orientalisms*. Ithaca, NY: Cornell University Press, 1991.

Macfarlane, Alan. *Marriage and Love in England: Modes of Reproduction 1300–1840*. London: Blackwell, 1986.

MacKenzie, John M. *The Empire of Nature: Hunting, Conservation and British Imperialism*. Manchester: Manchester University Press, 1988.

MacKenzie, John M. *Propaganda and Empire: The Manipulation of British Public Opinion, 1880–1960*. Manchester: Manchester University Press, 1984.

MacKenzie, John M., ed. *Imperialism and Popular Culture*. Manchester: Manchester University Press, 1986.

Mackerras, Colin. *Western Images of China*. Oxford: Oxford University Press, 1989.

Macleod, Dianne Sachko. *Art and the Victorian Middle Class: Money and the Making of Cultural Identity*. Cambridge: Cambridge University Press, 1996.

Magnus, Philip. *King Edward the Seventh*. London: William Clowes & Sons, 1964.

Marchand, Roland. *Advertising the American Dream: Making Way for Modernity, 1920–1940*. Berkeley: University of California Press, 1985.

Marchese, Ronald T. "Material Culture and Artifact Classification." In *American Material Culture: The Shape of Things around Us*, edited by Edith Mayo,

11–23. Bowling Green, OH: Bowling Green State University Popular Press, 1984.

Marcus, Shanon. "Reflections on Victorian Fashion Plates." *Differences: A Journal of Feminist Cultural Studies* 14, no. 3 (2005): 4–33.

Marcuse, H. *One Dimensional Man*. London: Ark, 1986.

Marquet, Jacques. "Objects as Instruments, Objects as Signs." In *History from Things: Essays on Material Culture*, edited by Steven Lubar and Kingery W. David, 30–40. Washington, DC: Smithsonian Institution Press, 1993.

McBride, Eeresa M. *The Domestic Revolution: The Modernisation of Household Service in England and France 1820–1920*. New York: Holmes and Meier, 1976.

McClintock, Anne. *Imperial Leather: Race, Gender and Sexuality in the Colonial Conquest*. New York: Routledge, 1995.

McClintock, Anne. "Soft-Soaping Empire: Commodity Racism and Imperial Advertising." In *Imperial Leather: Race, Gender and Sexuality in the Colonial Contest*, 207–31. New York: Routledge, 1995.

McCracken, Grant. *Culture and Consumption: New Approaches to the Symbolic Character of Consumer Goods and Activities*. Bloomington: Indiana University Press, 1990.

Mehta, Unday Singh. *Liberalism and Empire: A Study in Nineteenth-Century British Liberal Thought*. Chicago: University of Chicago Press, 1999.

Meikle, Jeffrey L. *American Plastic: A Cultural History*. New Brunswick, NJ: Rutgers University Press, 1995.

Meredith, Martin. *Africa's Elephant: A Biography*. London: Hodder and Stoughton, 2001.

Miller, Daniel. *Material Cultures: Why Some Things Matter*. London: University College London Press, 1997.

Miller, Elizabeth Carolyn. *Framed: The New Woman Criminal in British Culture at the Fin de Siècle*. Ann Arbor: University of Michigan Press, 2008.

Milne-Smith, Amy. *London Clubland: A Cultural History of Gender and Class in Late Victorian Britain*. Houndmills: Palgrave Macmillan, 2011.

Mire, Amina. "Skin-Bleaching: Poison, Beauty, Power and the Politics of the Colour Line." *New Feminist Research* 28, nos. 3&4 (2001): 13–38.

Montgomery, Charles F. "The Connoisseurship of Artifacts." In *Material Culture Studies in America*, edited by Thomas J. Schlereth, 143–52. Nashville: American Association for State and Local History, 1982.

Moore, Doris Langley. *Fashion through Fashion Plates, 1771–1970*. New York: Clarkson N. Potter, 1971.

Morgan, Marjorie. *Manners, Morals and Class in England, 1774–1858*. Houndmills: Macmillan, 1994.

Mossman, S.T.I. "Parkesine and Celluloid." In *The Development of Plastics*, edited by S.T.I. Mossman and P.J.T. Morris, 10–25. Cambridge: Royal Society of Chemistry, 1994.

Musgrove, F. "Middle-Class Education and Employment in the Nineteenth-Century." *Economic History Review*, 2nd series XII (August 1959): 91–111.

Nelson, Claudia. *Family Ties in Victorian England*. Westport, CT: Praeger, 2007.

Nevett, T. R. *Advertising in Britain: A History*. London: Heinemann, 1982.

Newman, Louise Michele. *White Women's Rights: The Radical Origins of Feminism in the United States*. New York: Oxford University Press, 1999.

Orvell, Miles. *The Real Thing: Imitation and Authenticity in American Culture, 1880–1940*. Chapel Hill: University of North Carolina Press, 1989.

Orwell, George. *Down and out in Paris and London*. Harmondsworth: Penguin Books, 1974.

Oxford English Dictionary. 2nd ed. Oxford: Oxford University Press, 1989.

Pagden, Anthony. *Lords of All the World: Ideologies of Empire in Spain, Britain and France c. 1500–c. 1800*. New Haven, CT: Yale University Press, 1995.

Pedersen, Joyce Senders. "Schoolmistresses and Headmistresses: Elites and Education in Nineteenth-Century England." *The Journal of British Studies* 15, no. 1 (1975): 135–62.

Peiss, Kathy. *Hope in a Jar: The Making of America's Beauty Culture*. New York: Metropolitan Books, 1998.

Perkin, Harold James. *The Rise of Professional Society: England since 1880*. London: Routledge, 1989.

Perrot, Philippe. *Fashioning the Bourgeoisie*. Translated by Richard Bienvenu. Princeton, NJ: Princeton University Press, 1981.

Phillips, Ruth B., and Christopher B. Steiner, eds. *Unpacking Culture: Art and Commodity in Colonial and Postcolonial Worlds*. Berkeley: University of California Press, 1999.

Pickering, M. "White Skin Black Masks: 'Nigger' Minstrelsy in Victorian Britian." In *Music Hall: Performance and Style*, edited by J. Bratton, 70–91. Milton Keynes: Open University Press, 1986.

Pool, Daniel. *What Jane Austen Ate and Charles Dickens Knew: From Fox Hunting to Whist—the Facts of Daily Life in 19th-Century England*. New York: Touchstone, 1994.

Porter, Bernard. *The Absent-Minded Imperialists: Empire, Society, and Culture in Britain*. Oxford: Oxford University Press, 2004.

Prown, Jules. "Mind in Matter: An Introduction to Material Culture Theory and Method." *Winterthur Portfolio* 17 (1982): 1–12.

Ramamurthy, Anandi. *Imperial Persuaders: Images of Africa and Asia in British Advertising*. Manchester: Manchester University Press, 2003.

Rappaport, Erika. " 'The Bombay Debt': Letter Writing, Domestic Economies and Family Conflict in Colonial India." *Gender and History* 16, no. 2 (2004): 233–60.

Rappaport, Erika. "Introduction: Shopping as Women's Pleasure and Women's Work." *Defining Gender, 1450–1910*. http://www.gender.amdigital.co.uk/essays/content/rappaport.aspx. Accessed June 29, 2010.

Rappaport, Erika Diane. *Shopping for Pleasure: Women in the Making of London's West End*. Princeton, NJ: Princeton University Press, 2000.

Reay, Barry. *Watching Hannah: Sexuality, Horror and Bodily De-Formation in Victorian England*. London: Reaktion Books, 2002.

Reedy, Sapna. "Be Sure to Get under Your *Ombra*: Ever Wonder about the Umbrella? A Glance at How People down the Ages Used It." *The Hindu: Online Edition of India's National Newspaper*, August 26, 2005. http://www.hindu.com/yw/2005/08/26/stories/2005082600150200.htm. Accessed September 6, 2011.

Retallack, G. Bruce. "Razors, Shaving and Gender Construction: An Inquiry into the Material Culture of Shaving." *Material Culture Review* 49 (Spring 1999): 4–19.

Richards, Thomas. *The Commodity Culture of Victorian England: Advertising and Spectacle, 1851–1914*. Stanford, CA: Stanford University Press, 1990.

Riello, Giorgio, and Peter McNeil. *Shoes: A History from Sandals to Sneakers*. London: Palgrave, 2006.

Ritvo, Harriet. "Destroyers and Preservers: Big Game in the Victorian Empire." *History Today* 52, no. 1 (2002): 33–39.

Roberts, M.J.D. "The Concept of Luxury in British Political Economy: Adam Smith to Alfred Marshall." *History of the Human Sciences* 11, no. 1 (1998): 23–47.

Roediger, David. *The Wages of Whiteness: Race and the Making of the American Working Class*. London: Verso, 1992.

Ross, Ellen. *Love and Toil: Motherhood in Outcast London, 1870–1918*. New York: Oxford University Press, 1993.

Russett, Cynthia Eagle. *Sexual Science: The Victorian Construction of Womanhood*. Cambridge, MA: Harvard University Press, 1989.

Ryan, Mary P. *Civic Wars: Democracy and Public Life in the American City during the Nineteenth Century*. Berkeley: University of California Press, 1998.

Ryan, Mary P. *Women in Public: Between Banners and Ballots, 1825–1880*. Baltimore: Johns Hopkins University Press, 1990.

Said, Edward. *Culture and Imperialism*. London: Chatto & Windus, 1993.

Said, Edward W. *Orientalism*. New York: Vintage Books, 1994.

Sanders, Lise. *Consuming Fantasies: Labour, Leisure, and the London Shopgirl, 1880–1920*. Columbus: Ohio State University Press, 2006.

Saxton, Alexander. *The Rise and Fall of the White Republic: Class Politics and Mass Culture in Nineteenth-Century America*. London: Verso, 1990.

Schlebecker, J. T. "The Use of Objects in Historical Research." *Agricultural History* 51 (1977): 200–208.

Schorman, Rob. *Selling Style: Clothing and Social Change at the Turn of the Century*. Philadelphia: University of Pennsylvania Press, 2003.

Searle, G. R. *Morality and the Market in Victorian Britain*. Oxford: Clarendon Press, 1998.

Sekora, John. *Luxury: The Concept in Western Thought, Eden to Smollett*. Baltimore: Johns Hopkins University Press, 1977.

Severa, Joan, and Merrill Horswill. "Costume as Material Culture." *Dress* 15 (1989): 51–64.

Shammas, Carole. *The Pre-Industrial Consumer in England and America*. Oxford: Clarendon Press, 1990.

Shannon, Brent. *The Cut of His Coat: Men, Dress and Consumer Culture in Britian, 1860–1914*. Athens: Ohio State University Press, 2006.

Shannon, Brent. "Refashioning Men: Fashion, Masculinity, and the Cultivation of the Male Consumers in Britain, 1860–1914." *Victorian Studies* 46, no. 4 (2004): 598–99.

Sheriff, Abdul. *Slaves, Spices and Ivory in Zanzibar: Integration of an East African Commercial Empire into the World Economy, 1770–1873*. London: James Currey, 1987.

Shuttleworth, Sally. *Charlotte Brontë and Victorian Psychology*. Cambridge: Cambridge University Press, 1996.

Simmel, Georg. "Fashion." *International Quarterly* X (1904): 130–41.

Simmel, Georg. *On Women, Sexuality and Love*. Translated by Guy Oakes. New Haven, CT: Yale University Press, 1984 [1911].

Smith, Bonnie G. *Ladies of the Leisure Class: The Bourgeoises of Northern France in the Nineteenth Century*. Princeton, NJ: Princeton University Press, 1981.

Snow, Michael R. *Brushmaking: Craft and Industry*. Oxford: Oxford Polytechnic Press, 1984.

Somers, Margaret R. "The Narrative Constitution of Identity: A Relational and Network Approach." *Theory and Society* 23, no. 5 (1994): 605–49.

Stearns, Peter N. *Consumerism in World History: The Global Transformation of Desire*. London: Routledge, 2006.

Steele, Valerie. "Appearance and Identity." In *Men and Women: Dressing the Part*, edited by Claudia Brush Kindwell and Valerie Steele, 6–21. Washington, DC: Smithsonian Institution Press, 1989.

Steele, Valerie. *The Corset: A Cultural History*. New Haven, CT: Yale University Press, 2001.

Steele, Valerie. *Fashion and Eroticism: Ideals of Feminine Beauty from the Victorian Era to the Jazz Age*. New York: Oxford University Press, 1985.

Steele, Valerie. *Shoes: A Lexicon of Style*. London: Scriptum Editions, 1998.

Stone, Lawrence. *The Family, Sex and Marriage in England, 1500–1800*. New York: Harper & Row, 1991.

Stowe, David W. "Uncolored People: The Rise of Whiteness Studies." *Lingua Franca* 6, no. 6 (1996): 68–77.

Swann, June. *Shoes*. London: B. T. Batsford, 1982.

Tait, Malcolm, and Edward Parker. *London's Royal Parks.* London: Think Publishing, 2006.

Tarrant, Naomi A. E. *Great Grandmother's Clothes: Women's Fashion in the 1880s.* Edinburgh: The National Museums of Scotland Edinburgh, 1986.

Taylor, Graham D., and Patricia E. Sudnik. *DuPont and the International Chemical Industry.* Boston: Twayne, 1984.

Temkin, Owsei. *"On Second Thought" and Other Essays in the History of Medicine and Science.* Baltimore: Johns Hopkins University Press, 2002.

Thirsk, Joan. *Economic Policy and Projects: The Development of a Consumer Society in Early Modern England.* Oxford: Clarendon Press, 1978.

Thompson, Christine. "Disruptive Desire: Medical Careers for Victorian Women in Fact and Fiction." *Nineteenth-Century Contexts* 15, no. 2 (1991): 181–96.

Thornton, Arland. "The Developmental Paradigm, Reading History Sideways, and Family Change." *Demography* 38, no. 4 (2001): 449–56.

Tickner, Lisa. *The Spectacle of Women: Imagery of the Suffrage Campaign, 1907-14.* London: Chatto & Windus, 1987.

Tiersten, Lisa. *Marianne in the Market: Envisioning Consumer Society in Fin-de-Siècle France.* Berkeley: University of California Press, 2001.

Tosh, John. "Gentlemanly Politeness and Manly Simplicity in Victorian England." *Transactions of the Royal History Society* 12 (2002): 455–72.

Tosh, John. "New Men? Bourgeois Cult of Home." In *Victorian Values: Personalities and Perspectives in Nineteenth-Century Society*, edited by Gordon Marsden, 77–88. London: Longman, 1998.

Tozer, Jane, and Sarah Levitt. *Fabric of Society: A Century of People and Their Clothes 1770-1870.* Manchester: Laura Ashley, 1983.

Trentmann, Frank, ed. *The Making of the Consumer: Knowledge, Power and Identity in the Modern World.* Oxford: Berg, 2006.

Turbin, Carole. "Collars and Consumers: Changing Images of American Manliness and Business." In *Beauty and Business: Commerce, Gender, and Culture in Modern America*, edited by Philip Scranton, 87–108. New York: Routledge, 2001.

Valverde, Mariana. "The Love of Finery: Fashion and the Fallen Woman in Nineteenth Century Social Discourse." *Victorian Studies* 32, no. 2 (1989): 169–88.

Van Wyhe, John. *The History of Phrenology on the Web.* http://www.historyofphrenology.org.uk/literature.html. Accessed June 29, 2010.

Van Wyhe, John. *Phrenology and the Origins of Victorian Scientific Naturalism.* Burlington: Ashgate, 2004.

Verplaetse, Jan. *Localising the Moral Brain: Neuroscience and the Search for the Cerebral Seat of Morality, 1800-1930.* London: Springer, 2009.

Vicinus, Martha. *Independent Women: Work and Community for Single Women, 1850-1920.* Chicago: University of Chicago Press, 1985.

Vickery, Amanda. "Golden Age to Separate Spheres? A Review of the Categories and Chronology of English Women's History." *The Historical Journal* 36, no. 2 (1993): 383–414.

Visser, Margaret. *The Way We Are*. Toronto: HarperCollins, 1994.

Volpe, Andrea. *The Middling Sorts: Explorations in the History of the American Middle Class*. New York: Routledge, 2001.

Wahrman, Dror. *Imagining the Middle Class: The Political Representation of Class in Britain, c. 1780–1840*. Cambridge: Cambridge University Press, 1995.

Walkowitz, Judith R. *City of Dreadful Delight: Narratives of Sexual Danger in Late-Victorian London*, Women in Culture and Society. Chicago: University of Chicago Press, 1992.

Walkowitz, Judith R. "The Indian Women, the Flower Girl, and the Jew: Photojournalism in Edwardian London." *Victorian Studies* 42, no. 1 (1998): 3–46.

Ware, Vron. *Beyond the Pale: White Women, Racism and History*. London: Verso, 1996.

Ware, Vron. "Island Racism: Gender, Place, and White Power." In *Displacing Whiteness: Essays in Social and Cultural Criticism*, edited by Ruth Frankenberg, 35–59. Durham, NC: Duke University Press, 1997.

Warren, John T. "Whiteness and Cultural Theory: Perspectives on Research and Education." *The Urban Review* 31, no. 2 (1999): 185–203.

Washburn, Wilcomb E. "Manuscripts and Manufacts." *American Archivist* 27, no. 2 (1964): 245–250.

Watanabe, Toshio. *High Victorian Japonisme*. Bern: P. Lang, 1991.

Waters, Karen Volland. *The Perfect Gentleman: Masculine Control in Victorian Men's Fiction, 1870–1901*. New York: P. Lang, 1997.

Webb, Beatrice. "The Diary of Beatrice Webb: 1873–1892." Edited by Norman MacKenzie and Jeanne MacKenzie. Cambridge, MA: Belknap, 1982.

Wellman, David. "Minstrel Shows, Affirmative Action, and Angry White Men: Marking Racial Otherness in the 1990s." In *Displacing Whiteness: Essays in Social and Cultural Criticism*, edited by Ruth Frankenberg, 311–31. Durham, NC: Duke University Press, 1997.

West, Candace, and Don H. Zimmerman. "Doing Gender." *Gender and Society* 1, no. 2 (1987): 125–51.

West, Candace, and Sarah Fenstermaker. "Doing Difference." *Gender and Society* 9, no. 1 (1995): 8–37.

Wexler, Laura. *Tender Violence: Domestic Visions in an Age of U.S. Imperialism*. Chapel Hill: University of North Carolina Press, 2000.

Whorton, James C. *The Arsenic Century: How Victorian Britain Was Poisoned at Home, Work, and Play*. Oxford: Oxford University Press, 2010.

Willis, F. *101 Jubilee Road: A Book of London Yesterdays*. London: Phoenix House, 1948.

Wilson, Robert A., and David E. Jordan. *Personal Exemptions and Individual Income Tax Rates, 1913–2002*. Bulletin prepared for the Internal Revenue Service, Publication 1136. Washington, DC: Government Printing Office, 2002.

Winter, Janet, and Carolyn Savoy. *Victorian Costuming*. Vol. I, *1840 to 1865*. Oakland, CA: Other Times Publications, 1980.

Worsnop, Judith. "A Reevaluation of 'The Problem of Surplus Women' in Nineteenth-Century England: The Case of the 1851 Census." *Women's Studies International Forum* 13, nos. 1/2 (1990): 21–31.

Yarwood, Doreen. *English Costume from the Second Century* B.C. *to 1967*. London: B. T. Batsford, 1967.

Yarwood, Doreen. *Fashion in the Western World 1500–1990*. New York: Drama Book Publishers, 1992.

Yokoyama, Toshio. *Japan in the Victorian Mind: A Study of Stereotyped Images of a Nation 1850–80*. Houndmills: Macmillan, 1987.

Zandy, Janet. *Hands: Physical Labor, Class, and Cultural Work*. New Brunswick, NJ: Rutgers University Press, 2004.

Index

advertising, 155–9, 161–7, 173n95
anxiety, 10, 49, 75
aristocracy, 4, 5, 37, 140
  and coquette, 63
  and umbrella, 125–9
arm *see* hand
arts and crafts movement, 150–2,
  170n48, 170n50

Bailey, Peter, 63, 81
Beamish, Richard, 52
Beeton, Isabella Mary, 50
Bernhardt, Sarah, 40, 41f
bodies, 31–32, 47
  critique of, 32
  management of, 54
  standardized, 37
Bourdieu, Pierre, 124, 140, 19n22
Braxton Hicks, Dr., 71, 98n51
British Xylonite Company, 148, 155–9,
  149f
brushmakers *see* celluloid, United
  Society of Brush Makers; United
  Society of Brush Makers
Butler, Judith, 9, 32, 54

Campbell, Lady, 37–38
celluloid, 13, 180
  and camphor, 147, 181, 169n28
  and colonialism, 147–50
  chemical makeup, 147–8
  dangers of, 147–8, 153–4, 172n73
  price of, 149–50, 157
  select committee on, 150, 154
  substitute for ivory, 148–9, 154,
  157, 158–9
  United Society of Brush Makers,
  150, 152–4
census
  of 1851, 64–5, 75
  of 1881, 64, 67
character, 1–2, 33, 34, 51, 52, 75–6,
  83, 141, 159–60, 161–2, 165, 166
  men, 36, 124–31

class
  and ivory, 141–7
  and umbrellas, 32, 124–31, 18n15
  colonialism, 8, 11–12, 86, 180,
  25n51, 26n55, 133n21
  definitions of, 3–6, 18n11
  elephant hunting, 143–6
  masculinity 107
  passing, 44, 45, 130
  slippage, 31, 38, 48–54, 140, 160
  see also celluloid, and colonialism;
  performance, class
Combe, George, 52
companionate marriage, 87–8
consumption
  and colonialism, 26n54
  and women, 47, 85, 141, 163
  conspicuous, 6, 8, 19n22
  consumerism, 1, 3, 4, 5, 6–7,
  13–14, 16, 34, 54
  consumer society, 33–4
coquette *see* flirt
corset, 8, 36, 38
Crawford, Sir Homewood, 71, 76
Cullwick, Hanna, 50
cultural capital, 19n22

Darwin, Charles, 52
Davidoff, Leonore and Catherine Hall,
  4, 5, 9, 33
De Medici, Catherine, 66
democracy, 8, 140, 150–1, 180
  and parasols, 12, 106–7, 109, 117,
  119, 124
Department of Practical Art, 65, 97
Department of Science and Art, 71
diet, 39–40, 48
Disraeli, Benjamin, 78
domestic ideology *see* separate
  spheres
domestic servant, 9, 33, 49, 50,
  29–30, 23n42, 137n83
domestic sphere *see* separate
  sphere

DuPont Company *see* E. I. Du Pont de Nemours and Company
Duvelleroy *see* Maison Duvelleroy
Duvelleroy, Louis, 77

E. I. Du Pont de Nemours and Company, 139, 155, 156–9, 161–7, 176n119
eating habits *see* diet
Edict of Nantes, 94n24, 96n32
effeminacy, 36, 115–17
elephant, 141, 143, 146, 147
employment for women *see* fan, design
etiquette manual, 1–2, 13, 33–4, 51, 120, 159–60
excess profits tax, 156
exhibition, 86, 91, 145
  fan, 69, 71–4, 76
  Great International of 1862, 155
  Great of 1851, 64, 67
  International of 1871, 71

fan, 2–3, 9, 12–13, 15–16, 78–80, 86, 89–90, 91–2, 142, 179–80, 181–2, 41, 42f, 94n22
  as weapon of seduction, 84–5
  design, 12, 64, 67–8, 71
  exhibitions *see* exhibitions fan
  flirtation, 12, 63, 64, 65, 76–8, 83
  history, 66, 93n17
  Japanese women 12, 85–92
  language of the, 3, 77–8, 101n100
  manufacture, 65–7, 69, 71–4, 94n23
fan making
  France, 66–7, 74, 94n24, 95n25
  warehouse and manufactory of Louisa Avant & Co., 67, 69, 96n32
  working class, 67
  see also Worshipful Company of Fan Makers
fashion plate, 41, 43, 78–9
fashion system, 13
Female School of Design, 67, 68, 69–71, 96n44
feminist, 9, 12, 65, 85
flapper, 163–4
flirt, 9, 14, 75, 80, 82, 88–90, 139, 180
  coquette, 7–9, 82–3, 80–2, 85–6, 181, 122n110

definition, 83
parasol, 107, 122
working class, 81
see also fan, language of the; parasol, courtship; umbrella, courtship

Gall, Franz Joseph, 51
gender
  differentiation, 9
  performance, 9, 32, 54, 75–6, 180
  roles, 33, 65
  see also separate spheres
glove, 4, 13, 15, 31, 179, 181
  color, 46
  cotton, 44–5
  hide labor, 3, 9, 31, 38–9
  industry, 34, 46–7
  kid/leather, 44, 47
  men, 35, 36–7
  opera or evening, 40
  pointing, 46
  silk, 44
  size, 46
  stretchers, 44
  wearing etiquette, 34–5, 56n15
  working class, 45
  worn out, 39, 43–4, 45, 46
  see also hand
Great Exhibition of 1851 *see* exhibition

hair, 2, 160, 163, 182
  brushing, 9
  style, 139, 166
hand, 31
  and labor, 33, 37–8, 42, 48–9, 50–2
  aristocratic, 37–8, 42–3, 54, 59n51
  arm, 39–40
  care of, 35
  elbows, 39–40, 48
  fingers, 38, 40, 42, 44, 47, 50, 52
  gestures, 41–2
  knuckles, 39–40, 44, 48
  naked, 34–6
  shape, 32, 38
  thumb, 52
  veins, 31, 46
  white, 39, 181
  working class, 40, 48–50, 52, 54

Hanway, Jonas, 116
Hyatt, John Wesley, 148

imitation, 3, 5, 140–1, 149, 150–2,
    157, 159
inner/outer self *see* character
interconnections of race class and
    gender, 9, 10–11, 32
ivory, 3, 4, 12, 13, 66, 140, 141–3,
    145–7, 180
  masculinity, 146
  price of, 168n14
  Pyralin, 148–9
  rate of imports, 141, 147, 149

Japan, 7, 12, 65–6, 70, 73, 85–92,
    148, 180, 181
  see also fan, Japanese women;
    Russo-Japanese War;
    separate spheres, Japanese
    women; women, Japanese
Jouvin, Xavier, 46–7

Lavater, J. C., 52
leisure, 3, 9, 16, 38, 40, 43, 48, 69,
    86, 91, 179
London, Jack, 10–11
Loudon, Jane C., 38–9
Lucite, 164–7
luxury, 3, 6–7, 139, 151, 181

Mclan, Fanny, 70
Maison Duvelleroy, 74, 77
manufacturing, 13–14
masculinity 105, 107, 115–17,
    124–31, 146, 180, 19n22
  see also character, men; glove, men
material culture, 8, 13–16, 21n34
Mayhew, Henry, 10–11, 25n47
metanarrative, 106, 107, 109, 119
middle class, 1, 3–6, 17n10, 18n16
  definitions of, 48–9
  employment, 20n24
  formation of, 19n20
  income, 17n9
  lower-middle-class, 6, 10, 33, 69,
    157–8
  see performance, class
Mikado, 14, 88–90
Mill, John Stuart, 107

modernism, 140, 166
Munby, Arthur, 49–50
music hall, 45–6

Nash, Edward Barrington, 71

Orvell, Miles, 150

parasexuality, 63
parasol, 13, 180
  Africa, 107, 110
  ancient Greece and Rome, 105–6,
    113, 114, 119
  Asia, 109–10, 112–13
  as imperial spoils, 110
  as symbol of power, 105, 106,
    107–9, 119
  Christianity, 111, 113–14
  colonization, 105
  courtship, 122–3
  East Asia, 107, 109, 111
  Fiji Islands, 107
  history, 106, 134n33
  material makeup, 117
  Middle East, 107
  price, 118
  rain, 105, 111–12, 116, 118
  royalty, 12
  sumptuary laws, 107
  sun, 105, 108, 111–12, 116, 118
  Turkey, 109
  women, 115–16
  youth, 120–2
  see also flirt, parasol; democracy,
    and parasol; masculinity; Prince
    of Wales, Edward; umbrella
Parkensine Company Limited *see*
    British Xylonite Company
Parkes, Alexander, 148, 155
performance
  class, 9, 10, 46, 48, 49, 54, 180
  gender, 48–9, 63, 77
phrenology, 10, 51–3, 57n34
plastic *see* celluloid
posture, 39, 41, 48
press, 3, 7, 33
Prince of Wales, Edward, 105, 144
Pyralin, 140, 155, 157–9, 161–4,
    176n119
  see also celluloid

Queen Victoria, 70, 71, 110, 119, 145

race, 1,10, 106
  vagabond savage, 10–11
redundant women, 64–6, 69–70, 71–3, 75, 85–6, 91, 120, 180, 17n9, 97n45
Revenue Act of 1918, 157
Russo-Japanese War, 86

Schreiber, Lady Charlotte, 72
Sears Roebuck & Co., 157
select committee, 70, 150
self, outer and inner state see character
self-fashioning see character
separate sphere, 64–6, 71, 87, 75, 78, 79, 85, 82, 86, 92, 55n11, 101n108
  Japanese women, 87
servant see domestic servant
sexuality, 78, 81, 85, 139, 103n120
Simmel, George, 83, 89
skin, 6, 10, 181
  damage, 39, 48, 120, 37f
  health, 2–3
  ointment, 3, 47
  race, 11, 32
  white, 2, 32–3, 88, 106
Smiles, Samuel, 5
Somers, Margaret R., 106
South Kensington Museum see Victoria and Albert Museum
Spill, Daniel, 155, 172n78
spinster see redundant women
Spurzheim, Johann Kaspar, 51
surplus women question see redundant women

thrift, 5, 6
Treaty of Edo, 86

umbrella, 12
  courtship, 123–4, 136n71
  imperial spoil, 144

middle class, 129
  sword, 125
  working class, 130–1
  see class, and umbrellas
United Society of Brush Makers, 14, 171n61, 171n65

vanity set, 3, 9, 13, 139–41, 180–2, 17n7
  disappearance of, 166–7
Veblen, Thorstein, 4, 9, 19n14
Victoria and Albert Museum, 65, 72
vulgar, 44, 81, 152,

Watteau, 67, 77, 165
woman question, the see redundant women
women
  employment, 12
  Japanese, 65, 86–92
  modern, 92
  passive, 64, 75, 77, 78–80, 82 85–6, 101n108
  question, the see redundant women
  workers' directory, 68
  see also consumption, and women; fan, Japanese women; fan, design; parasol, women; performance, gender; redundant women; separate spheres, Japanese women
working class, 5, 10–11, 33, 160, 161f
  definitions of, 48–9
  see also fan making; flirt; glove; hand; umbrella, working class
Working Ladies' Guild, the, 67–8
World War I, 3, 155, 163, 179, 180–1
Worshipful Company of Fan Makers 66, 67, 69, 71–4, 76

youth, 2, 120